D1177487

ICON

JOHN SCHREINER

Icon

FLAGSHIP WINES *from* BRITISH COLUMBIA'S BEST WINERIES

Photography by
Christopher K. Stenberg

TOUCHWOOD
EDITIONS

TO WINEMAKER JOHN SIMES,
who created Oculus in the 1997 vintage at Mission
Hill Family Estates, continually refining it until
it became the Okanagan's premier icon wine.

Contents

JOHN SCHREINER

Introduction

The judgments and notes in this book reflect a lifetime of tasting wine, beginning in the 1960s, when very few wine courses were offered in Vancouver. Wine was learned bottle by bottle, with plenty of surprises. I did not expect to find a cork when I first cut the capsule on a bottle of Sauternes and discovered—on a Sunday afternoon—that I needed a corkscrew. The neighbourhood pharmacy had one, but the design was so poor that I shoved the cork into the bottle. The wine, however, was delicious, beginning my appreciation for sweet wines and good corkscrews.

In lieu of wine courses, my friends and I organized wine tastings in our homes. That led me to join numerous local wine-tasting clubs dedicated to French, German, Italian, Australian, Spanish, and South African wines. A club organized in the 1980s to taste BC wines failed because the wines then were mediocre; nothing being made was remotely iconic. Twenty-five years later, however, I was able to join a new club called the BC Wine Appreciation Society. It has thrived because the wines from this province now meet world standards of quality.

In 1975, my curiosity about wine led me to join a winemaking club and become a home vintner. While I never produced any icons of my own, what I learned about grapes and wine production proved extremely useful when I began interviewing winemakers and writing about their wines. I might have rounded out this self-instruction by actually buying a vineyard. I was tempted once when I spent a sun-drenched summer afternoon with a grower on Black Sage Road, absorbing what seemed to me to be the magical details of grape growing. At the end of the afternoon, he proposed building a winery if I would make the wine. I spent a weekend thinking about it before realizing my strength lay in writing about (and drinking) the wines others made. But that shows how seductive wines and wine-growing can be.

I supported my passion (and my family) through a 40-year career as a business reporter with a national newspaper. In my free time, I wrote extensively about wine, and I expanded my knowledge with travels to wineries in both Europe and the New World. It is not entirely accurate to say there were no wine courses available to me: in 1983, I travelled to Germany and took the excellent German Wine Academy course, a concentrated week-long course with an examination at the end. I came second in a class of 40, beaten by one point by the son-in-law of a California vintner, who clearly had a head start.

It has always been important to taste wines from other wine regions, if only to measure how Canadian wines have been progressing and to avoid what the industry calls "cellar palate." I was brought up short once in 1990 when I took a Canadian Merlot from a new producer to France and offered it to a tasting in a venerable Bordeaux château.

The wine was embarrassingly poor, not deserving of the acclaim it was being given by its home winery. Canadian wines have improved so much since then that there would be little risk of being humiliated today. But this shows the merit in tasting wines from other countries and broadening one's palate.

Wine writing led to numerous invitations to judge wines, if only because it was assumed writers had developed discerning palates and the ability to recognize superior wines. Today, such skills can be acquired through, for example, the excellent training for professional sommeliers. I have worked on judging panels with sommeliers, and I admire their technical competence. But I have also judged with many people who learned the art of wine adjudication the way I did: bottle by bottle. This background has armed me with the ability to recommend wines that you should consider for your cellar.

Perhaps your favourite wine is not included here. All that proves is that wine preference is subjective. When I was a business journalist, I organized occasional wine tastings in the boardrooms of our corporate readers, with the hosts inviting their friends. During a tasting of 10 California Zinfandels in a financial company's elegant boardroom, the host was the only taster who picked the simplest wine as his favourite. Most wines eventually find a champion. Continue to champion your favourites while you explore mine.

ICON WINES

An icon wine is the very best wine a producer can make. It is the rising tide that lifts all boats in terms of the calibre of wines the winery produces. Icon wines (also called luxury wines) are made by producers all over the world. "The Icon market accounts for one per cent of the global wine market," writes Michael Beverland, a marketing professor at Australia's Monash University. "These wines sell for over US $50 per bottle, are generally consumed by connoisseurs and are relatively scarce."

Many of the icon wines discussed in this book cost in the range of $30 a bottle, the majority are $40 to $60 a bottle, and a few exceed $100. They are necessarily expensive: they are made with a winery's best grapes, aged in the winery's most expensive barrels, and then aged another several years in bottle before release. Production volumes are often limited, with scarcity being another reason for aggressive pricing. I do not agree with critics who dismiss icons as wines merely driven by the winemaker's ego. Wine blogger Jamie Goode, in what he called a rant in 2011, suggested an end to "these icon wines, driven by ego, with their heavy bottles and silly price tags and sweet, inky, oaky concentrated flavours. They achieve nothing positive." It was a provocative dig at a lot of fine wines that most of us would enjoy.

I have chosen what I consider to be the flagship wines at just under 100 wineries. Not all the collectible wines recommended here are premium-priced. They are, in my view, wines with a track record of rising quality that are more accessible and entirely suitable for cellaring. Some sell for as little as $20 a bottle and would hardly be considered icons. Such wines may not live as long nor be as complex as the $50 to $100 wines, yet they also will mature to deliver more flavour and aroma than when they were young. A $20 wine can be expected to peak in seven years (in a good cellar). Most icon wines are constructed to age at least 10 years, improving and becoming more complex as they age. Indeed, the wines will likely cellar longer than that. As vines in this province have grown older and winemaking has become more skilled, the best wines are living 15 or more years.

My objective with this book is to encourage readers to collect verticals (a vertical is a succession of vintages) of favourite wines, red and white. There is no better way to understand a wine than to taste and compare, preferably with friends, five or more vintages of it. The wine profiles in this book include information on each vintage to let you drill down to a wine's essentials.

THE ICON WINE'S ROLE

The icon or "flagship" wine has a particular role in a winery's portfolio. The discipline required to grow quality grapes and make quality wine shapes how all the grapes are grown and how all the wines are made. The vineyard that produces a $50 wine grows its best blocks of grapes to reach that quality. Vineyards can be farmed to produce $15 wines, typically by growing more clusters on each vine. But good viticultural practices that yield icon wines will lift quality throughout an entire vineyard.

The prestige of an icon wine cascades across a winery's entire portfolio. The Okanagan's first $50 wine was a red blend from Sumac Ridge called Pinnacle. The wine was ahead of its time and was eventually discontinued when the subsequent owner of Sumac Ridge decided to focus on producing lower-priced (but excellent) varietals. In its day, Pinnacle lifted the sales of Sumac Ridge's $25 Meritage because consumers concluded—correctly—that the

other premium wines sharing a portfolio with an icon were also likely to be of high quality.

THE ABSENCE OF WHITE VARIETIES

With the exception of Rieslings, Chardonnays, and sparkling wines, there are no white wines in this book. Generally, collectors are more likely to cellar red wines than whites, believing that reds live longer. However, with wines there are no absolute rules. During research for this book, I tasted a 2005 Pinot Gris at Averill Creek Vineyard—a stunning wine with fresh, slightly honeyed fruit flavours held together with bright acidity. A decade of age had given it a richness and complexity that was quite satisfying.

"For me, Pinot Gris from Vancouver Island is such a wonderful wine to hang on to," Averill Creek proprietor Andy Johnston said. "It ages impeccably." The key is the relatively high acidity often found in the Island's wines; the whites may be austere when young but mellow and full with age. Other white varieties also age well. Most Chardonnay can be cellared for at least five years. Viognier, which has more tannin in its skins than other whites, can be expected to develop expressively up to seven years. Sémillon and Chenin Blanc, both varieties with good acidity, have a similar ability to age.

ICEWINES AND SWEET WINES

The age-worthiness of icewine is contentious. The small and slender bottles in which these wines are packaged are less than ideal for aging. My preference is to drink icewine within a year or two of the vintage, when the wines are bursting with tropical fruit flavours. It is true that the concentration of sugar and acidity will enable icewines to age almost indefinitely. But with age, the aromas and flavours develop the maderized character of sherry. That can be pleasing, but not as pleasing as the exuberant flavours of young icewine.

Sweet wines made with botrytis-affected grapes age better than icewines. However, the Okanagan's dry climate usually prevents the misty mornings at harvest that foster the growth of botrytis spores. Quails' Gate Totally Botrytis Affected Optima is a rare example of this style of wine; it is produced most vintages because of a special terroir in the Quails' Gate vineyard beside Okanagan Lake. The wine is typically packaged in half-bottles, again not ideal for long-term aging.

FORMAT AND STORAGE

Wines age more gracefully and significantly longer in large-format bottles. The 750 mL bottle is the standard size (and the size for which most wine cellars are designed). However, many producers have begun to offer limited releases of magnums (with the capacity of two standard bottles), double magnums or jeroboams (four bottles), and occasionally methuselahs (eight bottles). It is worth adding large-format bottles to your wine collection because wines age more slowly in large formats and can be cellared for several additional years.

The ideal wine cellar is a cool, dark room free of deleterious odours. You cannot store wine and snow tires in the same room. The optimal cellar temperature is 13°C; if the cellar is not underground or is not air-conditioned, the temperature should at least be stable. Dramatic spikes in the storage temperature or an overly warm temperature will result in the premature aging of wines.

Temperature-controlled wine cabinets are effective but are seldom large enough to house sizable collections. Wine collectors living in condos with limited storage should consider commercial wine-storage options.

ABOUT THE BOOK

Under my comments on each winery and icon wine, I have generally reproduced the tasting notes written by the winery on release of the wine. Since wines evolve as they age, you should expect to find changed flavours and textures in older wines. Unless stored too long, a well-cellared older wine will have developed nuances that enhance the enjoyment of the wine. While researching this book, I was able to do a number of vertical tastings. However, it was impractical to taste every vertical and produce entirely new notes. For that reason, I have chosen to include winery notes written at the time of release. In some cases, I have added my own tasting notes if winery notes were unavailable or inadequate. A surprising number of wineries merely post the same tasting notes vintage after vintage. One winery owner told me, quite rightly, that it makes "no sense" to do that—unaware his staff had done just that through several vintages of his flagship red.

There are gaps in the tasting notes for certain individual wines. Not every winery archives this information, however critical it is to their customers. Perhaps that reflects a lack of staffing; to me, it suggests that it has not occurred to some of BC's young wineries that a growing number of consumers might want to collect their wines—or would do so with some encouragement.

The recommendations given on when to drink the wines occasionally come from the wineries. I have given guidance on when, in my judgment, you should drink the wines you are cellaring. Many wineries now provide such guidance. Invariably, the advice is conservative, perhaps because this is a young wine industry with limited experience in cellaring wines. I have usually tacked a few more years to what the wineries suggest, based on my experience and on the structure of the wines. I have suggested "drink now" for some wines and "mature" for older wines. "Drink now" means now and during the next few years. "Mature" means drink the wines very soon before they begin their inevitable decline.

The price is given only for the most recent vintage and generally includes taxes. Older vintages are seldom available to consumers, so their prices wouldn't be relevant if available. As well, percentages of varietals, names of vineyards, and numbers of cases produced are not disclosed by every winery.

HAT TIP TO JOHN LEVINE

The first consumer to foster the emerging icon wines of BC was the late John Levine, who died in 2012. A passionate collector of wines from France and California, he became an influential champion of BC wines. He founded the Vancouver International Wine Festival and was a member of every important wine society in Vancouver. In his restaurants, he featured BC wines. When his friend Simon Wosk opened Sip Wines, a VQA store in Richmond, in 2004, John became his mentor.

When Simon asked whether there were enough premium Bordeaux red blends from the Okanagan for a special tasting, John took on the research that identified the wines. In 2008, Sip sponsored the first in-store tasting of icon wines. It became a major annual tasting, open to the first 100 or so people who bought tickets. After the 2016 tasting, Simon sold the Sip Wines business and closed the store. However, he has revived the icon tasting under different auspices, keeping alive an event that served to establish the icon-wine concept in British Columbia. It is now tradition at each icon tasting to honour John Levine, whose portrait and hat are near the head table, by toasting him with sparkling wine.

Arrowleaf Cellars

SOLSTICE RESERVE

The inspiration for this wine came from the many Austrian red blends that include Zweigelt, arguably the leading red variety in Austria. As former residents of Switzerland, Joe and Margrit Zuppiger, the owners of Arrowleaf, were familiar with Austrian wines before they came to Canada in 1986. After running a dairy farm in Alberta, they purchased a vineyard in 1997 in the North Okanagan that was planted primarily with Gewürztraminer, Pinot Gris, Auxerrois, and Bacchus.

When the Zuppigers moved into wine production, they recognized the need for full-flavoured red wines, planting Merlot in 1998 and Zweigelt in 1999. Their son, Manuel, who went to study at the Swiss winemaking school at Wädenswil, had suggested Pinot Noir, but his father wanted varieties capable of producing more robust wines. Pinot Noir was added to the vineyard several years later.

Manuel, who was born in 1976, acquired practical winemaking experience at Wädenswil, where students spend most of the year apprenticing in wineries with periodic breaks to study theory. He worked the 2001 vintage in the Barossa Valley with Grant Burge, who was then a leading Australian winemaker. In BC, he worked briefly at Tinhorn Creek before beginning to make Arrowleaf's wines in 2001. Burge wanted him back in Australia for the 2002 vintage, but with the new winery under development, Manuel stayed in the Okanagan.

He made the first Solstice blend in 2003, anchoring the wine with Merlot and Zweigelt. In a true reflection of Austrian red blends, he was able to include Lemberger in both this and the 2004 vintage. That variety has not been available to Arrowleaf since. Manuel uses grapes only from Arrowleaf's Suncrest Vineyard and from the nearby Ritchie Vineyard, which is managed by the Zuppiger family.

The two varieties in the blend are generally fermented and aged separately. The final blend is assembled from a selection of the best barrels. Solstice Reserve is made only in the best vintages. (The first two vintages, while excellent, were not called Reserve.) Since 2006, screw cap closures have been used, accounting for the freshness of the flavours. The ageability of the wine is due also to Zweigelt's naturally bright acidity.

2013 ($22)

Merlot 63%, Zweigelt 37%. Alcohol 13.5%. Suncrest and Ritchie vineyards. Aged 15 months in French and American oak. Production 370 cases.

WINERY TASTING NOTES "[The wine begins with] rich dark cherry and plum aromas with subtle notes of vanilla, coffee, and dark chocolate. The palate is full-bodied and generous, providing plenty of ripe fruit through to the finish." Drink by 2023.

2012

Merlot 58%, Zweigelt 42%. Alcohol 13.7%. Suncrest and Ritchie vineyards. Aged 15 months in French and American oak (50% new). Production 444 cases.

WINERY TASTING NOTES "Rich and dense, [the wine] displays aromas of raspberry, cherry, and plum with supple notes of vanilla, coffee, and dark chocolate. The palate is full-bodied and generous, providing plenty of ripe fruit through to the finish." Drink by 2022.

2010

Merlot 65%, Zweigelt 35%. Alcohol 14%. Suncrest Vineyard. Aged 12 months in American oak.

AUTHOR'S TASTING NOTES "Reflecting a cool vintage, the wine has a hint of greenness mingling with cherry aromas. On the medium-bodied palate, there are flavours of cherry, blackberry, and raspberry." Drink by 2020.

2009

Merlot 60%, Zweigelt 40%. Alcohol 14.5%. Suncrest Vineyard. Aged 12 months in French oak. Production 220 cases.

AUTHOR'S TASTING NOTES "Reflecting a ripe vintage, this full-bodied wine has aromas and flavours of raspberry, cherry, and plum. The tannins are polished and the finish is silky." Drink by 2019.

2007

Zweigelt 54%, Merlot 46%. Alcohol 13.9%. Suncrest Vineyard. Aged 12 months in French and American oak. Production 220 cases.

AUTHOR'S TASTING NOTES "The Zweigelt comes through with vibrant aromas and flavours of cherry, blackberry, and raspberry. The structure is age-worthy." Drink by 2020.

2006

Merlot 63%, Zweigelt 37%. Alcohol 14.8%. Suncrest Vineyard. Aged 12 months in French oak.

AUTHOR'S TASTING NOTES "The wine is bold and ripe, with aromas of blackberry and raspberry. The fruit flavours on the palate—cherry and blackberry—are lively and generous, with its freshness preserved under screw cap closures." Drink by 2018.

2004

Merlot 60%, Zweigelt 34%, Lemberger 6%. Alcohol 13.9%. Suncrest and Branch vineyards. Aged 12 months in French oak.

AUTHOR'S TASTING NOTES "Whether due to bottle variation or an ineffective cork closure, this wine is slightly oxidized." Mature.

2003

Merlot 41%, Zweigelt 39%, Lemberger 20%. Alcohol 13.5%. Suncrest and Branch vineyards.

AUTHOR'S TASTING NOTES "Tasted in 2015, this wine showed some browning but still delivered a delicious core of sweet fruit, including cherry. The wine has a dusty, spicy finish. In this wine, the cork closures are still doing the job." Drink now.

Averill Creek Vineyard
PINOT NOIR

More than once, Averill Creek proprietor Andy Johnston has declared that he intends to produce the best Pinot Noir in Canada at his vineyard in the Cowichan Valley on Vancouver Island. Whether he has achieved that is for consumers to decide. Without a doubt, however, he makes consistently fine and long-lived Pinot Noirs in a challenging climate.

"You cannot make a formulaic wine in the Cowichan Valley because there is so much variation in the years," Andy has discovered. Note the dramatic production swings of this wine from year to year, from a low of 350 cases in 2007 to 1,220 cases in 2009, plus another 220 cases so bold that the wine received a rare reserve designation. "That is totally what the weather gives me," Andy says. "You are cropping anywhere from three tons to less than one, depending very much on the year." In 2011, a very cool growing year, the production of Pinot Noir had to be reduced to 0.75 tons an acre so that the vines could ripen the grapes. "I really had to agonize whether to make a Pinot Noir," he recalls. "I am happy with what we have got. It is not as big as the other wines, but it is a very complete wine."

The Pinot Noir passion is Andy's second career. A medical doctor who was born on a Welsh farm in 1947, Andy came to Canada in 1973 and practised medicine in Alberta for about 30 years. Deciding that "there are only so many patient visits in me," he eased into winemaking by working the 1998 vintage at Villa Delia in Tuscany. That opened the door to working the 1999 vintage at McGuigan Wines in Australia, then a vintage in the south of France in 2000, followed by vintages in New Zealand, including one with a Pinot Noir specialist, Escarpment Vineyard in Martinborough. While doing that, he acquired a property north of Duncan, on the fairly steep southward slope of Mount Prevost. He began planting vines in 2002, devoting a third of the 12-hectare (30-acre) vineyard to four Pinot Noir clones. From time to time, he debates replacing most of the other varieties with Pinot Noir.

"I think it is fantastic that we can make these wines in the Cowichan Valley," Andy says. "I feel they have more elegance and complexity than most Okanagan Pinots. The style is very different from the Okanagan." Andy's views have mellowed: he once argued that the Okanagan was too hot for Pinot Noir. He now admits admiration for several Okanagan Pinot Noir producers.

The Averill Creek Pinot Noirs, even with the vintage variation caused by climate, show a familial style. The elegant wines are medium-bodied, with bright acidity giving vibrancy to the red berry flavours and longevity to the wines. The 2005 Pinot Noir, Averill Creek's first and made with fruit from three-year-old vines, was very much alive a decade later. No doubt the screw cap closures that Andy has always used help retain the freshness of aroma and flavour. More recent vintages from maturing vines have the structure to age even longer.

2013 ($22)

Alcohol 13.2%. Production 500 cases.

WINERY TASTING NOTES "Delicate but intense. Elegant yet earthy. Our Pinot Noir opens with an alluring bouquet of dark berries and violets, leather and butterscotch. The silky, medium-bodied palate features rich black cherry and ripe plum flavours, finished with a touch of spice and soft, supple tannins." Drink by 2023.

2012

Alcohol 12.9%. Production 689 cases.

WINERY TASTING NOTES "This silky, medium-bodied red is expressive and alluring on the nose with layered aromas of roses, cherries, white pepper, and tobacco leaf. On the palate bright red berry flavours mingle with delicate clove spice, earthy minerality, and soft tannins to finish with length and finesse." Drink by 2022.

2011

Alcohol 13.2%. Production 470 cases.

WINERY TASTING NOTES "Delicate but intense. Elegant yet earthy. Our Pinot Noir opens with an alluring bouquet of dark berries and violets, leather and butterscotch. The silky medium-bodied palate features rich black cherry and ripe plum flavours with a touch of spice and soft, supple tannins." Drink by 2021.

2010

Alcohol 13.2%. Production 950 cases.

AUTHOR'S TASTING NOTES "Ruby in colour, the wine begins with dramatic aromas of cherries and pepper, which are echoed in the bright flavours. The texture manages to be both firm and silky." Drink by 2020.

Reserve 2009 ($70)

Alcohol 13.5%. Production 220 cases.

AUTHOR'S TASTING NOTES "The wine, which was aged 15 months in French oak, begins with those complex aroma notes— tea, spice, cherry—that sometimes are called barnyard, a positive descriptor with Pinot Noir. On the palate, there are flavours of cherry and raspberry, with a spicy (cloves, nutmeg) finish. The texture is silky." Drink by 2019.

2009

Alcohol 12.5%. Production 1,220 cases.

WINERY TASTING NOTES "In the glass it has a deep ruby colour with aromas of violets, black cherries, leather, and tobacco. The silky medium-bodied palate offers flavours of strawberry and plum with soft, seductive tannins followed by a lasting, well-balanced finish." Drink by 2019.

2008

Alcohol 12%. Production 660 cases.

WINERY TASTING NOTES "The nose is fragrant with layers of dried cherry, plum, and violets opening to overtones of smoke, leather, and soft clove spice. On the palate, flavours of wild strawberry and raspberry give way to an earthy minerality with hints of tobacco and orange zest." Drink by 2018.

2007

Alcohol 12.7%. Production 350 cases.

AUTHOR'S TASTING NOTES "The wine begins with aromas of toasted oak and plum, which carry through to the flavour along with hints of chocolate. There is also a complex note of forest floor on the quite Burgundian finish." Drink now.

2006

Alcohol 12.9%. Production 680 cases.

WINERY TASTING NOTES "The wine is a dark ruby/magenta colour with a soft, almost perfumed black cherry nose overlaid with tobacco and leather. The entry is soft and fruity with a mouth-filling complex middle palate and nicely balanced tannins." Drink by 2018.

2005

Alcohol 12.8%. Production 460 cases.

AUTHOR'S TASTING NOTES "The wine begins with alluring aromas of strawberry and raspberry, which are echoed in the bright and vibrant fruit flavours. The elegant polish of the silky textures owes something to the wine having been fined with egg whites." Drink now.

Baillie-Grohman Estate Winery
PINOT NOIR

The signature variety at Baillie-Grohman, Pinot Noir, accounts for more than half the vines in the 9.5-hectare (23.5-acre) vineyard. It is an intelligent choice for Creston, a relatively cool growing region with an average high temperature in July of 26°C. Dan Barker, Baillie-Grohman's consulting winemaker from New Zealand, says it reminds him of Central Otago in that country, where Pinot Noir also produces premium wines.

The vineyard was developed starting in 2007 by Bob Johnson and Petra Flaa, Baillie-Grohman's owners, who had previously pursued business careers in Alberta. Petra had managed information technology projects, while Bob was a reservoir engineer with Sproule Associates, an oil-industry consultancy. They have always been drawn to agriculture. They lived on a small farm near Calgary and, after being attracted to Creston for family reasons, they invested in a cherry orchard before switching to grapes. Baillie-Grohman, named in honour of Creston pioneer William Baillie-Grohman, was the city's second winery when it made its first vintage in 2009.

Creston's first winery, Skimmerhorn, which had opened three years earlier, blazed the trail by hiring a New Zealand winemaker willing to work the vintage in Creston during the off-season in the southern hemisphere. Baillie-Grohman did the same after failing to recruit an experienced Canadian winemaker. "We had some very junior applications, but we weren't willing to bet the farm on someone who had a little bit of education and no experience," Petra says. They were fortunate to recruit Barker. He had been named New Zealand Young Winemaker of the Year in 2003. He operates Moana Park Winery in Hawkes Bay, which he has owned since 2008. In addition to working Baillie-Grohman's vintage every year, Dan also mentored Wes Johnson, Bob and Petra's son. In 2014, Wes completed his Bachelor of Science in Oenology at a New Zealand university and is now assistant winemaker at Baillie-Grohman.

It is a credit to Petra's skill in the vineyard and Bob's marketing talents that Baillie-Grohman's full production target, about 6,000 cases, was reached in 2014. While the winery buys Merlot and Cabernet Franc from an Osoyoos vineyard, most of its wine is produced from Creston grapes. Three of the best Pinot Noir clones—115, 667, and 777—flourish here.

The Pinot Noir grapes enable the winery to produce a rosé, an easy-drinking red blend called Récolte Rouge, an estate Pinot Noir, and a reserve Pinot Noir. The reserve is a rigorous selection of the best French oak barrels in each vintage.

Estate 2013 ($25)

Pinot Noir. Alcohol 13%. Cold-soaked 7 to 10 days, inoculated with Burgundy yeasts, fermented at temperatures peaking at 30°C. Aged 12 months in French oak (15% new). Production 535 cases.

WINERY TASTING NOTES "Deep carmine in colour with a purple hue. Aroma—lifted notes showing wild red and black fruit, with truffle and game. Palate—a rich textural palate, medium-bodied with a long finish, great balance, and concentration displaying notes of blackberry, plum, and spice." Drink by 2020.

Reserve 2012 ($45)

Pinot Noir clones 115, 667, 777. Alcohol 13%. At crush, 20% of the juice was drained off before a 7-day cold soak. Fermentation is done with Burgundy yeasts. The wine was aged in French oak (30% new) and bottled unfiltered. Production 98 cases.

WINERY TASTING NOTES "The 2012 Reserve Pinot Noir is a deep carmine colour with a purple hint. The style has lifted notes of ripe wild red and black fruit with cedar and game. It has a rich textural palate, medium-bodied with a long finish, great balance and concentration displaying notes of blackberry, plum, and spice." Drink by 2020.

Estate 2012

Pinot Noir. Alcohol 12.5%. Cold-soaked 7 to 10 days, inoculated with Burgundy yeasts, fermented at temperatures peaking at 30°C. Aged 12 months in French oak (10% new). Production 404 cases.

WINERY TASTING NOTES "[The wine] is a deep carmine colour with a purple hue. The style has lifted notes of ripe red and black fruit with spice and truffle. The palate has a vibrant bouquet of cassis, red berries with truffle and thyme . . . Spicy and earthy notes accompany the silky tannins." Drink by 2020.

Estate 2011

Pinot Noir clones 115, 667, 777. Alcohol 13.5%. Aged in French oak (30% new). Production 700 cases.

WINERY TASTING NOTES The wine has aromas of "wild red and black fruits, cedar and game [with flavours of] blackberry, lavender, and plum with truffle and spice." Drink by 2019.

Reserve 2009

Pinot Noir clones 667, 777. Alcohol 13.5%. Aged in French oak (30% new).

WINERY TASTING NOTES "Colour: dark carmine with purple hints; aroma: wild red and black fruits, cedar, and game. A rich textural palate, medium-bodied with a long finish, displaying notes of blackberry, lavender, and plum with cigar box and leather." Drink by 2019.

Estate 2009

Pinot Noir. Alcohol 13.3%. Aged in French oak for 8 months. Production 105 cases.

WINERY TASTING NOTES "[The wine] is a deep cherry colour with a ruby hue. The style is fruit driven, with spicy berry and concentrated red fruit . . . with notes of mushroom, red currant aromas, and notes of beetroot." Drink by 2018.

Bartier Bros.

THE GOAL

When they began selling wine under their own label, Don and Michael Bartier crafted a winery slogan to celebrate their Okanagan Valley roots: "This is what 30 years has led to . . ." The sons of an accountant, they were both born in the valley, Don in 1958 and Michael in 1967, and they initially pursued careers outside of wine. Don, after becoming an accountant, began working in the oil and gas industry in Alberta in 1978. He planted a small block of Gewürztraminer in 2010 at a Summerland vineyard after he and his brother agreed to develop a winery.

Michael has a degree from the University of Victoria in recreational administration. "I wasn't interested in the recreational field," he admits. "By the time I realized that, I was too far along in my degree to stop those studies." On graduation, he joined a Victoria wine agency for five years before returning to the Okanagan as a rock climbing guide. He discovered his métier in 1995 when he joined the cellar crew at Hawthorne Mountain Vineyards. He enrolled in winemaking courses and, in 1998, worked the vintage at the Thomas Hardy winery in Australia. Since 2002, he has honed his winemaking craft at Stag's Hollow, Township 7, Road 13, and Okanagan Crush Pad, where he made the debut vintages for Bartier Bros. In 2015, he and Don began building their own winery on the Cerqueira Vineyard on Black Sage Road.

The Goal, their premium red wine, was launched with a 50-case production in the 2009 vintage. In the first two vintages, the grapes were sourced from several vineyards. Since 2011, the grapes have been from the Cerqueira Vineyard, a terroir that Michael considers quite special for its minerality.

It is a vineyard with mature vines growing on a calcium-rich gravel bar laid down by a retreating glacier perhaps 10,000 years ago. Michael began using the grapes more than a decade ago, when he was at Township 7 and negotiated a long-term contract with grower Joe Cerqueira. Michael then took over the contract for Bartier Bros. Subsequently, he and Don bought the 6-hectare (15-acre) property.

Michael believes the vineyard's mineral content makes it singular. "All our rocks are crusted white [with calcium] and the small feeder roots from the vines are 'hugging' those rocks," Michael says. "Every vintage, the wines are fresh, fruity, and minerally . . . That limestone ends up in every glass of our wine." The terroir is further accentuated by fermenting many of the wines with the wild yeasts found in the vineyard.

The name of the wine was inspired by a legendary triumph in hockey by a team from the brothers' hometown. "In 1954, Canada's tradition of sending their top amateur hockey team to face national teams at the World Hockey Championships was severely tested," Michael recounts. Canada's representatives, the East York Lyndhursts, suffered a devastating, embarrassing 7–2 loss to the Russian team. In 1955, Canada's team would need to beat Russia to bring the title back and restore Canada's hockey pride; the Penticton Vees were that team. "In 1955, Penticton was a small town of just over 12,000 people—a town of orchard farmers and ranchers. The odds were definitely against the Vees; not even the Canadian hockey executives and media thought they would win. A team made up of homegrown boys with a few ex-pros, the Vees played a rough style of hockey that completely dominated the tournament. Appropriately, the gold medal game had the Vees playing the rival Russian team, which the Vees defeated 5–0."

2013 ($30)

Merlot 45%, Cabernet Franc 35%, Syrah 20%. Alcohol 14.1%. Cerqueira Vineyard. Production 187 cases.

WINERY TASTING NOTES "Dark chocolate and blackberries dominate the nose and palate. Present but soft tannins are followed by a long, smoky, cordite finish. This is a big wine yet it still presents with incredible elegance." Drink by 2023.

2012

Merlot 71%, Cabernet Franc 29%. Alcohol 14%. Cerqueira Vineyard. Production 174 cases.

WINERY TASTING NOTES "Combining the weight and dark fruit of Merlot with the bright fruit and vibrant tannins of Cabernet Franc, this wine is defined by its elegance and balance. Minerality in the forms of wet stone and slate, and chalky aromas persist through its finish and make it refreshing and complex." Drink by 2022.

2011

Merlot 90%, Cabernet Franc 10%. Alcohol 14.5%. Cerqueira Vineyard. Production 345 cases.

WINERY TASTING NOTES "Elegant, bright and complex. Medium to full-bodied with red berry fruit characters, slightly gripping tannins, and just enough acidity to keep the wine refreshing." Drink by 2021.

2010

Merlot 40%, Cabernet Franc 30%, Syrah 30%. Alcohol 13.9%. Production 241 cases.

WINERY TASTING NOTES "Red and black fruits are front and centre with vanillin and stoney characters in the background. The wine is uncompromisingly fresh—very Okanagan. The tannic structure is definitely there, with very fine-grained tannins, which are still quite approachable even in the wine's youth." Drink by 2020.

2009

Merlot 41%, Cabernet Franc 22%, Syrah 19%, Cabernet Sauvignon 18%. Alcohol 13.5%. Production 50 cases.

Tasting notes unavailable.

Black Hills Estate Winery

NOTA BENE

Nota bene suggests that a person should "take notice." That is exactly what happened with the very first vintage of Nota Bene in 1999. The acclaim from critics and consumers gave it a cult status that the wine has enjoyed ever since.

The founders of Black Hills were two couples who left city jobs in 1996 to plant 36,000 vines, mostly Bordeaux red varieties, in a vineyard on Black Sage Road. Senka Tennant, one of the quartet, was tasked with making the wine. She made the first three vintages of Nota Bene with advice from Rusty Figgins, a Washington state winemaker who had made numerous Bordeaux-style blends at prestigious Leonetti Cellars.

There was a jarring disconnect between Nota Bene's image and the original winery. The production facility was a homely Quonset hut more appropriate for tractor storage than winemaking. The tasting room, when open, was a plank across two upended barrels. However, the success of Nota Bene enabled the partners to build a new and well-equipped winery in 2006.

To allow one of the founding couples to retire, Black Hills was sold in late 2007 to a group of investors called Vinequest Wine Partners Limited Partnership. Many of the investors were Nota Bene collectors who now had an even more compelling reason to buy the wine. Senka Tennant's final Nota Bene was the 2008 vintage, and she has been succeeded in the cellar by Graham Pierce.

Vinequest has since expanded Black Hills with the purchase of a neighbouring vineyard in 2011 on which, in the following year, a $1 million wine shop was built. The winery at last had a tasting room commensurate with Nota Bene's prestige.

Black Hills has the ability to produce more than 5,500 cases from its two vineyards. The volume of Nota Bene, however, is capped at 3,500 to 4,000 cases. The wine's quality is consistent; it is always made with three estate-grown Bordeaux varieties. It was aged in oak for a year until the 2014 vintage, when the winery extended barrel-aging to 16 months. The current oak regime is 80% French, 20% American; one-third of the barrels are new, one-third are a year old, and the remaining third are two years old. The red wines remaining after each Nota Bene blend is assembled go into a solid second label called Cellar Hand.

2014 ($52.09)

Cabernet Sauvignon 52%, Merlot 33%, Cabernet Franc 15%. Alcohol 14.9%. Aged 16 months in barrels. Production 3,300 cases.

WINERY TASTING NOTES "This new release of Nota Bene shows its tantalizing signature of raspberries, plum, and fruit leather complemented by dusty, mushroom, and earthy components. Rich velvety-smooth tannins coat the palate resulting in a well-balanced, elegant, and delicate lingering finish of raspberries and spice." Drink by 2024.

2013

Cabernet Sauvignon 49%, Merlot 40%, Cabernet Franc 11%. Alcohol 13.7%. Production 3,200 cases.

WINERY TASTING NOTES "Its tantalizing signature of sweet, ripe cherry complemented by its dusty earth undertones is salivating. Rich, smooth tannins coat the palate resulting in a juicy mouth feel with an alluring gilt of violets, flowery undertones, and a lingering finish reminiscent of a sweet cigar box." Drink by 2023.

2012

Merlot 57%, Cabernet Sauvignon 35%, Cabernet Franc 8%. Alcohol 14.5%. Production 3,800 cases.

AUTHOR'S TASTING NOTES "The wine has sage and herbal notes on the aroma and the finish. The fruit flavours include black cherry, plum, coffee, and chocolate. The texture is rich and ripe, with long tannins." Drink by 2022.

2011

Cabernet Sauvignon 50%, Merlot 40%, Cabernet Franc 10%. Alcohol 14%. Production 3,080 cases.

WINERY TASTING NOTES "This complex and delicious blend comes charging out of the glass with a bouquet of blackberry, cherry, plum, and chocolate. The palate delivers rich dark fruits with a hint of sage brush and notes of fine cocoa tannins." Drink by 2020.

2010

Cabernet Sauvignon 57%, Merlot 32%, Cabernet Franc 11%. Alcohol 14%. Production 3,115 cases.

AUTHOR'S TASTING NOTES "The wine begins with aromas of raspberries and pepper and tastes of cola, coffee, and vibrant red berry notes. It has the classic cigar box notes on the finish that signal the Bordeaux heritage of this wine." Drink by 2020.

2009

Cabernet Sauvignon 46%, Merlot 38%, Cabernet Franc 16%. Alcohol 14.1%. Production 3,265 cases.

AUTHOR'S TASTING NOTES "The wine has dramatic aromas of vanilla and cassis, followed by flavours of blackcurrant, coffee, mocha, and cedar. There is also vanilla, eucalyptus, and dark fruits on the nose, with flavours of plum, black cherry, and chocolate." Drink by 2020.

2008

Cabernet Sauvignon 48%, Merlot 41%, Cabernet Franc 11%. Alcohol 14.2%. Production 4,350 cases.

AUTHOR'S TASTING NOTES "This begins with appealing aromas of red fruit, vanilla, and mocha. It is rich and ripe on the palate with flavours of plums, black cherries, and vanilla. On the finish, there are hints of chocolate, red berries, and spice." Drink by 2018.

2007

Cabernet Sauvignon 46%, Merlot 39%, Cabernet Franc 15%. Alcohol 14.7%. Production 3,900 cases.

AUTHOR'S TASTING NOTES "The firm structure and power of this vintage marks it as a good candidate for further cellaring. However, it is appealing with spice and cassis aromas and with earthy plum flavours." Drink now.

2006

Cabernet Sauvignon 47%, Merlot 37%, Cabernet Franc 16%. Alcohol 14.7%. Production 3,600 cases.

WINERY TASTING NOTES The wine is "appealing for its layers of dark fruit with a hint of spice, olives, and cedar on the nose; full-bodied and balanced with silky, velvety tannins and a great, lengthy, rich finish." This wine is a milestone for Black Hills, which had replaced its challenging Quonset hut winery with a new winery equipped with all the tools needed for modern winemaking. Drink now.

2005

Cabernet Sauvignon 43%, Merlot 37%, Cabernet Franc 20%. Alcohol 14.6%. Production 2,900 cases.

AUTHOR'S TASTING NOTES "This begins with a seductive aroma of vanilla and cassis. The wine delivers a big spoonful of sweet fruit to the palate (lingonberry, cherry, raspberry) with long silky tannins and with a persistent finish." Drink now.

2004

Cabernet Sauvignon 46%, Merlot 36%, Cabernet Franc 18%. Alcohol 14.6%. Production 2,800 cases.

AUTHOR'S TASTING NOTES "The wine begins with spicy berry aromas, leading to flavours of blackcurrant, plum, and cigar box." Drink now.

2003

Cabernet Sauvignon 46%, Merlot 34%, Cabernet Franc 20%. Alcohol 14.5%. Production 2,400 cases.

AUTHOR'S TASTING NOTES "This was a hot Okanagan vintage and the atmosphere was saturated with smoke from the forest fires. There is just a touch of smoke on the aroma and in the flavour of this wine, along with notes of plum, black cherry, and olives." Drink now.

2002

Cabernet Sauvignon 48%, Merlot 37%, Cabernet Franc 15%. Alcohol 14.5%. Production 2,200 cases.

AUTHOR'S TASTING NOTES "This is a satisfying wine, beginning with dark hue and a texture that is big and bold. On the palate, the ripe plum flavours are juicy and generous. The wine is at its peak. I reviewed this wine when it was released and wrote that it was the best Nota Bene to date." Drink now.

2001

Cabernet Sauvignon 46%, Merlot 35%, Cabernet Franc 19%. Alcohol 14%. Production 2,100 cases.

AUTHOR'S TASTING NOTES "The aroma is smoky and spicy but the mid-palate is lean and dried out. It reminded me very much of an old Chianti, with its short, dusty finish." Mature.

2000

Cabernet Sauvignon 52%, Cabernet Franc 25%, Merlot 23%. Alcohol 14%. Production 1,800 cases.

AUTHOR'S TASTING NOTES "The wine has delicate truffle aromas, with flavours of plum, cassis, and cigar box. The texture is polished and elegant." Mature.

1999

Merlot 64%, Cabernet Sauvignon 26%, Cabernet Franc 10%. Alcohol 13%. Production 1,600 cases.

AUTHOR'S TASTING NOTES "This was tasted during vertical tastings in 2013, 2015, and 2016. The fruit aromas and flavours had matured, developing earthy notes and ephemeral fruit flavours typical of a well-aged wine. The complexity recalled an aged Italian red from Tuscany. While there was bottle variation, the wine in 2016 was deliciously sweet up front with a spicy berry note on the finish. It was beyond its peak, but still showed elegance." Fully mature.

Black Sage Vineyard
CABERNET SAUVIGNON

This is the storied vineyard where the South Okanagan's Bordeaux renaissance began in 1993. Harry McWatters, the founder in 1989 of Sumac Ridge Estate Winery, rejected the conventional wisdom that Bordeaux varietals could not survive Okanagan winters. In 1992, he and his partners bought a 46.5-hectare (115-acre) site on the Black Sage Bench that had previously grown French hybrid varieties. Harry planted primarily Bordeaux vines the following year. By their third leaf, the vines were producing award-winning wines and other producers were hurrying to plant Bordeaux and other vinifera vines on the rest of the bench.

Ownership of Black Sage Vineyard rested half with Harry and half with Sumac Ridge Estate Winery. After Constellation Brands acquired Sumac Ridge in 2007, it kept half of the vineyard along with the name. (Harry's half was renamed Sundial Vineyard and was sold in 2016 to Chinese investors now developing a winery of their own.) In 2005, Constellation planted the nearby Black Sage Two Vineyard entirely with red varieties. In 2013, Black Sage Vineyard, formerly a Sumac Ridge brand, was elevated into a brand of its own, showcasing the exceptional grapes. Collectors should also consider the Merlot and the Cabernet Franc from this producer.

The winemaker with the opportunity to work with these grapes is Ontario-born Jason James. He first did an honours degree in biology at the University of Guelph. In 2001, he got a certificate in oenology and viticulture at Brock University, did a crush in New Zealand in 2002, and worked as a cellar hand and then winemaker at Thomas & Vaughan Estate Winery in Ontario. He moved to Sumac Ridge in 2005 because he "was keen to experience winemaking in British Columbia."

 Black Sage Vineyard, formerly a Sumac Ridge brand, was elevated into a brand of its own, showcasing the exceptional grapes.

2014 ($25)

Alcohol 14.09%. Aged 14 months in French (65%) and American (35%) barrels (20% new).

WINERY TASTING NOTES "This 100% Cabernet Sauvignon has a bouquet of blackberry, blackcurrant, vanilla notes, and a hint of graphite. Flavours of dark berries, soft toasted oak, and some vanilla on the palate, with semi-soft tannins and a long, lingering finish." Drink by 2024.

2013

Alcohol 13.5%. Aged 12 months in French and American oak (20% new).

WINERY TASTING NOTES "This Cabernet Sauvignon exhibits ripe raspberry and blackberry with hints of vanilla on the nose. The dark fruit continues on the palate with blackberry, some warm spice, and natural oak sweetness. The tannins are plentiful but they are soft and mouth-coating." Drink by 2023.

2012

Alcohol 13.4%. Aged 12 months in French and American oak.

WINERY TASTING NOTES "[The] Cabernet Sauvignon displays black cherry and currant flavours, enhanced by hints of eucalyptus and cedar on the finish. The vines for this wine dig deep in the parched Canadian landscape to produce a robust red wine brimming with flavour and character." Drink by 2022.

2011

Alcohol 13%. Aged 12 months in French and American oak.

WINERY TASTING NOTES "The 2011 Black Sage Vineyard Cabernet Sauvignon displays black cherry and currant flavours, enhanced by hints of eucalyptus and cedar on the finish." Drink by 2021.

2010

Alcohol 13.75%. Aged 12 months in French and American oak.

WINERY TASTING NOTES "The 2010 Black Sage Vineyard Cabernet Sauvignon displays black cherry and currant flavours, enhanced by hints of eucalyptus and cedar on the finish." Drink by 2020.

Black Widow Winery

HOURGLASS

Dick Lancaster, who operates Black Widow with his wife, Shona Lancaster, began making wine at home when he was 18. Born in Montreal in 1953, he acquired an interest in wine from his father, Graham, who was a manager of food services for Air Canada. Dick became an award-winning amateur winemaker. To this day, he shows many of those medals in a display frame in the Black Widow wine shop.

Dick's favourite varietals for home winemaking were Merlot and Cabernet Sauvignon, so it is no surprise that he planted those varieties in this Naramata Bench vineyard. The vineyard was already growing 1.6 hectares (4 acres) of white varieties when he and Shona bought it in 2000. They almost doubled the vineyard by adding Merlot and a small block of Cabernet Sauvignon.

"We dreamed of having a winery one day, but when we bought the property there was no firm plan for a winery," Dick says. "It was just that we wanted someplace in the Okanagan to vacation, and if I could get some grapes from it for my amateur winemaking, that would be great." He made the first commercial wines for Black Widow in 2005 in a neighbour's winery and built the Black Widow winery in 2006.

Clearly confident in his abilities, Dick has had Hourglass, his icon wine, in the portfolio from the beginning. It is always a Merlot/Cabernet Sauvignon blend made exclusively from estate-grown grapes. The only exception was in 2012, when he was offered a small lot of premium Cabernet Franc grapes, enough to add five percent to the Hourglass blend. Dick concluded that the impact on the flavour was not significant, and he dropped that varietal from subsequent vintages. The consistent style of Hourglass—ripe, spicy, and elegant—reflects the fact that the grapes come from the same terroir each year. While the winery generally recommends drinking the wine within 10 years, they will certainly age beyond that.

We wanted someplace in the Okanagan to vacation, and if I could get some grapes from it for my amateur winemaking, that would be great.

2014 ($42)

Merlot 70%, Cabernet Sauvignon 30%. Alcohol 14.6%. Aged 21 months in French oak (mostly new). Unfiltered. Production 190 cases.

WINERY TASTING NOTES "An elegant Bordeaux-style blend with aging potential up to 8 years from vintage." Drink by 2024.

2013

Merlot 70%, Cabernet Sauvignon 30%. Alcohol 13.8%. Aged 21 months in French oak. Production 175 cases, 30 magnums, six double magnums.

WINERY TASTING NOTES "Not fined or filtered, the wine is concentrated with dark cherry colour. Aromas of chocolate and berries. Rich cherry, toasty oak, plum, and a touch of licorice on the palate with a lingering finish augmented by fine tannins." Drink by 2023.

2012

Merlot 82%, Cabernet Sauvignon 13%, Cabernet Franc 5%. Alcohol 14.4%. Aged 21 months in French oak (mostly new). Production 200 cases.

AUTHOR'S TASTING NOTES "Made from a strong Okanagan vintage, this wine shows abundant red berry aromas and flavours in its youth, built around a structure of ripe tannins. There is a note of spice on the finish." Drink by 2022.

2011

Merlot 77%, Cabernet Sauvignon 23%. Alcohol 13%. Production 92 cases, six magnums, six double magnums.

AUTHOR'S TASTING NOTES "The second cool vintage in a row resulted in the grapes achieving ripeness at lower sugar levels, as the alcohol level indicates. The wine is bright and vibrant, with aromas of blackberry and blackcurrant and flavours of blackcurrant and vanilla. The finish is spicy—a hallmark of the Hourglass wines that collectors have remarked on." Drink by 2020.

2010

Merlot 80%, Cabernet Sauvignon 20%. Alcohol 14.5%. Production 87 cases, 24 magnums, six double magnums.

AUTHOR'S TASTING NOTES "The cool 2010 vintage gives this wine bright acidity and firm tannins that will prolong its life in the cellar. The wine begins with rich cassis aromas. On the palate, there are bright berry flavours including black and red currant." Drink by 2020.

2009

Merlot 62%, Cabernet Sauvignon 38%. Alcohol 15.2%. Production 94 cases, six double magnums.

AUTHOR'S TASTING NOTES "One of the best Hourglass wines in the decade. An early October frost required careful selection of grapes, reducing the production. The result is still a gloriously ripe and densely concentrated wine with aromas and flavours of blackcurrant and black cherry. The spice and cedar notes on the finish give the wine a Bordelaise personality." Drink by 2020.

2008

Merlot 95%, Cabernet Sauvignon 5%. Alcohol 14.9%. Production 225 cases.

AUTHOR'S TASTING NOTES "This is a wine with a generous texture. It begins with a medley of aromas, including cassis, black cherry, blueberry, blackberry, and vanilla and then cascades those onto its ripe, juicy palate." Drink by 2019.

2007

Merlot 93%, Cabernet Sauvignon 7%. Alcohol 14.5%. Production 350 cases.

AUTHOR'S TASTING NOTES "This wine begins with aromas of blackcurrant and blackberry and delivers those berry flavours to the palate, mingled with mocha and red licorice. The finish lingers." Drink by 2018.

2006

Merlot 85%, Cabernet Sauvignon 15%. Alcohol 14.9%. Production 220 cases.

AUTHOR'S TASTING NOTES "Tasted in 2014, this had achieved an impressive peak, with aromas and flavours of cassis, black cherry, and vanilla. Bottle age has polished the tannins and the concentrated texture." Drink now.

Blasted Church Vineyards

NOTHING SACRED

Whimsical wine labels have perhaps had an unintended consequence for Blasted Church Vineyards: collectors tend to view these as popular wines but not as collectible wines. And that's a mistake.

This winery opened in 2000 under the name of its founder, Dan Prpich. When Chris and Evelyn Campbell bought it in 2002, they renamed the winery (with the help of consultant Bernie Hadley-Beauregard) Blasted Church Vineyards. The inspiration was a church that was moved from a deserted mining camp to nearby Okanagan Falls in 1929—the movers set off a small dynamite blast to loosen the nails inside the building so that it could be taken apart before the relocation.

Hadley-Beauregard embellished both the history and the clerical allusions in naming a number of the wines. Hatfield's Fuse, the winery's most popular white blend, is named for the moving crew's foreman. Big Bang Theory, a red blend, recalls the dynamite explosion. He was most creative when Blasted Church began making reserve-quality wines. This tier, called the Revered Series, includes Bible Thumper, Cross to Bear, Holy Moly, OMG, Swear to God, and Amen (for a port-style wine). That has had an unintended result: even a winery principal once told me that Blasted Church had no icon wine.

In fact, it does: a Meritage blend called Nothing Sacred, which was launched in the excellent 2007 vintage. The wine is anchored on Merlot and Cabernet Sauvignon. Grapes are drawn from the winery's own vineyard as well as other vineyards in the South Okanagan. Each variety is fermented separately and aged in oak for up to two years. The blend is put together just before bottling, and the wine is bottle-aged another two years before release. One is tempted to call this wine Nothing Spared.

Given the limited quantities of Nothing Sacred—which isn't made every year—Blasted Church Merlot is also collectible and is more accessible, with 714 cases produced in 2012. Nothing is spared here either to make an excellent wine: the 2012 is a blend of 87% Merlot, 10% Malbec, and 1.5% each of Cabernet Sauvignon and Syrah. The wine is aged for 20 months in French and American oak before release. The price is $26.50.

The inspiration [for the vineyard's name] was a church that was moved from a deserted mining camp to nearby Okanagan Falls in 1929.

2014 ($45)

Merlot 40%, Cabernet Sauvignon 20%, Petit Verdot 20%, Malbec 20%. Alcohol 13.5%. Aged 20 months in new oak (75% French, 25% Hungarian). Production 100 cases.

AUTHOR'S TASTING NOTES "This is a full-bodied wine with aromas and flavours of blackcurrant, blackberry, and spicy fruit cake." Drink by 2024.

2011

Merlot 53%, Petit Verdot 24%, Malbec 23%. Alcohol 12.5%. Production 200 cases.

WINERY TASTING NOTES Aromas of "berry, cassis, blackberry, oak, vanilla, and tobacco along with coffee. Palate: Full-bodied and velvety with a long finish. Silky tannins, with great concentration. Supple and mouth-coating." Drink by 2021.

2010

Merlot 46%, Cabernet Sauvignon 25%, Petit Verdot 20%, Malbec 9%. Alcohol 13.7%. Production 200 cases.

AUTHOR'S TASTING NOTES "The wine begins with rich aromas of cassis, vanilla, and mocha. On the palate there are flavours of plum, black cherry, red currants, and mocha, with notes of cedar and tobacco on the finish. The freshness of the wine when tasted in 2016 speaks to the benefit of its screw cap closure." Drink by 2020.

2009

Cabernet Sauvignon 44%, Petit Verdot 22%, Cabernet Franc 22%, Merlot 12%. Alcohol 14%. Production 229 cases.

WINERY TASTING NOTES "Berry, cassis, oak. Palate: Full-bodied, rich with a long finish."

2008

Merlot 50%, Cabernet Sauvignon 40%, Malbec 5%, Petit Verdot 5%. Alcohol 14.5%. Production 195 cases.

WINERY TASTING NOTES "Bouquet: Berry, cassis, cedar. Palate: Earthy flavours are rich, delicious, and appealing."

2007

Merlot 33.5%, Cabernet Sauvignon 33.5%, Malbec 22%, Cabernet Franc 11%. Alcohol 14%. Aged in new French oak barrels. Production 216 cases.

WINERY TASTING NOTES "Bouquet: Soft, sweet, toasty vanilla, ripe black fruit, spicy tobacco, hints of mint, cloves, eucalyptus, and leather. Palate: Black cherry, cedar, cranberry, vibrant blackberry framed by nicely integrated oak and soft tannins."

Blue Mountain Vineyard and Cellars

THE RESERVES

The style and consistency of Blue Mountain's estate-grown wine is such that everything in the portfolio has the cellar longevity that collectors look for. It begins in the 32-hectare vineyard that the Mavety family has farmed for 45 years. "The approach that we take is to treat all the vineyard blocks like a grand cru vineyard," winemaker Matt Mavety says. "We spend all our time working hard in the vineyards, and we spend time in the cellar to look after all of the wines. Every grape that is brought into here gets handled such as it could be reserve wine."

Ian and Jane Mavety, Matt's parents, planted this picturesque Okanagan Falls vineyard in 1971, initially with the hybrid varieties then in demand for winemaking. They began replanting with vinifera in 1985, focusing on the varieties of Burgundy and Alsace, the French terroirs they believed to be most similar to their vineyard. The winery opened in 1992 with Pinot Blanc, Pinot Gris, and Pinot Noir from the 1991 vintage, followed shortly by the 1991 Blue Mountain Brut and a 1993 Chardonnay.

The winery soon began making its eminently collectible reserves, beginning with a 1992 Vintage Reserve sparkling wine (subsequently phased out). Striped labels were designed to differentiate the reserve wines from the regular wines, released with cream-coloured labels. The winery released its first reserve table wines in 1996—a 1994 Pinot Noir, and a Chardonnay and Pinot Gris from the 1995 vintage.

Blue Mountain gained international recognition when it was the first Canadian winery invited to the prestigious International Pinot Noir Celebration in Oregon, to pour its 1994 Pinot Noir Reserve.

Since then, Blue Mountain has produced reserve table wines virtually every vintage. The typical volume is 600 to 800 cases of Pinot Noir and about 350 cases of Chardonnay. The reserve sparkling wine was replaced in the 2005 vintage with the R.D.—or "recently disgorged"—which is on the lees for six or seven years before being disgorged. Volumes range from 100 to 200 cases.

No Reserve Chardonnay was made in 2009 (for a 2010 release), a cool vintage, when isolating the reserve fraction would have caused an unacceptable drop in the quality of the cream label Chardonnay. "If it turns out that we cannot take away any of the components to make a reserve without compromising what's left, we don't make a reserve," says Matt Mavety, who became involved in making the wine after completing winemaking studies at Lincoln University in New Zealand in 1997.

The grapes from each vineyard block at Blue Mountain are fermented and aged separately. About nine months after the harvest, the lots are assessed to determine which wines will be blended as reserves and which are destined for the cream label. "We are looking for a little bit more structure, a little bit more body," Matt says about the reserve level wines. "At the time of blending, it may not necessarily be as powerful, but in time it'll get there. It really is a fine-tuning exercise."

Vintage variation aside, the wines are consistent in style and quality. This reflects that Blue Mountain only uses estate-grown grapes. From the very first vintage until 2013, when he died, Blue Mountain employed the same winemaking consultant from California, French-trained Raphael Brisbois. Matt has been the hands-on winemaker in the Blue Mountain cellar for nearly two decades.

The consistency extends to the winery's choice of oak barrels, which have come almost exclusively from a family-owned cooperage in France, Tonnellerie de Mercurey. "In 1997, I had three or four different cooperages in here," Matt recalls. "It was decision-making time; do we carry on with this approach? The reality is we were happy with the Mercurey barrels, so we continue to use them."

Reserve Pinot Noir 2013

($39.90)

Clones 113, 114, 115, 667, 777. Alcohol 13.5%. Fermented 100% with indigenous yeast. Aged 10 months in French oak.

AUTHOR'S TASTING NOTES "The wine begins with appealing aromas of cherry mingled with toasty oak; these are echoed on the complex palate and on the spicy finish. The texture is elegantly silky." Drink by 2022.

Reserve Pinot Noir 2012

Clones 113, 114, 115, 667, 777. Alcohol 13.5%. Fermented 100% with indigenous yeast. Aged 10 months in French oak.

AUTHOR'S TASTING NOTES "Dark ruby in colour, the wine begins with aromas of lightly toasted oak mingled with red fruit. On the palate, there are rich flavours of strawberry and plum supported by toasty oak. The texture is silky and the finish is spicy. The wine is seductive and delicious." Drink by 2021.

Reserve Pinot Noir 2011

Clones 113, 114, 115, 667. Alcohol 13.5%. Fermented 100% with indigenous yeast. Aged 10 months in French oak.

WINERY TASTING NOTES The wine "is a rich, ruby-coloured wine with complex layers of red fruit, spice, and integrated oak." Drink by 2020.

Reserve Pinot Noir 2009

Clones 113, 114, 115, 667. Fermented 50% with indigenous yeast. Aged 10 months in French oak.

AUTHOR'S TASTING NOTES "Subtle and elegant, this wine begins with aromas of spice and strawberries, leading to flavours of cherry with a touch of raspberry and mocha. The wine has developed the classic silky texture of the variety." Drink by 2018.

Reserve Pinot Noir 2008

AUTHOR'S TASTING NOTES "This wine begins with an alluring aroma of strawberries and cherries. Dark in colour, it has flavours of raspberries and strawberries. The elegant texture includes some firm tannins, allowing this wine to age into a great Burgundy." Drink by 2018.

Reserve Chardonnay 2013 ($29.90)

Alcohol 13.5%. Fermented 50% in French oak and aged 10 months in barrel; fermented 50% and aged about 11 months in stainless steel.

WINERY TASTING NOTES The wine is "complex and full-bodied, displaying delicate citrus blossom and fruit flavours, with sweet lemony spice and *sur lie* character." Drink by 2020.

Reserve Chardonnay 2012

Alcohol 13.5%. Fermented 50% in French oak, 50% in stainless steel.

AUTHOR'S TASTING NOTES "The wine begins with aromas of citrus mingled with lightly toasted oak and notes of lees. Half of this wine was fermented and aged in French oak. The texture is full, almost fleshy, with flavours of lemon, tangerine, and peach that linger on a lightly spicy finish." Drink by 2019.

Reserve Chardonnay 2011

Alcohol 13.5%. Fermented 50% in French oak, 50% in stainless steel.

WINERY TASTING NOTES "The 2011 Reserve Chardonnay is complex and full-bodied, displaying delicate citrus blossom and fruit flavours, with sweet lemony spice and *sur lie* character." Drink by 2018.

Reserve Chardonnay 2009

Alcohol 13.5%. Fifty-five percent barrel fermented and aged 8 months in French oak; 45% fermented in stainless steel.

AUTHOR'S TASTING NOTES "This wine has developed a creamy elegance with aromas and flavours of tangerine and toast." Drink now.

Reserve Brut 2008 R.D. ($40)

Chardonnay 50%, Pinot Noir 50%. Alcohol 12.5%. Six and a half years on the lees.

WINERY TASTING NOTES "The Reserve Brut has a fine mousse, with a fresh, complex aroma of red fruit/citrus and a toasty character on the nose and across the palate with a long, rich strawberry finish." Drink now.

Reserve Brut 2007 R.D.

Chardonnay 50%, Pinot Noir 50%. Alcohol 12.5%. Seven years aging on lees.

WINERY TASTING NOTES "The Reserve Brut has a fine mousse, with a fresh, complex aroma of red fruit and citrus. [There is a] toasty character on the nose and across the palate with a long, rich strawberry finish." Drink now.

Reserve Brut 2006 R.D.

Chardonnay 70%, Pinot Noir 30%. Seven years *en tirage*.

AUTHOR'S TASTING NOTES "It is almost creamy on the palate with toasty notes on the nose. The flavours include appealing hints of strawberry and citrus. The wine, which finishes dry, is exceptional in its elegance." Drink now.

Reserve Brut 2005 R.D.

Pinot Noir 60%, Chardonnay 35%, Pinot Gris 5%. Alcohol 12%. Seven years *en tirage*.

WINERY TASTING NOTES "The Reserve Brut has a fine mousse, with a fresh, complex aroma of red fruit; strawberry and a toasty character on the nose and across the palate with a long, rich strawberry finish." Drink now.

Blanc de Blancs 2009 R.D. ($40)

Chardonnay 100%. Alcohol 12.5%. Five and a half years *en tirage*.

WINERY TASTING NOTES "The Blanc de Blancs 2009 has a fine mousse, with lemon, nutty, and toasty character on the nose and across the palate." Drink now.

Blanc de Blancs 2008 R.D.

Chardonnay 100%. Alcohol 12.5%. Six years *en tirage*.

WINERY TASTING NOTES "The Blanc de Blancs 2008 has a fine mousse, with lemon, nutty, and toasty character on the nose and across the palate." Drink now.

Blanc de Blancs 2007 R.D.

Chardonnay 100%. Six years *en tirage*.

AUTHOR'S TASTING NOTES "The prolonged time on the lees has given this wine toasty, nutty aromas and flavours, and very fine bubbles. The finish is crisply clean and dry." Drink now.

Blanc de Blancs 2006 R.D.

Chardonnay 100%. Alcohol 12%. Six years *en tirage*.

WINERY TASTING NOTES "The Blanc de Blancs has a fine mousse, with lemon, nutty, and toasty characters on the nose and across the palate." Drink now.

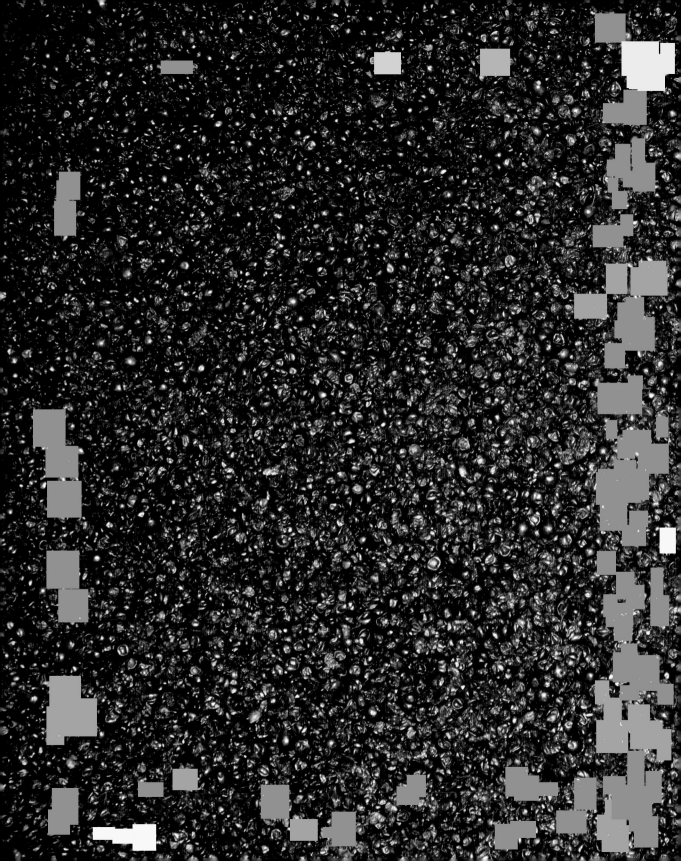

Bonamici Cellars

BELVIAGGIO

Philip Soo and Mario Rodi are old friends—hence the winery's name—with a shared passion for wine. Mario, who was born in 1957 in northern Ontario, was just 12 when he started helping his immigrant Italian father crush grapes for the family's wine. Philip was born in Vancouver in 1969, the son of immigrants from Hong Kong with negligible wine culture. "We had family celebrations, but they never encouraged kids to drink," Philip remembers. "I was 12 or 13 when my first sip of alcohol, Baby Duck, was at a Christmas party."

It seems that was enough to get Philip interested. After doing degrees in microbiology and food engineering, he was offered jobs at a pharmaceutical firm and a company that produced gourmet salads, but, having been a good amateur beer maker while in college, he took a job with a manufacturer of wine kits "because it was in line with my hobby." Subsequently, Andrew Peller Limited bought the wine kit company and soon promoted Philip to the Peller winery in Port Moody in 2000. When the winery closed five years later, he moved to the Okanagan to become a consulting winemaker.

Mario spent about 20 years in food and soft-drink sales before joining Peller in 1995 as general manager of Wine Experts, as the kit company was called. He and Philip, who reported to him, became close friends. Mario left Peller in 2009. Wanting to stay in the wine business, he proposed Bonamici to Philip. "He is a great winemaker," Mario says. "I focused on the sales and marketing for my entire career. I thought this might be an opportunity for us to get together and build something great."

Taking advantage of a good vintage in 2012, they bought grapes from Philip's favourite growers and rented space in an existing winery to make about 1,000 cases of wine, including 199 cases of Belviaggio. Still getting established in the market, they skipped Belviaggio in 2013 but did make 180 cases in 2014. In this blend, Malbec replaced Merlot.

"The template for creating Belviaggio is Tuscan red wine," Philip says. "With Bonamici, I am more leaning toward Italian wines. Instead of a big, bold, in-your-face wine, I am more for finesse and varietal fruit character. I am looking for a lot more sophistication in the wine." Future vintages of Belviaggio may include Petit Verdot or Sangiovese if those varieties become available. Philip wants to give the blend a distinctive character to differentiate it from standard Meritage blends.

In the spring of 2017, Bonamici established a tasting room and began planting a vineyard beside Oliver Ranch Road, not far from one of Philip's leading clients, Noble Ridge Vineyards.

2012 ($34.90)

Cabernet Franc 60%, Syrah 30%, Merlot 10%. Alcohol 14.7%. Aged 15 months in French oak. Production 199 cases.

WINERY TASTING NOTES The wine is "rich with aromas of blackcurrant, black pepper, and raspberry, with subtle notes of anise, vanilla and cocoa; bursting with flavours on the palate, with notes of tobacco, toffee, and blueberries with silky-smooth tannins." Drink by 2020.

Burrowing Owl Estate Winery
MERITAGE

Since the release of its first wines from the 1997 vintage, Burrowing Owl has enjoyed a cult following. All of the winery's red wines are collected, including Cabernet Sauvignon, Cabernet Franc, Merlot, Syrah, and a field blend (Cabernet Sauvignon and Syrah) called Athene. However, the Meritage has first place in many cellars. The fact that it is a blend guarantees remarkable consistency vintage to vintage.

The Burrowing Owl red wines are among the biggest in the South Okanagan because they are grown in a sunbathed vineyard. Winery founder Jim Wyse, a successful real-estate developer, began acquiring this Black Sage Bench acreage in 1993. The hybrid varieties that had flourished there previously had been pulled out in 1988, leaving just blocks of mature Pinot Blanc. Under Jim's direction, the vineyard was revived primarily with classic vinifera vines. When the winery was being developed, Burrowing Owl retained Bill Dyer, a consulting winemaker from California. He crafted the winery's house style of big, ripe reds, taking advantage of the terroir's ability to ripen flavour-packed grapes.

The Meritage program began in 2000 with a production of just 248 cases. "The wine was given wonderful reviews," Jim wrote later, "so that the 2001 vintage was increased to 500 cases." Production since then has ranged from about 1,000 to 1,500 cases a year.

The production protocol was established under Bill Dyer's hand. In a letter in 2005 announcing new releases, Jim explained: "After fermentation, all the Meritage components are barrel-aged separately for approximately one year, at which time the winemaker decides on the blend proportions. Individual barrels are then earmarked to be used in the mix based on their flavour and smell. After blending, the wine is returned to barrels for another full year of aging and development." Alain Sutre, the Bordeaux consultant now working with Burrowing Owl, has changed the protocol slightly but the basic approach has been maintained.

Earlier vintages were blends of Cabernet Sauvignon, Merlot, and Cabernet Franc. Minor, but still important, percentages of Malbec and Petit Verdot have usually been included since 2004. Tasting notes since 2008 have been written for the winery by Rhys Pender, Master of Wine.

2013 ($45)

Merlot 39%, Cabernet Sauvignon 28%, Cabernet Franc 20%, Petit Verdot 10%, Malbec 3%. Alcohol 14.5%. Aged separately 18 months in French oak (76%), Hungarian oak (12%), American oak (10%), and Russian oak (2%). Thirty percent of the barrels were new.

WINERY TASTING NOTES The wine "opens on aromas of cassis, red currant, roasted red pepper, chocolate, paprika, and some pretty violet floral notes in the background along with a hint of toasty oak. The palate is firmly structured with a full body and genuine intensity. There is toast, creamy oak, a mixture of red and black cherry, blueberry, black plum, and some complexity added with baking spice and a little marzipan." Drink by 2026.

2012

Cabernet Franc 43%, Merlot 28%, Cabernet Sauvignon 20%, Petit Verdot 9%. Alcohol 14.5%. Aged 18 months in French oak (86%), American oak (10%), and Hungarian and Russian oak (2% each). Twenty-five percent of the barrels were new.

WINERY TASTING NOTES "Vibrant and complex nose with everything from ripe raspberry, cassis, blackberry, and prune plum through to dried sage brush, orange zest, clove, black olive, marzipan, dusty vanillin, oak, and malt. The structure for aging is framed by . . . dark chocolate, black plum, black cherry, spiced berry compote, citrus peel, and a touch of fig, raisin, and leather." Drink by 2025.

2011

Merlot 33%, Cabernet Franc 32%, Cabernet Sauvignon 31%, Malbec 2%, Petit Verdot 2%. Alcohol 14.5%.

WINERY TASTING NOTES ". . . Aromas [of] cassis, vanilla, blackberry, and black plum through roasted nut, smoke, black olive, chocolate ice cream, burlap, dried sage, cocoa, and some sweet blue floral notes. The palate is youthful and structured with plenty of acidity and tannin for long aging and lots of cassis, blueberry, plum raspberry, cedar, cigar box, paprika, and a subtle saffron note." Drink by 2021.

2010

Cabernet Franc 55%, Merlot 25%, Cabernet Sauvignon 15%, Malbec 2.5%, Petit Verdot 2.5%. Alcohol 14.5%.

WINERY TASTING NOTES "The nose is subtle but multifaceted with cassis, mixed red berry, plum, cherry, cocoa, blueberry, burlap, tobacco, and cedar. The palate is refined and stylish with a silky textured body, ripe tannins, and crisp acidity. The intense flavours of plum, cherry, and raspberry along with the tobacco, burlap, and spice linger on a long, graceful finish." Drink now.

2009

Merlot 38%, Cabernet Sauvignon 33%, Cabernet Franc 23%, Malbec 4%, Petit Verdot 2%. Alcohol 14.5%.

WINERY TASTING NOTES "An intense explosion of red and black fruit on the nose leads into layers of complexity in this engaging wine. The ripe blackberry, blueberry compote, raspberry, plum, and black cherry aromas are joined by sweet spices, chocolate, and the alluring earthy scent of an autumn morning. The palate is well crafted, with intense brambly fruit, refreshing acidity, ripe tannins, and well-integrated coffee, cocoa, and oak notes. The finish is long with the savoury roasted sage element of the south Okanagan desert terroir lingering." Drink now.

2008

Merlot 50%, Cabernet Sauvignon 24%, Cabernet Franc 24%, Malbec 1%, Petit Verdot 1%. Alcohol 14.9%. Production 969 cases.

WINERY TASTING NOTES "This wine has a lovely deep, dark, purple core with a vivid, violet rim. On the nose, aromas of cassis, blackcurrants, blackberry, truffles, and complex earth tones are prevalent with a hint of tobacco and clove. The silky, elegant tannins complement the earthy cassis, currants, and truffles on the palate, while hints of chocolate and ripe, red fruits also shine through." Drink by 2020.

2007

Cabernet Franc 36%, Merlot 35%, Cabernet Sauvignon 23%, Malbec 5%, Petit Verdot 1%. Alcohol 14.5%. Aged 22 months in French, Hungarian, and Russian oak (50% new).

WINERY TASTING NOTES "A floral nose with beautiful ripe red fruit, luscious cassis, blackberries, and plums with clean forest aromas along with an allusion of pepper, mint, clove, and tobacco. The palate has rich smooth tannins, an elegant and silky finish with forest fruit and dark chocolate." Drink by 2018.

2006

Merlot 53.8%, Cabernet Franc 27.5%, Cabernet Sauvignon 12.5%, Malbec 3.7%, Petit Verdot 2.5%. Alcohol 14.5%. Aged 22 months in French, American, Hungarian, and Russian oak (two-thirds new).

WINERY TASTING NOTES "This wine displays outstanding complexity with loads of black fruits and cassis, accentuated by aromas of mint, vanilla, cedar, and tobacco. On the palate . . . the abundant silky tannins are supported by opulent primary black fruits and a slight mintiness." Drink now.

2005

Merlot 64%, Cabernet Franc 25%, Cabernet Sauvignon 10%, Malbec 1%, Petit Verdot 1%. Alcohol 14.4%. Production 1,455 cases.

WINERY TASTING NOTES "Aromas of heady, smoky mixtures of violets, cassis, blackberry, plums, vanilla, cloves, and toasty oak. The wine is firm yet subtle, offering big rich flavours." Drink now.

2004

Merlot 65%, Cabernet Franc 20%, Cabernet Sauvignon 13%, Malbec 1%, Petit Verdot 1%. Alcohol 14%. Production 1,500 cases.

WINERY TASTING NOTES "Rich bouquet of blackberry, with hints of almond, mahogany, and beetroot. Smooth, lush berry fruit flavours are infused with chocolate . . ." Mature.

2003

Aged 20 months in Russian oak (new, 1-year-old, and 2-year-old). Alcohol 14%.

WINERY TASTING NOTES "A deep, dark cherry red colour with seductive aromas of blackcurrant, vanilla, and chocolate. The palate dry, full-bodied with high but fine tannins." Mature.

2002

Cabernet Franc 60%, Merlot 30%, Cabernet Sauvignon 10%. Alcohol 14%. Production 1,000 cases.

WINERY TASTING NOTES "A classic full-flavoured Bordeaux-style wine that features rich berry fruit . . . outgoing berry flavours knit with fully integrated oak." Mature.

2001

Cabernet Franc 40%, Merlot 40%, Cabernet Sauvignon 20%. Alcohol 13.5%. Production 497 cases.

WINERY TASTING NOTES "The aromas are earthy and peppery and the bright fruit flavours—cherries, currants, and even cranberries—make this quite a vivacious wine on the palate." Mature.

2000

Cabernet Franc 40%, Merlot 40%, Cabernet Sauvignon 20%. Alcohol 13.5%. Production 248 cases.

Tasting notes unavailable.

Cassini Cellars

THE GODFATHER

Adrian Cassini, who opened this winery in 2009, has a notebook in which he jots down ideas for wine names. When the winery's first icon wine was getting close to bottling, he thumbed through his book and found "Godfather." It was clearly the right name for a wine that makes a statement. "It's big," he says. "I want a full-bodied wine. I want a steel fist in a velvet glove."

The powerful red wines preceding The Godfather include Nobilus, a bold Merlot, and Maximus, now a blend of Cabernet Franc and Merlot. "I am a perfectionist, so I have to go to the next level," Adrian says. "I want to do better, and it is possible to do better." The Godfather is aimed at über-collectors willing to pay for a top wine structured to age at least 10 years under good cellaring conditions.

Born in Romania, Adrian developed his wine knowledge when, as a young immigrant to Canada, he worked in restaurants. Strongly entrepreneurial, he ran a series of successful businesses before he came to the Okanagan in 2006 to buy a lavender farm, which he converted to a vineyard the following year. Subsequently, he built a highly visible winery right on the highway. He honed his winemaking skills under the mentorship of several consultants.

The Godfather is a blend selected from the best barrels of each variety, after 22 to 24 months in barrel. The prolonged barrel-aging (Maximus gets only 14 months) makes the Godfather even bigger. About 10 percent of the volume is lost to evaporation; this is what winemakers call the angel's share.

The four varietals in the 2010 the Godfather all played a role in the blend. "The Cabernet Sauvignon creates the pillar," Adrian says. "The Merlot and the Cabernet Franc are the mid-palate, and Syrah is the glue of the whole blend." He deviated from that in 2011 and came back to it in 2012. Adrian stresses that the wine is not made to a recipe. "I want people to look forward to what I come up with the next year," he says. "It is always going to be good. We are dancing a little bit with the varietals."

He believes that estate-grown Cabernet Franc will eventually anchor the Godfather blend. He has a model in mind: Bordeaux's Château Angélus, whose $200-plus red is built around Cabernet Franc. That's also one of the best varieties in the Cassini vineyard. "My goal is to do all the wines in Cassini's upper tier with fruit that I control and grow," he says.

2012 ($70)

Cabernet Sauvignon 41.78%, Cabernet Franc 33.33%, Merlot 16.6%, Syrah 8.29%. Alcohol 14%. Production 150 cases.

AUTHOR'S TASTING NOTES "The wine begins with aromas of cassis, black cherry, and vanilla. The wine has a lusciously ripe, almost chewy texture with flavours of blackcurrant and black cherry and a hint of mint." Drink by 2022.

2011

Cabernet Sauvignon 86%, Cabernet Franc 14%. Alcohol 13.6%. Production 150 cases.

AUTHOR'S TASTING NOTES "This is a remarkably ripe wine for a cool vintage. The Cabernet Sauvignon expresses a core of sweet fruit, including blackcurrant and cherry. The flavours also include dark chocolate and coffee. The texture is firm." Drink by 2021.

2010

Cabernet Sauvignon 33%, Merlot 33%, Cabernet Franc 17%, Syrah 17%. Alcohol 14.5%. Aged in French oak for 23 months. Production 120 cases.

WINERY TASTING NOTES "Nice integration of oak and dark fruit flavours like cherry, blackcurrant, and plums gives this wine a rich and complex taste with silky tannins to round out the wine." Drink by 2020.

C.C. Jentsch Cellars

THE CHASE
SYRAH

Collectors accumulating verticals of red wine from C.C. Jentsch Cellars face a dilemma: should they collect The Chase (a Bordeaux blend) or the Syrah?

"The Syrah started out to be our *tête de cuvée*," says winemaker Amber Pratt. "It is always barrel-aged, primarily in American oak." The gold and platinum medals gained by the winery's second Syrah, the 2013 vintage, support its primacy in the portfolio.

On the other hand, The Chase is Jentsch's flagship red in volume (about 7,500 cases in 2013) and perhaps in potential. "I am excited about The Chase," Amber says. "It is on an upward trajectory of quality; it is a hidden gem. It gives you everything you could want from a red wine, especially at the price."

What should attract collectors is C.C. Jentsch's practice of bottling significant quantities in large-format bottles. Some 300 jeroboams (3-litre bottles) of the 2013 The Chase and 100 jeroboams of the Syrah were released. These are ideal for long-term aging, even for wines that, like these, are made primarily for early consumption.

Chris Jentsch, who owns the winery with his wife, Betty Jentsch, is a third-generation Okanagan fruit grower with a massive 1,115-square-metre (12,000-square-foot) packing house. He started with apples, but the declining economics of apples propelled him into cherries. When the returns on cherries dropped, he converted his orchard between 2005 and 2008 to 19 hectares (47 acres) of grapes. The major winery buying his grapes decided in 2012 that it no longer needed them. Chris had Okanagan Crush Pad make an initial 2,000 cases for his winery in 2012. Then he plunged in with both feet. "I got forced into doing my own thing," he says. "But really, it fits me better. I would rather die by my own action, right or wrong."

He promptly turned the packing house into a winery and, in 2013, recruited Amber, formerly an assistant winemaker at Black Hills Estate Winery. She found herself with ample good fruit, since the Jentsch vineyards grow the five major Bordeaux reds required for a blend like The Chase. And there is also Syrah and Viognier.

"I love that we make this wine," Amber says of The Chase. "I have had the good fortune to work with some great red blends. I think The Chase can stand up with any one of them. Many people say we priced it too low. Maybe that has been to our disadvantage because people's psychology is such that, unless you are in the icon price range, people discount you. At the same time, we want everyone to have access to this wine on a regular basis."

The Chase 2013 ($19.90)

Cabernet Franc 32.5%, Cabernet Sauvignon 32.5%, Merlot 30%, Petit Verdot 3%, Malbec 2%. Alcohol 13.9%. Aged 6 months American and French oak (new). Production 7,488 cases, 300 jeroboams.

WINERY TASTING NOTES "This well-balanced beauty of a blend has it all; gushes of juicy red raspberry and cherry fruit, a hint of cocoa and vanilla, all enrobed with a wisp of smoke." Drink by 2018.

The Chase 2012

Merlot 35%, Cabernet Sauvignon 34%, Petit Verdot 12.5%, Cabernet Franc 11%, Malbec 7.5%. Alcohol 13%.

AUTHOR'S TASTING NOTES "The wine is made in a soft and approachable style for early drinking. It has aromas and flavours of cassis and blueberry." Drink now.

Syrah 2014 ($26.29)

Syrah 91%, Viognier 9%. Alcohol 14.4%. Aged 16 months in French and American oak barrels. Production 511 cases.

WINERY TASTING NOTES "Our juicy, full-bodied Syrah was co-fermented with 9% Viognier, lending aromas of apricot skins and violets. Flavours of blueberry, blackberry, sweet spice, and black pepper combine with a velvety texture, medium tannins, toasty oak, and balanced acidity." Drink by 2021.

Syrah 2013

Alcohol 13.8%. Aged 6 months in barrel. Production 1,358 cases, 100 jeroboams.

WINERY TASTING NOTES "A meaty, full-bodied Syrah with enticing aromas of blackberries and liquorice. The palate carries a complex combination of dark fruit, pepper, and wood." Drink by 2020.

Syrah 2012

Alcohol 13%. Co-fermented with 6% Viognier and aged 6 months in thin-staved American oak barrels.

WINERY TASTING NOTES "Dark ruby in colour, this medium-bodied wine has aromas and flavours of rich mocha, dark chocolate, and ripe black fruits intermingled with notes of pepper and toasty oak. Soft and subtle on the palate, our Syrah has a finely grained structure and excellent length."

CedarCreek Estate Winery

PLATINUM BLOCK 2 PINOT NOIR
PLATINUM BLOCK 4 PINOT NOIR

In the summer of 1998, Kevin Willenborg left the venerable Louis M. Martini winery in California to become the winemaker at CedarCreek. Impressed with the quality of the grapes that vintage, he ordered new French oak barrels (the winery was using mostly American oak) in order to produce reserve-tier wines. That included 300 cases of Platinum Pinot Noir released at $35 a bottle, an audacious price at the time.

CedarCreek's reserves are always dubbed Platinum. The reason: at a 1992 Okanagan wine competition, a CedarCreek Merlot so impressed the judges that they insisted on giving it a platinum medal, not just a gold medal. Over the years, the winery has made (and still makes) long-lived, collectible Bordeaux reds from its two vineyards near Osoyoos. However, Pinot Noir has become the winery's pre-eminent red because of the quality of the fruit produced by the old vines (20 years or older) on its Home Vineyard next to the winery in East Kelowna. The 20-hectare (49-acre) vineyard is located on a southeast-facing slope; half is devoted to Pinot Noir.

"There are a lot of advantages for old vines," says Darryl Brooker, the Australian-born winemaker who joined CedarCreek in 2010 (and moved to Mission Hill in 2014 after the two wineries came under joint ownership). At CedarCreek, he noted that two Pinot Noir blocks in the vineyard were producing very good and also quite different wines. Since 1998, with one exception, the Platinum Pinot Noir was either a single-block wine or a blend of the blocks (with some fruit from Greata Ranch, a Peachland vineyard developed by CedarCreek). Darryl believed the individual blocks made better wines.

"I could see there was a difference in the vineyard," Darryl says. In 2010, he kept the Block 2 and Block 4 wines separate until bottling, when they were blended. The subsequent wines from 2011 and 2012 conclusively confirmed that each block delivers distinctive and different flavours and should be bottled separately. He describes the Block 2 Pinot Noir as "feminine," while the Block 4 Pinot Noir is dark and brooding. The difference is astonishing, given that the blocks are on the same slope; Block 4 is about 200 metres further up.

"We dug some really big pits in the soil last year," Darryl said in a 2014 interview. "I needed to know where the difference is." The soil difference: the clay base is eight feet below the surface at Block 2 and about 11 feet down at Block 4. Vine roots reach down to the clay in both blocks, but Block 4 does not hold as much water. The Block 4 vines struggle more, producing a smaller quantity of darker, more tannic grapes. Block 4 also ripens a week to 10 days later. Since the 2011 vintage, Darryl has kept the wines separate.

The winemaking is classic Burgundy. "We ferment them 100 percent with wild yeast now," Darryl says, referring to the spontaneous fermentation brought on by the native yeasts in the vineyard and winery. He puts the wines into French oak for 14 to 18 months, with less than 20 percent of it new, so that the barrel flavours do not overpower the wine. His favourite barrels include ones from François Frères, which also provides the barrels for Domaine de la Romanée-Conti, the pre-eminent Burgundy.

The wines, if well cellared, will age at least eight to 10 years. The first release of a single-block Pinot Noir (248 cases from Block 4), in 2005, was priced at $55. Bottles in CedarCreek's wine library remained sound a decade later.

The differences between the wines usually result in collectors buying both. "We never open one without the other," Darryl says of the practice at CedarCreek's wine shop. "They should always be poured together."

When Darryl moved to Mission Hill, he passed the CedarCreek cellar to his assistant, Taylor Whelan, who has been at CedarCreek since in 2012. He shares Darryl's passion for Pinot Noir.

Platinum Block 2 Pinot Noir 2013 ($51.99)

Alcohol 14.1%. Fermented 23 days on the skins and aged 16 months in French oak. Production 325 cases.

WINERY TASTING NOTES "Our Block 2 Pinot Noir vines, at 22 years old, are just entering their prime—their root depth beginning to tap the true character of our soil. The Block 2 Pinot Noir is floral, pretty, and almost feminine. We crop to just one cluster per shoot to intensify its personality—leaving as much fruit on the ground as we harvest each year." Drink by 2021.

Platinum Block 4 Pinot Noir 2013 ($55.99)

Alcohol 13.8%. Fermented 25 days on the skins and aged 15 months in French oak. Production 420 cases.

WINERY TASTING NOTES "Planted in 1995, our Block 4 Pinot Noir marches to the beat of its own drummer. Structured. Rich. Deeply flavoured and masculine. We further enhanced the Block 4 Pinot's iconoclastic nature by choosing to use wild yeast in its fermentation, letting the yeast that occurs naturally at CedarCreek further develop this Pinot's sense of place." Drink by 2021.

Platinum Block 2 Pinot Noir 2012

Alcohol 13.6%. Fermented 25 days on the skins and aged 16 months in French oak. Production 380 cases.

WINERY TASTING NOTES "What we smell: dry flowers. What we taste: ripe raspberries and violets." Drink by 2020.

Platinum Block 4 Pinot Noir 2012

Alcohol 13.7%. Fermented 25 days on the skins and aged 16 months in French oak. Production 376 cases.

WINERY TASTING NOTES "What we smell: nutty dark chocolate. What we taste: dark plums and a little spice." Drink by 2020.

Platinum Block 2 Pinot Noir 2011

Alcohol 13.8%. Fermented 25 days on the skins and aged 16 months in French oak. Production 354 cases.

WINERY TASTING NOTES "What we smell: violets. What we taste: bright red fruit like cherries and strawberries." Drink by 2019.

Platinum Block 4 Pinot Noir 2011

Alcohol 13.8%. Fermented 25 days on the skins and aged 16 months in French oak. Production 426 cases.

WINERY TASTING NOTES "What we smell: blackberry. What we taste: dark plums." Drink by 2019.

Platinum Home Block Pinot Noir 2010

Alcohol 13.8%. Fermented 14 to 21 days on the skins and aged 16 months in French oak. Production 559 cases.

WINERY TASTING NOTES "What we smell: violets. That's Block 2. Dark plums. That's Block 4. What we taste: raspberry. It's all Block 4 on the palate." Drink by 2018.

Platinum Home Block Pinot Noir 2008

Clones 114, 115, 667, 777. Alcohol 13.9%. Home Block and Greata Ranch vineyards. Aged 16 months in French oak. Production 759 cases.

WINERY TASTING NOTES "What we smell: strawberry, raspberry, and red cherry. What we taste: all of the above plus cloves and silky tannins." Drink now.

Platinum Reserve Pinot Noir 2007

Alcohol 13.8%. Home Block and Greata Ranch vineyards. Aged 17 months in French oak. Production 667 cases.

WINERY TASTING NOTES "What we smell: strawberry, raspberry, and red cherry. What we taste: all of the above plus cloves and silky tannins." Drink now.

Platinum Reserve Pinot Noir 2006

Clones 114, 115, 667, 777. Alcohol 13.9%. Home Block and Greata Ranch vineyards. Aged 15 months in French oak. Production 1,372 cases.

WINERY TASTING NOTES "Medium ruby red in colour with aromas of cherry, coffee, mocha, and spice. Medium-bodied with silky tannins and balanced acidity." Drink now.

Platinum Reserve Pinot Noir 2005

Alcohol 13.9%. Home Block and Greata Ranch vineyards. Aged 15 months in French oak (67% new, 33% 1-year-old). Production 704 cases.

WINERY TASTING NOTES "Medium ruby red in colour with concentrated aromas of cherry, coffee, mocha, and spice. Medium-bodied . . . silky smooth texture with a long velvety finish and a hint of subtle French oak." Drink now.

Platinum Reserve Block 4 Pinot Noir 2005

Alcohol 14.4%. Aged 15 months in French oak (71.4% new, 28.6 1-year-old). Production 248 cases.

WINERY TASTING NOTES "Medium ruby red in colour with delicate yet concentrated aromas of cherry, coffee, mocha, and spice. The palate is dry and medium-bodied . . . The French oak adds complexity without being overbearing." Drink now.

CheckMate Artisanal Winery

CHARDONNAYS
MERLOTS

One of the most focused wineries in the Okanagan, CheckMate Artisanal Winery produces only ultra-premium Chardonnay and Merlot table wines. Anthony von Mandl, the owner, had a model in mind. "I happen to love Burgundian Chardonnays," he remarks. "I believed we could produce Chardonnays of similar sophistication." The wines, five Chardonnays from the 2013 vintage, were launched first in New York to make the point that these are truly international wines.

It could be argued that Mission Hill Family Estate, Anthony's largest Okanagan winery, was already making sophisticated Chardonnays. Mission Hill and the Okanagan were put on the map with a 1992 Chardonnay that won one of the first major international awards, the Avery Trophy for the best Chardonnay at the 1994 International Wine & Spirits Competition in London.

That wine was made with an unknown, but quite special, clone of Chardonnay from a vineyard near Oliver. The CheckMate project was born in 2012 when Anthony bought that vineyard, now called Heritage Vineyard, along with a dormant neighbouring winery. After a worldwide search, he recruited an intellectual Australian winemaker, Phil McGahan, to manage CheckMate. Formerly a

lawyer, Phil graduated in 2006 with a wine science degree from Charles Sturt University. His career took him to the Williams Selyem Winery in Sonoma in 2010 and to CheckMate two years later.

The 10 blocks of Chardonnay in the Okanagan owned by Mission Hill and associated wineries are what inspired this winery's name. "If you look at a chessboard and you think each of the individual squares being a block in a vineyard, it allows us to really dial in on specific blocks and make some very limited-edition wines," Anthony explains.

For the debut wines, Phil selected grapes from just three of those blocks. The winemaking is elegantly simple. The grapes are picked at night and are pressed while still cool and fresh. Individual blocks are fermented separately and aged about 18 months in French oak before being bottled. One of the initial five wines is a blend of several vineyards; the rest are single-vineyard wines. All are complex and age-worthy, like fine Burgundy.

The Merlot wines are equally sophisticated. The grapes are from premium vineyards near Osoyoos and Oliver as well as from the Black Sage Bench. The wines are all fermented with wild yeast and aged 21 months in new French oak.

Attack 2013 ($115)

Chardonnay. Alcohol 14.2%. Barn Vineyard. Aged 18 months in a new French *foudre*. Unfined and unfiltered. Production one 1,700-litre *foudre*.

WINERY TASTING NOTES "Winemaking and *foudre* combine to impart aromas of Asian spice with wet stones and flint on the nose. The palate has a zesty entry with a hint of richness and minerals followed by a lingering flavour of lychee, ginger, and spice." Drink by 2020.

Capture 2013 ($90)

Chardonnay. Alcohol 14.2%. Border Vista Vineyard. Fifty percent wild-fermented. Aged 18 months in French oak barrels (53% new). Production 7 barrels.

WINERY TASTING NOTES "A struggling, natural ferment contributes a lifted, perfumed nose reminiscent of mandarin blossom with a wild element. The palate opens with spice and creamy stone fruits, which are overtaken by minerals and a keen acidity, smoothly interwoven with an oak influence." Drink by 2020.

Fool's Mate 2013 ($80)

Chardonnay. Alcohol 14.5%. Barn Vineyard (64%), Border Vista Vineyard (25%), Heritage Vineyard (11%). Aged 17 months in French oak (50% new). Production 17 barrels.

WINERY TASTING NOTES "An extremely complex wine with a nose of brioche, herbs, hints of melon, yellow peach, and *sur lie* notes. The palate is rich and reminiscent of almond croissant and brioche. The finish is long and round with a touch of mocha, vanilla, and spice." Drink by 2020.

Little Pawn 2013 ($110)

Chardonnay. Alcohol 14.4%. Barn Vineyard. Fifty percent wild-fermented. Aged 18 months in French oak barrels (57% new). Production 17 barrels.

WINERY TASTING NOTES "Captivating floral nose with hints of rose petal and cinnamon spice. On the palate, subtle richness, hints of cream, and beautiful oak integration create, a wine of restrained elegance, with substantial length." Drink by 2020.

Queen Taken 2013 ($125)

Chardonnay. Alcohol 14.3%. Heritage Vineyard. Fifty percent wild-fermented. Aged 17 months in French oak barrels (36% new). Production 9 barrels.

WINERY TASTING NOTES "This wine has essences of citrus peel, honeydew melon, and white peach combined with aromas of freshly toasted brioche, rose hip, wet stone, and floral notes. The palate has a generous, broad entry, rich mid-palate, and good acidity, providing a long, complex, textured finish." Drink by 2020.

Black Rook Merlot 2013 ($85)

Alcohol 14.4%. Production 9 barrels.

WINERY TASTING NOTES "A lifted nose of roses, aniseed, and bramble fruit. The palate is rich with dark fruits, cassis, and savoury tannins, coating the mouth." Drink by 2023.

Opening Gambit Merlot 2013 ($85)

Alcohol 14.5%. Production 13 barrels.

WINERY TASTING NOTES "An elegant nose of blackcurrant and black fruits with creamy undertones. The palate is charming, with dark, ripe fruits, supple tannins, and well-integrated oak." Drink by 2023.

Silent Bishop Merlot 2013 ($85)

Alcohol 14%. Production 12 barrels.

WINERY TASTING NOTES "A nose of intense red fruits and floral notes, with a fresh palate of well-balanced acidity, fruit, and oak, producing a wine of harmony and length." Drink by 2023.

End Game Merlot 2013 ($85)

Alcohol 14.5%. Production 12 barrels.

WINERY TASTING NOTES "A complex, lifted nose, showcasing sassafras, spices, and aromatic oak. The palate is rich, with savoury notes, good weight, firm tannins, and immense length." Drink by 2023.

Church & State Wines
QUINTESSENTIAL

Even the name says it: this red blend, created in the 2005 vintage, is the crowning wine at Church & State. "From our first vintage in 2005 to that of the present day, you can see the progression of improvement—yet this big, soft, complex red has remained constant in its style, and has consistently been amongst the best in the country," proprietor Kim Pullen asserts.

Jeff Del Nin, who made the wines until leaving in 2016, elaborates: "With our Quintessential, every year we try to make the best wine possible. That could come from the best vineyard parcels. It could also come from certain barrels within certain batches. We try to make a limited quantity of 400, 500 cases every year. In 2009, we had such a great year that we made roughly 750 cases."

Almost every vintage has won gold or double gold medals in national and international competitions. The exceptions are the 2010 and 2012 vintages, which had not yet been released when this was written. Prior to its release, the 2012 Quintessential garnered an award of excellence in the prestigious lieutenant-governor's competition in BC.

Kim decided to launch the wine when Bill Dyer, a legendary consulting winemaker from Napa, was working with Church & State. The winery had opened in 2002 under different owners as Victoria Estate Winery on the Saanich Peninsula on Vancouver Island, but it failed two years later.

Kim acquired the winery, renamed it, and initiated a turnaround that included hiring Dyer. He also moved the winery to the South Okanagan and purchased 48.5 hectares (120 acres) of vineyard to supply premium grapes. "Great wine begins in the vineyard," Kim says.

Jeff Del Nin, who was born in Canada but trained in Australia, made the Quintessential vintages from 2009 until 2015. It is more than a trophy wine; growing grapes for a super-premium wine elevates the entire Church & State portfolio. "We start out with trying to make everything Quintessential quality if we possibly can," Jeff says. "Of course, it might be hard to sell 12,000 cases of $55 wine." He had stamped a style on Quintessential by the time he moved to Road 13 Vineyards in 2016.

Every year we try
to make the best
wine possible.

2013 ($55)

Merlot 35%, Cabernet Sauvignon 20%, Petit Verdot 20%, Cabernet Franc 15%, Malbec 10%. Alcohol 14.2%. Each parcel of fruit was aged separately in French oak for 22 months, with the final blend assembled just before bottling. Production 475 cases.

WINERY TASTING NOTES "Very dark red in colour, this wine has an intoxicating mixture of black cherry, blackberry, and cassis aromas complexed with subtle savoury/meaty notes and creamy vanilla. On the palate, this is a deep, dense, black-fruited wine with a full, rich texture and impeccable balance. This wine confidently threads the needle between structure and smoothness. A very seductive, complex wine." Drink by 2026.

2012

Cabernet Sauvignon 45%, Merlot 45%, Cabernet Franc 3.33%, Malbec 3.33%, Petit Verdot 3.33%. Alcohol 14.3%. Aged 22 months in French oak (33% new). Production 150 cases.

AUTHOR'S TASTING NOTES "The wine is generous in texture and in flavours. It begins with aromas of black cherry, blackcurrants, vanilla, and truffles. On the palate, there are flavours of plum, mulberry, black cherry, and dark chocolate." Drink by 2025.

2011

Merlot 70%, Cabernet Franc 15%, Cabernet Sauvignon 5%, Malbec 5%, Petit Verdot 5%. Alcohol 13.5%. Aged 20 months in French oak (30% new). Production 550 cases.

TASTING NOTES by Anthony Gismondi on GismondiOnWine.com: "The 2011 is very hedonistic in style and well, more California than Okanagan at this point. There is a ripeness you don't often see in BC Bordeaux blends; this red has all five grapes: Cabernet Sauvignon, Cabernet Franc, Merlot, Malbec, and Petit Verdot. All grown on the Black Sage Bench. The nose is more South Okanagan, fragrant, savoury, dried herbs mixed with ripe cassis. The attack is skinny and warm with more dark fruits, tobacco, cedar, and a hint of dried tomatoes. This needs another three years to put some fat on to balance off the fruit and spice." Drink by 2022.

2010

Cabernet Sauvignon 40%, Petit Verdot 25%, Malbec 15%, Merlot 10%, Cabernet Franc 10%. Alcohol 14.5%. Aged 20 months in French oak (20% new). Production 535 cases.

WINERY TASTING NOTES "Extremely dark blue/black in colour, the wine has an intoxicating mixture of primary black cherry, blueberry, and cassis aromas mixed with prominent savoury cedar, meaty, peppery complexity, and a hint of spice, iodine, and creamy vanilla. A deep, dark, dense, black-fruited powerhouse with fullness, impeccable balance, and amazing length of flavour. Vibrant, explosive, alive, intense, and electric." Drink by 2022.

2009

Cabernet Sauvignon 40%, Cabernet Franc 30%, Merlot 20%, Malbec 5%, Petit Verdot 5%. Aged 20 months in French oak (30% new). Alcohol 14.5%. Production 750 cases.

WINERY TASTING NOTES "Dense and dark in colour, with ultra black cherry and cassis aromas complexed by notes of coffee, baker's chocolate, pencil shavings, and graphite aromas. On the palate, there is dark concentrated black cherry fruit and gorgeous tannin structure producing great richness and length, but with impeccable balance. The wine coats and totally fills your mouth, and a staggering array of complex flavours continue to linger in your mouth long after swallowing." Drink by 2020.

2008

Cabernet Sauvignon 58%, Cabernet Franc 17%, Merlot 17%, Malbec 4%, Petit Verdot 4%. Alcohol 14.5%. Aged 24 months in French oak (33% new). Production 500 cases.

AUTHOR'S TASTING NOTES "Each varietal was aged separately in French oak for 12 months and then, after the wine was blended, it spent another 12 months in French oak. The wine soaked up the wood very well; it does not intrude on the vibrant aromas and flavours of red fruit (raspberry, cherry), with hints of mocha and red licorice. The fine-grained tannins give the wine a supple, accessible texture." Drink by 2019.

2007

Merlot 32%, Cabernet Franc 28%, Cabernet Sauvignon 23%, Petit Verdot 9%, Malbec 8%. Alcohol 14.5%. Aged 22 months in French oak (33% new). Production 547 cases.

AUTHOR'S TASTING NOTES "This is a blend of all five Bordeaux grape varieties. It begins with aromas of cherry and chocolate that reminded me, pleasantly, of Black Forest cake, enhanced with a touch of oak. On the palate, there are sweet, even jammy flavours of plum and cherry, with lingering fruit on the finish of this delicious wine." Drink by 2018.

2006

Merlot 36%, Cabernet Franc 28%, Cabernet Sauvignon 16%, Petit Verdot 12%, Malbec 8%. Alcohol 14.5%. Aged 22 months in French oak (33% new). Production 500 cases.

WINERY TASTING NOTES The wine has "layers of wild berry, currant, and sage mingled in a framework of toasty oak and rich supple tannins with a finish that goes to eternity." Drink by 2018.

2005

Merlot 38%, Cabernet Franc 31%, Petit Verdot 19%, Cabernet Sauvignon 6%, Malbec 6%. Alcohol 14.6%. Aged 22 months in French oak (33% new). Production 364 cases.

The winery released this wine with an assessment by Vancouver wine writer Anthony Gismondi: "Quintessential is a mix of all five Bordeaux varieties in this case assembled by winemaker Bill Dyer. It has all the Dyer hallmarks. Ripe round and elegant with fine acidity and freshness. Liquorice and black fruit with a touch of smoke and oak carry the current palate. Looks to have fine potential in the years to come. A fine start." Drink by 2018.

Clos du Soleil Winery
SIGNATURE

The winemaking aesthetic at Clos du Soleil is an echo of Bordeaux. "But while we talk about our French philosophy, our wines are never going to taste like Bordeaux, and they shouldn't," cautions Michael Clark, the managing partner and winemaker. "They should taste like Upper Bench Keremeos in the Similkameen Valley, and I think they do."

The founding partners, all lovers of French wines, planted just Bordeaux varieties—five reds, two whites—on a 4-hectare (10-acre) farm purchased in 2006. Formerly a honey-producing farm, the property's lean soils lie on a moderate south-facing slope against a mountainous rock face. The vines are grown under both organic and biodynamic disciplines.

The Bordeaux-inspired wines were initially crafted by Ann Sperling, a consulting winemaker of national repute and one of the owners of Sperling Vineyards in Kelowna. And before Clos du Soleil built its own winery in 2015, the wines were made at the Sperling winery. Winemaking was taken over in 2013 by Michael Clark, who grew up in a home where the wine cellar included classified growth Bordeaux wines.

Born in Cambridge, Ontario, in 1972, Michael began reading wine books when he was 10. Initially, he pursued careers in science (he has two degrees in theoretical physics) and finance (he holds a master of business administration). After managing hedge-fund portfolios in Switzerland, he surrendered to his passion for wine, studying viticulture there and making wine in Bordeaux. When he returned to Canada to join Clos du Soleil in 2012, he had also received a winemaking certificate from the University of California. "Anybody will tell you that I am a bit of a detail person," he says. "I think that plays well in winemaking, because it is the sum of a million little details that add up to the final wine."

Michael believes that "the star of our vineyard is Cabernet Sauvignon, which is planted right below the rock face. The Similkameen terroir is expressed in the Cabernet Sauvignon, which is so unique. It doesn't taste like an Okanagan Cabernet or a California Cabernet or a Bordeaux Cabernet. It really tastes of here. It has a spicy, floral, violet component. It has density, lots of complexity, but it isn't heavy."

That defines the style of Signature, the winery's flagship Bordeaux red, and also the limited-production Estate Reserve, first produced in the 2010 vintage.

"To me, delicacy matters," Michael says. "My philosophy is that our best wines demonstrate their quality in ways other than bigness or heaviness. A great wine, whether you are talking about Clos du Soleil or a classified growth in Bordeaux, is determined by elegance, complexity, layers and ageability, not by huge, chewy fruit or aggressive tannins."

Signature 2013 ($45)

Merlot 51%, Cabernet Sauvignon 34%, Cabernet Franc 11%, Malbec 2%, Petit Verdot 2%. Alcohol 13.8%. Aged 17 months in French oak barrels.

WINERY TASTING NOTES "The taster is immediately enveloped in the dense and layered perfumes of this wine, with notes of cedar, fresh blackberry and cassis, and a hint of cracked black pepper. On the palate the wine bursts with ripe fruit flavours—blackberry, raspberry, and red currant—expressed through an elegant, mouth-filling structure and soft, round tannins." Drink by 2026.

Signature 2012

Cabernet Sauvignon 48%, Merlot 42%, Cabernet Franc 9%, Petit Verdot 1%. Alcohol 13.6%. Aged 18 months in French oak barrels.

WINERY TASTING NOTES "The nose opens with aromas of cassis, blueberry, and dark cherry, on a background of spice and mixed herbs. On the palate the wine is full, long, and elegant. Bright fruit flavours of cherry and black and red currant flow seamlessly into a long finish with notes of tobacco and black pepper. Enjoyable in its youth, the fine tannins and beautiful balance of this wine ensure its ability to age for a decade." Drink by 2025.

Signature 2011

Merlot 44%, Cabernet Sauvignon 23%, Cabernet Franc 22%, Malbec 6%, Petit Verdot 5%. Alcohol 13.4%.

WINERY TASTING NOTES written in 2013 by Rhys Pender, MW: "The 2011 vintage is a perfect union of fruit and spice. Black cherry, raspberry, and ripe fig notes drift from the bouquet. First sips show vibrant notes of juicy red fruits, plum, mocha, and black pepper. Because of the climatic variation this season, green harvesting took place in order to achieve the best fruit with ripeness and flavours." Drink by 2024.

Signature 2010

Merlot 48%, Cabernet Sauvignon 34%, Malbec 9%, Petit Verdot 9%. Alcohol 14%. Production 375 cases.

WINERY TASTING NOTES "Unfiltered and unfined, there are notes of cassis and blackberry that greet the nose. They are echoed on the palate with a soft note of oak that complements the dark berry fruit balanced with good acidity and black plum freshness. Decanting this wine opens up multiple layers of ripe black fruits in addition to darker essences of cocoa and espresso." Drink by 2020.

Signature 2009

Merlot 41%, Cabernet Franc 28%, Cabernet Sauvignon 20%, Petit Verdot 7%, Malbec 4%. Alcohol 14.2%.

WINERY TASTING NOTES written in 2013 by Rhys Pender, MW: "As a result of the Petit Verdot being added to this vintage, less red fruit is detectable. It is still very plummy and engaged with black fruit notes. The tannins are well structured and there is good flavour concentration in this wine. Cola, spices, dark chocolate, and ripe berries all combine to create this well-layered red." Drink by 2020.

Signature 2008

Merlot 52%, Cabernet Sauvignon 26%, Cabernet Franc 13%, Malbec 9%. Alcohol 14.5%.

WINERY TASTING NOTES written in 2013 by Rhys Pender, MW: "Cordial cherry, brilliant raspberry, sweet honeyed figs, and cola notes predominate this bouquet. Sounds sweet, but this dry wine is merely still showing its fruit-forwardness. Leaning toward pronounced intensity on the palate, this bold red was made from grapes that had particularly good acid and sugar levels. In the mouth, mocha, black fruits, rosemary, and an exciting chalky minerality create a lively wine that will cellar for years to come." Drink by 2019.

Red 2007

Cabernet Sauvignon 45%, Merlot 35%, Cabernet Franc 20%. Alcohol 13.3%. Production 450 cases.

WINERY TASTING NOTES written in 2013 by Rhys Pender, MW: "Still developing, the bouquet possesses layers of red berries, very ripe blackberry, plum, wet tobacco, and a hint of toast. In the mouth, cassis, earth, red and black fruits, and leather dominate. It is holding its acid and tannins nicely, and provides an unrelenting length filled with a hint of peppercorn spice." Drink by 2018.

Red 2006

Cabernet Sauvignon 60%, Merlot 22%, Cabernet Franc 18%. Alcohol 13.8%. Production 75 cases.

WINERY TASTING NOTES in 2013 by Rhys Pender, MW: "Striking notes of dried pitted fruits, sweet tobacco, and dark chocolate are found in the bouquet. Still having potential for aging, this vintage is only growing better on the palate. Notes of tea leaves, currants, thyme and sage, and velvety vanilla." Drink by 2018.

Coolshanagh Vineyard

CHARDONNAY

Coolshanagh is a Celtic word that translates as "a meeting place of friends." For Skip and Judy Stothert, it had an excellent ring to it for the vineyard they began planting in 2004 on their property near the north end of Naramata Road. The name has been used by Judy's family, which has roots in Scotland and Ireland, for several generations to identify various homes.

"My grandmother always used to have Coolshanagh, with the address underneath, on her letterhead," Judy says. "My cousins continued with Coolshanagh and named their houses or their summer homes with it. It has continued with our family. When we decided on a name, we just liked 'meeting place of friends.'"

The vineyard and winery began when Skip decided to retire and turn over his business, Green Roads Recycling, to his sons. "We moved here in 2003," Skip says, referring to the 21 hectares (52 acres) of forest that he and his wife bought beside Naramata Road, attracted by the seclusion and the stunning views over Okanagan Lake. Skip, however, has energy to burn. "My sons were taking over the business, and I got bored. I researched grape varieties." He settled on Chardonnay and Pinot Noir, having grown up in a house with wine on the table regularly. Win Stothert, his father and owner of an international engineering firm,

belonged to the Opimian Society. "I grew up drinking Burgundian Chardonnays right from the get-go, when I was about 10 or 11," Skip says. "And there also was Burgundian Pinot Noir."

Trees were felled, land was prepared, and the first hectare of Chardonnay was planted in 2004. Since then, the vineyard has tripled in size. Between 2008 and 2011, Coolshanagh grapes were sold to Foxtrot Vineyards. Then in 2012, Skip and Judy discovered they could produce and sell wines under their own label by engaging Okanagan Crush Pad Winery to do the production. The target, when Coolshanagh is at full production, is to release about 1,500 cases of Chardonnay and 300 cases of Pinot Noir annually.

Okanagan Crush Pad's winemaking aims to put the minerality of the Coolshanagh vineyard into the bottle: "The site offers distinct regional flavours that emerge from the fertile, calcium carbonate-loaded silt, gravel, clay, and fractured glacial bedrock." No more than one-third of the Chardonnay is fermented in oak. The remainder is fermented in concrete, and the two lots are blended and aged in concrete. The resulting wines are generous in structure, with the fresh acidity and subtle minerality designed to make them as age-worthy as white Burgundy.

2014 ($36.90)

Alcohol 13.6%. Production 270 cases.

AUTHOR'S TASTING NOTES "Thirty-six percent of this was fermented in new oak puncheons, lightly toasted so that oak notes are minimal. The rest was fermented in a concrete egg. This wine has the textural richness that seems an attribute of concrete aging as well as aging on the lees for 11 months. It has rich flavours and aromas of tangerine and pineapple, with a hint of hazelnut. The bright acidity gives the wine a crisp and lingering finish." Drink by 2019.

2013

Alcohol 13.5%. Production 262 cases.

WINERY TASTING NOTES "This Chardonnay offers a vibrant and complex fruit profile with a lush, mouth-coating texture and very fine, juicy acidity. The finished wine offers a distinctive combination of bright, nimble acidity and solid weightiness. There's a distinctive sense of the vineyard in this wine, with its stony complexity and bright fruit evoking the rocky subsoils and cool mesoclimate. As of now, the wine tastes spectacular with great structure and mouth feel." Drink by 2018.

2012

Alcohol 13.8%. Production 220 cases.

AUTHOR'S TASTING NOTES "A third of this was fermented in new French oak. The remainder was fermented in stainless steel. The wine was then blended and aged on the lees in a concrete egg until bottling in 2013. The wine shows notes of citrus on the nose and the palate. The bright acidity and the spine of minerality give this elegant wine good ageability." Drink now.

Corcelettes Estate Winery

MENHIR

Menhir is the name for a type of stone obelisk erected throughout Europe for ceremonial purposes by prehistoric peoples. A menhir, the inspiration for this wine's proprietary name, stands on Corcelettes, the family farm in Switzerland where Urs Baessler lived until he and his wife, Barbara Baessler, moved to Canada in 1978. When they opened a winery in the Similkameen Valley in 2013, they adopted the name of the Swiss farm. And the Swiss fingerprints don't stop there: Chasselas, the leading white wine of Switzerland, grows in one Corcelettes vineyard.

The Baesslers came to Canada to grow wheat, not to make wine. For many years, they ran a grain farm in Manitoba as well as a buffalo farm in Wyoming. In 2007, having had enough of Prairie winters, they moved to an organic garlic farm in the Similkameen Valley. In the meantime, their son, Charlie, was completing a science degree at the University of Lethbridge. On graduating, he accepted a job with Lawrence Herder, then the owner of Herder Vineyards. The next year, 2009, he moved to the vineyards and cellar at Burrowing Owl Estate Winery, where he developed his skills as a viticulturist and a winemaker.

Once they recognized they had a wine grower in the family, the Baesslers in 2010 planted 1 hectare (2.5 acres) of grapes on their farm. These vines, along with purchased grapes, enabled them to begin making wines in 2011. Syrah and Cabernet Sauvignon were subsequently planted at a nearby vineyard. The initial intent was to produce between 1,000 and 1,500 cases of wine annually.

That changed in 2015, when Corcelettes took over the larger Herder winery and moved its production there. Herder had 2.6 planted hectares (6.5 acres), with another hectare to be planted in 2016. The varieties grown there (Malbec, Petit Verdot, Syrah, Cabernet Franc, Viognier, Chardonnay, Merlot, and Pinot Noir) significantly expand Charlie Baessler's repertoire and the production volume.

Menhir resembles Burrowing Owl's Athene, a co-fermented blend of Cabernet Sauvignon and Syrah. The similarity isn't a coincidence: Charlie honed his winemaking skills while being mentored by Burrowing Owl's winemakers.

 The inspiration for this wine's proprietary name stands on Corcelettes, the family farm in Switzerland.

2014 ($32)

Cabernet Sauvignon 62%, Syrah 38%. Alcohol 14.5%. Aged 17 months in barrel (primarily French). Production 205 cases.

WINERY TASTING NOTES "The nose of this wine is full of tobacco, black cherry and dried herbs. The chewy, layered palate echoes those same tobacco and black cherry notes along with dark, ripe plum, and coffee. The texture is rich and velvety, with a hint of slate minerality and a long finish." Drink by 2021.

2013

Cabernet Sauvignon 60%, Syrah 40%. Alcohol 14.2%. Aged 17 months in barrel (primarily French). Production 180 cases.

WINERY TASTING NOTES "The nose of this wine is full of pipe tobacco, black cherry, and dried herbs. The chewy, layered palate echoes those same tobacco and black cherry notes along with dark, ripe plum, and coffee. The texture is rich and velvety, with a hint of slate minerality and a long, spicy finish." Drink by 2020.

2012

Cabernet Sauvignon 60%, Syrah 40%. Alcohol 13%. Aged 17 months in barrel (primarily French). Production 90 cases.

AUTHOR'S TASTING NOTES "The wine begins with smoky red-berry aromas. On the palate, there are flavours of blackcurrant, mulberry, and plum. The Syrah adds a gamy, earthy note. The long, ripe tannins give this a generous texture." Drink by 2019.

2011

Syrah 55%, Cabernet Sauvignon 45%. Alcohol 13.5%. Aged 17 months in barrel (primarily French). Production 80 cases.

AUTHOR'S TASTING NOTES "The wine starts with intense and appealing aromas of black cherry, vanilla, and white pepper, all of which are echoed on the palate. The generous texture is rich and ripe." Drink by 2018.

Covert Farms Family Estate

AMICITIA RED

When third-generation farmer Gene Covert says that "winemaking is just an extension of farming," it reflects the storied history of Covert Farms.

The farm was established in 1961 by his grandfather, George. A former partner in a California tomato packing house, he bought 263 hectares (650 acres) of raw land on a plateau abutting McIntyre Bluff, north of Oliver. The farm became, and remains, a major producer of fruits, vegetables, and, at various periods in its history, grapes. From the early 1970s, Covert Farms had 73 hectares (180 acres) of vineyard and was one of the first Okanagan vineyards to test mechanical harvesting. The grapes were the hybrid varieties that were removed in the 1988 grape pullout, except for a block of table grapes. In 1996, Mike Covert, George's son, considered planting vinifera for a nearby winery. In 2005, Gene resumed growing wine grapes there and now farms 12 hectares (30 acres) of grapes for the Covert Farms winery.

The winery was initially called Dunham & Froese and was a partnership owned by two couples: Gene and his wife, Shelly, and winemaker Kirby Froese and his wife, Crystal. "I hadn't made wine before," says Gene (glossing over trials with beer and fruit wines). "But I have been growing things forever." The partnership broke up before the 2011 vintage. By that time, Gene, who was born in 1971 and has a degree in physical geography, had acquired the skills to make wine, with occasional help from a consultant.

Amicitia—Latin for "friendship" or "relationship"—was blended in 2006 and 2007 with purchased varietals that mirrored what Gene had planted. Since 2008, the wine has been made with grapes from the estate. The 2008 Amicitia is a remarkably concentrated wine, given that it is made with fruit from two-year-old vines. In some vintages, the winery has bottled magnums and double magnums, ideal for longer-term aging.

The Covert Farms vineyard is certified organic. In recent years, Gene has added a layer of biodynamic practices, consistent with his philosophy of farming.

"The big thing in growing anything is balance," he says. "If you are a small winery with a new vineyard and you want to take some fruit, you have to be very careful how you balance that fruit load so that the plant can fulfill its ultimate yield targets."

Covert Farms Family Estate Amicitia Red 2013
($28)

Merlot 52%, Cabernet Sauvignon 18%, Cabernet Franc 17%, Petit Verdot 6%, Syrah 5%, Malbec 2%. Barrel-aged for 12 months. Production 808 cases.

WINERY TASTING NOTES "Rich, warm notes of raisins, hazelnuts, and stewed cherries." Drink by 2024.

Covert Farms Family Estate Amicitia Red 2012

Merlot 40%, and 12% each of Cabernet Franc, Cabernet Sauvignon, Malbec, Petit Verdot, and Syrah. Alcohol 14.6%. Production 448 cases.

AUTHOR'S TASTING NOTES "This is a bold, ripe red with aromas of spice, plum, and blackcurrant. On the palate, the flavours recall a rich, spicy Christmas fruitcake, with notes of plum, fig, black cherry, and vanilla. The long, ripe tannins give the wine an almost silky finish, but with enough structure to age." Drink by 2023.

Covert Farms Family Estate Amicitia Red 2010

Merlot 40% and 12% each of Cabernet Franc, Cabernet Sauvignon, Malbec, Petit Verdot, and Syrah. Alcohol 13.7%. Production 400 cases.

AUTHOR'S TASTING NOTES "The tight, firm texture shows the vintage. The wine has cedar and graphite mingled with red fruits in the aroma. On the palate there are flavours of blackcurrant, black cherry, and leather." Drink by 2020.

Covert Farms Family Estate Amicitia Red 2009

Cabernet Sauvignon 47.22%, Cabernet Franc 18.85%, Syrah 11.8%, Petit Verdot 8.67%, Malbec 8.39%, Merlot 3.77%, Zinfandel 1.3%.

With the winery's change of name and ownership, a portion of the 2009 Amicitia was tweaked with a little Zinfandel and was filtered before bottling.

AUTHOR'S TASTING NOTES "The wine has dark, brooding fruit flavours including black cherry and blackcurrant, with hints of cedar and graphite. The texture is firm and age-worthy." Drink by 2019.

Dunham & Froese Amicitia Red 2009

Cabernet Sauvignon 48.57%, Cabernet Franc 18.8%, Syrah 11.8%, Petit Verdot 8.67%, Malbec 8.39%, Merlot 3.77%. Unfiltered.

AUTHOR'S TASTING NOTES "Dark in colour, the wine has aromas of plums, black cherries, and vanilla. The fruit flavours are echoed brightly on the palate, with a touch of mocha on the finish." Drink by 2019.

Dunham & Froese Amicitia Red 2008

Merlot 33%, Cabernet Sauvignon 30%, Syrah 20%, Cabernet Franc 11%, Malbec 3%, Petit Verdot 3%.

AUTHOR'S TASTING NOTES "The wine is bold and generous, beginning with dramatic aromas of spice and vanilla. It has flavours of blackcurrant, black cherry, coffee, and dark chocolate. The texture is concentrated." Drink by 2019.

Dunham & Froese Amicitia Red 2007

Blend of six Bordeaux red varieties plus Syrah. Alcohol 14%. Production 300 cases.

AUTHOR'S TASTING NOTES "Dark in colour, the wine has aromas of plums, figs, and cigars, with flavours of plums, black cherry, and spice." Drink now.

Dunham & Froese Amicitia Red 2006

Blend of major Bordeaux varieties and Syrah. Alcohol 14%. Production 200 cases.

AUTHOR'S TASTING NOTES "The wine has matured to show a core of sweet fruit flavours, including plum and black cherry, with an earthy, gamy finish. The tannins are soft." Drink now.

Culmina Family Estate Winery

HYPOTHESIS

This South Okanagan winery, which opened in 2013, got its name because it represents the culmination of a career in wine for Donald and Elaine Triggs and their daughter, Sara.

Donald's wine career began in 1972 with the wine division of John Labatt Ltd. He made a seven-year detour as a manager with a British agricultural chemicals company. But in 1989, he returned to Canada to lead the team that bought Labatt's wine assets. As chief executive, he built these into Vincor International, Canada's largest wine company. Vincor was taken over in 2006 by Constellation Brands, the world's largest wine company. The following year, at an age when most retire (Donald was born in Manitoba in 1944), he and Elaine plowed their life savings into Culmina. "*Retirement* to me is a nasty word because it implies stopping," Donald says. "I don't think life is about stopping. It is about continuing and doing what you love."

His ambition is to raise the bar for Okanagan wine quality, building on what Vincor achieved by enlisting Bordeaux's prestigious Groupe Taillan to develop the Osoyoos Larose Winery in 1998. For Culmina, Donald has engaged talent previously critical to the success of Osoyoos Larose, including winemakers Pascal Madevon and Jean-Marc Enixon, along with Bordeaux consultant Alain Sutre.

Culmina cultivates 22.6 hectares (56 acres) in three vineyards stacked one above the other on the slopes of a mountain. After detailed soil and climate studies, the vines were densely planted in 43 computer-monitored micro blocks, each averaging 1.25 acres in size. "Some of the blocks are smaller than the backyard of your house," Donald says. The intensive vineyard management aims to deliver superb-quality grapes to the winery.

The three vineyard benches, each with differing soils and elevations, provide many winemaking options. Merlot, Cabernet Franc, and Cabernet Sauvignon comprise the largest blocks, followed by Chardonnay, Riesling, Syrah, Malbec, and Petit Verdot. There is even one hectare of Grüner Veltliner, the Austrian white, planted on Margaret's Bench, the highest-elevation vineyard in the South Okanagan.

Vincor had operated wineries in Australia, New Zealand, California, and Ontario as well as in the Okanagan. Donald and Elaine drew on that knowledge to put leading-edge technology into both Culmina's gravity-flow winery and its vineyards. Proudly, they reveal it all to consumers who book the intensive tours and tastings that Culmina offers.

The winery's flagship red is called Hypothesis because the word's dictionary definition—"a provisional idea whose merit requires evaluation"—suggests that the Triggs family is somewhat tentative about its ambition to raise the bar once again. But most will agree there is nothing tentative about Culmina and its wines. Other collectible wines from Culmina include a Riesling called Decora, a Grüner Veltliner called Unicus, and a Chardonnay called Dilemma.

2013 ($38)

Merlot 38%, Cabernet Franc 36%, Cabernet Sauvignon 26%. Alcohol 14%. Arise Bench Vineyard. Aged 16 months in French oak barrels (60% new, 40% 1-year-old).

WINERY TASTING NOTES "Opulent cassis and freshly picked blackberry aromas are complemented by violets, cedar, and a pronounced minerality. The densely textured, savoury palate has lively acidity, succulent dark fruits, and polished, refined tannins. Combining generosity with elegance, the finish is long and persistent."

2012

Merlot 57%, Cabernet Sauvignon 24%, Cabernet Franc 19%. Alcohol 14%. Arise Bench Vineyard. Production 2,295 cases.

WINERY TASTING NOTES "A rich, bold, terroir-driven blend . . . displaying abundant spice, floral, and dark red fruit aromas, enveloping the palate with dense structure, toasted oak, fine tannins, red plum flavours, and a long, persistent finish." Drink by 2022.

2011

Cabernet Franc 40%, Merlot 36%, Cabernet Sauvignon 24%. Alcohol 13.5%. Arise Bench Vineyard. Production 550 cases.

WINERY TASTING NOTES "A rich, bold, terroir-driven blend . . . displaying abundant spice, floral, and dark red fruit aromas, enveloping the palate with a tight structure, toasted oak, velvety tannins, red cassis flavours, and a persistent finish." Drink by 2020.

Daydreamer Wines

MARCUS ANSEMS SHIRAZ

Two of the signature wines from Daydreamer are Shiraz (Syrah), a variety that practically runs in the veins of winemaker Marcus Ansems, the owner of this winery with his wife, Rachel Ansems. His family in Australia once owned a share of Mount Langi Ghiran, the legendary Shiraz producer in the state of Victoria, and his uncle, Trevor Mast, was a winemaker there.

"One of my favourite wines in the world was made at my family winery," Marcus says. "It is just unique to that site . . . an atypical Shiraz. That wine was what inspired me to get involved with the industry." Born in 1974, he graduated in 1996 with a degree in oenology from the University of Adelaide. He went abroad to gain experience, first with Simonsig in South Africa and then in Tuscany and the Rhône. He worked in Australia briefly before a Canadian wine entrepreneur, Peter Jensen, recruited him in 1999 to run wineries in Ontario and Nova Scotia. In the Niagara wine region, before he returned to Australia in 2002 as a consulting winemaker, he met Rachel, an accountant with talents in design and photography.

They moved to British Columbia in 2004, where Marcus became the winemaker first for Blasted Church Vineyards and, a year later, Therapy Vineyards. Since late 2008, he has been the buyer for Hemispheres Wine Guild, a Canadian club for wine collectors. In 2015, he became a Master of Wine after completing the rigorous studies necessary for joining this elite group of about 350 in the world.

Daydreamer is the culmination of a family winery dream that Rachel and Marcus share. The winery's Syrah-based blend is called Amelia, for their daughter. Daydreamer launched with about 1,000 cases, including Chardonnay and two Syrahs, one co-fermented with Viognier. "I like cool-climate Syrah," Marcus says. The wines come in two tiers, with the popular-priced wines under the Daydreamer label. For premium wines, he has revived the Marcus Ansems label he created while he was at Therapy.

Shiraz . . . was what inspired me to get involved with the industry.

2014 ($35)

Alcohol 13%. Matured 12 months in oak (70% French, 30% American). Production 115 cases.

AUTHOR'S TASTING NOTES "This wine is dark with muscular aromas of plum, black cherry, vanilla, and pepper. The texture is concentrated, supporting bold flavours of black cherry, delicatessen meats, Christmas spices, coffee, and black pepper." Drink by 2024.

2013

Alcohol 13%. Matured 12 months in oak (70% French, 30% American). Production 180 cases.

AUTHOR'S TASTING NOTES "The wine begins with aromas of black cherry and pepper. It delivers generous flavours of black cherry and spicy fruitcake, with black pepper, chocolate, and black cherry on the finish. There is a lot of Australian personality in this full-bodied wine." Drink by 2023.

Deep Roots Winery

SYRAH

This winery's name was prompted by the four generations of the Hardman family that have lived on the Naramata Bench. Bryan Hardman's grandfather came in 1919 after four years of military service, initially working with pioneer fruit grower Carl Aikins, who once owned about 250 hectares (618 acres).

The Hardmans became major fruit growers as well. Bryan, who was born in 1950, at one time owned 20 hectares (50 acres) of apple trees. He was also an industry activist, serving as president of BC Tree Fruits, the Okanagan's apple marketing organization. It is famously tough to make a living with apples, even for a grower as progressive as Bryan, who regularly embraced trendy new varieties like Gala and Fuji. Bryan planted 2 hectares (5 acres) of grapes in 1996 "just to see if I liked it." He did, and he gradually replaced his apple trees with vines and left the apple business entirely in 2010. Now he owns 8 hectares (20 acres) of vineyard and manages another 4 hectares (10 acres).

He began thinking about having a winery after his son, Will, who was born in 1983, began working in the vineyards in 2006. That propelled Will toward winemaking. In addition to taking courses at Okanagan College, Will has done crushes with wineries in New Zealand and South Africa. He has also worked with Robert Van Westen at Van Westen Vineyards. That is where Deep Roots made its 2012 vintage: a total of 13 barrels of Merlot, Malbec, and Syrah. The Deep Roots winery was built in 2013.

The red wines could all be collected, including the remarkable Gamay Noir. The cool-climate Syrah, while not as plump as those from the hot South Okanagan, is elegant with good acidity to ensure freshness of flavour with good aging potential.

> " It is famously tough to make a living with apples, even for a grower as progressive as Bryan, who regularly embraced trendy new varieties like Gala and Fuji. "

2014 ($34)

Alcohol 14.8%. Aged 18 months in French oak.

WINERY TASTING NOTES "Blueberry pie, shortbread, bacon, and lots of black pepper on the nose along with plum, paprika, and black cherry. The palate is dry, full-bodied with smoky meaty notes, toasty oak, blackberry, blueberry, and more black pepper, and a savoury dried herb complexity with firm tannins and a long spicy finish." Drink by 2024.

2013

Alcohol 13.9%.

WINERY TASTING NOTES "Spicy, peppery, and meaty on the nose along with some toasty vanillin oak, blueberry, blackberry, spiced cherry, and some savoury smoky, gamy notes. The palate has intensity and complexity, richness balanced by crisp acidity and flavours of black fruit, black pepper, paprika, coffee, leather, dried rosemary, and black olives with a long finish." Drink by 2023.

2012

Alcohol 14.5%. Aged 18 months in French oak.

WINERY TASTING NOTES "A ripe and brooding cool-climate Syrah with intense damson plum, violet, blueberry, and mulberry fruit as well as vanilla, coffee and Nutella. The palate is full-bodied with crisp acidity and ripe tannins; with flavours of dark chocolate, blackberry, black pepper, black plum, and dried raspberry with a long finish." Drink by 2022.

Desert Hills Estate Winery
MIRAGE

In the 2000 vintage, Desert Hills made its first red Bordeaux blend with just three varietals: Cabernet Sauvignon, Cabernet Franc, and Merlot. Sales began three years later, when the winery opened. Randy and Jesse Toor, the twin brothers who operate Desert Hills, called the wine "Meritage."

The term *Meritage* was coined in California in 1988 by the newly formed Meritage Alliance. The member wineries needed a suitable term for blends that could not be released under the name of the lead varietal, since there was less than 75 percent of that varietal in the blend. As well, it was not considered ethical (and subsequently became illegal) to label the wines with French geographical indicators like Médoc or Pomerol. In 1995 Harry McWatters, the founder of Sumac Ridge Estate Winery, struck an agreement with the Meritage Alliance to use the term in Canada.

The Toor brothers decided to do a five-variety blend, adding Malbec and Petit Verdot. They planted what was then only the second Malbec block on the Black Sage Bench because Randy admired bold Argentinian Malbec. And he was so impressed with Petit Verdot, an inky staple of many Bordeaux blends, that the brothers grafted that variety onto some of their 12-year-old Cabernet Sauvignon vines. "I think we were the first one to do a 'true' Bordeaux blend," Randy says

of the 2004 blend incorporating five varietals.

"Everybody had a Meritage," Randy observes, explaining why the name of the blend changed to Mirage. "We wanted to get away from that name. Desert Hills is a winery in the only pocket desert [in the Okanagan]. What do you see in a desert? A mirage!" The blend is always anchored with Cabernet Sauvignon. "I just love that grape," Randy says. "I love the taste of it."

The Toor brothers, who were born in Punjab in 1964, came to Canada with their family in 1982, moving first to Winnipeg and then to a struggling Okanagan apple orchard six years later. They began replacing the apple trees with vines in 1995 and succeeded first by selling fruit and then by opening Desert Hills.

They still have a few bottles of the 2000 Meritage. In 2015, Randy opened one and was pleasantly surprised to find not a tired wine but one still at its peak. "We can say that BC wines can hold up to 15 years," he says. That speaks to the longevity of Cabernet Sauvignon as well as the careful use of oak. The individual varietals are aged 14 to 18 months primarily in French oak, half of it new. Desert Hills also bottle-ages Mirage until it is ready, often releasing the wine close to its fifth birthday.

2011 ($36.90)

Cabernet Sauvignon 40%, Merlot 30%, Malbec 15%, Cabernet Franc 10%, Petit Verdot 5%. Alcohol 14.4%. Aged 18 months in French oak and blended prior to bottling. Production 450 cases.

WINERY TASTING NOTES "Rich blackcurrant, black cherry, and plum aromas lead to flavours of spice and dark chocolate, with a beautifully long finish." Drink by 2021.

2010 ($36.90)

Cabernet Sauvignon 40%, Merlot 30%, Malbec 15%, Cabernet Franc 10%, Petit Verdot 5%. Aged 18 months in French oak and blended prior to bottling. Production 300 cases.

Tasting notes unavailable.

2009

Cabernet Sauvignon 40%, Merlot 30%, Malbec 15%, Cabernet Franc 10%, Petit Verdot 5%. Alcohol 14.3%. Aged 18 months in French oak and blended prior to bottling. Production 833 cases.

AUTHOR'S TASTING NOTES "Firm and muscular; this wine begins with aromas of vanilla and cassis. On the palate, the concentrated texture opens to reveal flavours of blackcurrants, chocolate, and tobacco, with a note of licorice on the lingering finish." Drink by 2020.

2008

Cabernet Franc, Cabernet Sauvignon, Malbec, Merlot, Petit Verdot. Alcohol 14.3%. Three Boys and Eagle's Nest vineyards.

TASTING NOTES by *Food & Wine Trails*: "Aromas of cassis, cherry, and plum complement flavours of spice and dark chocolate." Drink by 2019.

Dirty Laundry Vineyard

BORDELLO

One needs to know the history of this Summerland winery to be comfortable with collecting a red wine called Bordello. It is just one of several double entendres in the portfolio.

The winery opened in 1995 as Scherzinger Vineyards. The owner was a German-born wood carver and carpenter who planted Gewürztraminer in 1978 after several years of losing money with cherries. When he retired in 2001, the winery was purchased by Ron and Cher Watkins. Showing respect to the former owner, they operated for several years under the Scherzinger name until they realized it was a liability: they could not sell more than 1,500 cases a year.

They hired Bernie Hadley-Beauregard, a Vancouver marketing consultant with a talent for creating provocative winery names based on local history. He struck pay dirt when he learned that Summerland once had a bordello that masqueraded as a laundry and was known as the "dirty laundry." This became the new name for the winery, which began selling wines with suggestive names such as Woo Woo Vines. Now the Watkinses had a new problem: they were sold out by June. The winery needed to expand, and they sold it in 2006 to a group of Albertans headed by lawyer Robert Campbell. Dirty Laundry has since grown to a 20,000-case winery.

Philip Soo, the consulting winemaker hired by the Campbell group, crafted the first Bordello in the 2008 vintage. It was (and remains) a blend of almost equal parts Cabernet Sauvignon and Merlot with just a dash of Cabernet Franc. Because the winery has other reds crafted for early drinking, Bordello has always been a red with grippy tannins that are designed to age. With a typical production usually between 300 and 500 cases, the wine was traditionally aged 18 months in French oak barrels and at least that long in bottle before release.

Mason Spink, who took over Dirty Laundry's winemaking in 2013, has changed the style by aging the wine up to 36 months in barrel and adding some Malbec to the blend. That is designed to give the wine a richer, more polished texture. It is still capable of long aging, but is expected to be a little more accessible on release.

> " Summerland once had a bordello that masqueraded as a laundry and was known as the "dirty laundry." "

2011 ($39.99)

Cabernet Sauvignon 49.5%, Merlot 49.5%, Cabernet Franc 1%. Alcohol 14.5%. Production 641 cases.

WINERY TASTING NOTES "A big red wine with aromas of meat spice, cocoa, vanilla, blackberry, blackcurrant, and anise. Firm tannins, finishes dry with lingering flavours of anise, cherry, toffee, and tobacco." Drink by 2022.

2010

Cabernet Sauvignon 49.5%, Merlot 49.5%, Cabernet Franc 1%. Alcohol 14.5%. Production 641 cases.

WINERY TASTING NOTES "A big red wine with aromas of meat spice, cocoa, vanilla, blackberry, blackcurrant, and anise. Firm tannins, finishes dry with lingering flavours of anise, cherry, toffee, and tobacco." Drink by 2021.

2009

Cabernet Sauvignon, Merlot, Cabernet Franc. Alcohol 14.5%.

AUTHOR'S TASTING NOTES "This is a dense and concentrated wine with aromas and flavours of plum, cassis, and black cherry, along with notes of coffee and tobacco. Tasted in 2015, the wine was vibrant and bright with polished, approachable tannins." Drink by 2020.

2008

Cabernet Sauvignon, Merlot, Cabernet Franc. Alcohol 14.9%.

TASTING NOTES by Gold Medal Marketing Inc. "A big red wine with aromas of meat spice, cocoa, vanilla, blackberry, blackcurrant, and anise. Firm tannins and finishes dry with long, lingering flavours of anise, cherry, toffee, and tobacco." Drink by 2018.

Eau Vivre Winery

PINOT NOIR

Eau Vivre is another winery posing a dilemma for collectors: whether to cellar the Pinot Noir or the Buddhafull, a Bordeaux blend better than its kitschy name. My choice is the Pinot Noir, with which the winery has won two Lieutenant Governor's Awards of Excellence, for its 2009 and 2010 vintages.

It turns out that Dale Wright, who owns the winery with his wife, Jeraldine Estin, has the same preference. In 2007, when they launched the winery, their original consultant asked them which wines they wanted in the portfolio. The top choice of the owners was Pinot Noir. "It has always been my favourite," says Dale. "My palate goes in that direction. The wine is a little lighter. It is nice and complex. When I get into the big Bordeaux wines, I will drink them but they are not my preference. I really am a Pinot drinker."

Dale and Jeraldine, both from Saskatchewan, came to the wine industry as business professionals with a love of wine. Jeraldine, who has an education degree, is a college-level teacher and counsellor. Dale is a geologist who has run his own oil-well drilling company since 1984. When they were attracted to the wine-growing lifestyle, they purchased a small winery near Cawston in the Similkameen Valley.

The winery's tiny vineyard was planted with Pinot Noir and Gewürztraminer. "We couldn't keep it alive," Dale says of the Pinot Noir. "It was in a frost pocket. After replanting it twice to Pinot Noir, I have Riesling in there now." The winery's success with Pinot Noir, especially after winning two Lieutenant Governor's Awards, has Eau Vivre sourcing multiple clones of the variety from Similkameen and Okanagan growers. The winery has made Pinot Noir every vintage except 2011, skipping that year just to balance inventory. But in the 2014 vintage, Eau Vivre, responding to the demand for its affordable, easy-drinking Pinot Noir, made 979 cases.

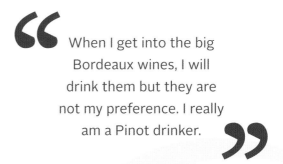

When I get into the big Bordeaux wines, I will drink them but they are not my preference. I really am a Pinot drinker.

Pinot Noir 2014 ($22)

Clones 114, 115, 777. Similkameen and Okanagan grapes. Alcohol 13.5%. Half was fermented with wild yeast. Aged in French oak for 16 months. Production 979 cases.

WINERY TASTING NOTES "The 2014 Pinot Noir is medium garnet in colour, featuring intense aromas of cherry, cranberry, and spice. Bright fruit flavors of fresh red berries, orange zest, and clove are complemented by the wine's lively acidity and subtle texture." Drink by 2020.

Pinot Noir 2013

Clones 114, 115, 777. Similkameen Valley grapes. Alcohol 13%. Aged in French oak barrels (21% new) for 10 months. Production 607 cases.

WINERY TASTING NOTES "[The wine has] a polished bright mid-red colour with lifted aromatics of freshly crushed cherries on the nose. Huge, intense notes of red fruits up front followed by spice and well-integrated oak. It finishes with a long silky texture and fresh acidity." Drink by 2018.

Pinot Noir 2012

Production 300 cases.
Tasting notes unavailable.

Pinot Noir 2010

Production 433 cases. Aged for 18 months in French and American oak barrels.

WINERY TASTING NOTES "Our 2010 Pinot Noir has delicate aromas of sour cherry, raspberry, and spice, complemented by wonderful notes of plum, dried herbs, and a touch of oak. Supple tannins and bright acidity round out the finish." Drink now.

Pinot Noir 2009

Production 203 cases.

AUTHOR'S TASTING NOTES "This is an elegant and polished wine, light in hue but silky in texture, with aromas and flavours of raspberry and mocha." Drink now.

Pinot Noir 2008

Alcohol 13.3%. Production 993 cases. Tasting notes unavailable. Drink now.

Pinot Noir 2007

Production 242 cases.

TASTING NOTES by Jurgen Gothe in the *Georgia Straight* in 2010: "A big red bite at the front, along with some smoky bacon, a little edgy, which will mellow away, and a full fruit-laden texture. A unique expression of BC Pinot." Drink now.

Buddhafull 2012 ($27)

Merlot 35%, Cabernet Franc 26%, Cabernet Sauvignon 26%, Petit Verdot 9%, Malbec 4%. Alcohol 13.5%. Aged 18 months in oak (French, American, and Hungarian). Production 550 cases.

WINERY TASTING NOTES "Notes of cherry, raspberry, and plum lead to mouth-coating blackberry, currants, and spice. This medium-bodied wine also exhibits a wide array of red and black fruits, violets, and fine chalky tannins." Drink by 2018.

Buddhafull 2010

Cabernet Franc 52%, Cabernet Sauvignon 27%, Malbec 15%, Syrah 6%. Alcohol 14.1%. Aged 16 months in oak (90% French, 10% American). Production 500 cases.

WINERY TASTING NOTES "This blend . . . is rich with dark fruit flavours and is encased with plush aromas of wild berries, plums, and tobacco. Wonderfully long on the finish, the silky tannins are softened by the natural acidity." Drink by 2020.

8th Generation Vineyard
RIESLING SELECTION

In 2011, 8th Generation Vineyard was already making two Rieslings—a dry one and an off-dry one—when winemaker Bernd Schales decided over dinner one early August evening to add an age-worthy premium Riesling to the portfolio. Stefanie, his wife, was not enthusiastic at first about extending an already large portfolio of wines. But the next day, Bernd went into the winery's Okanagan Falls vineyard and reduced the crop on four rows of vines. That settled the matter: those vines, now carrying less than two tons of grapes per acre, were destined to produce the more concentrated Riesling called Selection.

"The Selection is the one wine which I suggest my customers put into a decanter a few hours before tasting it," Stefanie says. "It shows so much more depth and texture." The lower-priced little brother, also a fine dry wine, is called Riesling Classic. That is the wine to open up with friends and neighbours, Stefanie says. "But you don't share the Selection. It is a special wine." She is joking, of course, just to make a point about the tiers of 8th Generation Rieslings.

The variety is in their blood. Stefanie, though trained in architectural drafting, has 10 generations of wine-growing in her family. Bernd, who was born in 1972, comes from a Rheinhessen family that has grown grapes and made wine for eight generations, since 1783. Rather than joining the siblings and relatives in family-owned Weingut Schales,

Bernd and Stefanie struck out on their own in the Okanagan. In 2003, they bought a vineyard near Okanagan Falls that had been planted in 1985 with, among other varieties, Riesling. The mature vines, all Clone 21B Riesling on their own roots, produce admirable wines with ripe flavours, crisp acidity, and a mineral backbone. "We were lucky," Stefanie says. "We knew the exposure was good, but we had no idea how the wine would taste."

They opened the 8th Generation winery in 2007. While establishing their brand, until 2011, they sold some of their grapes. Bernd introduced Selection in that vintage because he was able to keep all his grapes.

The intention is to make Selection every time a vintage produces a Riesling with exceptional flavour and texture. Bernd tried to make Selection in 2012 and 2014 but decided the wines were not quite at the Selection level. Those wines were added to the Classic blend, with a noticeable increase in the quality of the Classic. "It is a good year to buy Classic in a year when we don't have Selection," Stefanie says. "It all goes into the Classic."

The sophisticated 8th Generation Rieslings will blossom with age. Well-made Rieslings with this degree of minerality, acidity, and rich fruit typically develop honeyed aromas of marmalade (or petrol, if you wish) and will peak at about 10 years, and then hold that peak for who knows how long.

Riesling Selection 2015

($28.50)

Alcohol 13%. Fermented with indigenous yeast. Residual sugar 9.5 grams per litre. Production 180 cases.

WINERY TASTING NOTES "Zesty, refreshing, layered with apples and citrus and more finesse. My softest and richest Riesling, due to skin contact. You will discover notes of minerality at the long finish. Open the bottle at least four hours prior to dinner or give it a short swirl in a decanter." Drink by 2025.

Riesling Selection 2013

Alcohol 13.4%. Fermented with indigenous yeast. Residual sugar 8 grams per litre. Production 150 cases.

WINERY TASTING NOTES "Zesty, refreshing, layered with apples and citrus and more finesse. Soft and rich Riesling due to skin contact. Good notes of minerality at the end." Drink by 2024.

Riesling Selection 2011

Alcohol 12.3%. Fermented with indigenous yeast. Production 224 cases.

AUTHOR'S TASTING NOTES "The wine begins with a subtle and classic whiff of petrol—marmalade, if you prefer. On the richly textured palate, there are tangerine flavours lifted by bright acidity. The finish is dry." Drink now to 2023.

Riesling Classic 2015 ($21)

Alcohol 13.5%. Residual sugar 8 grams per litre. Production 600 cases.

WINERY TASTING NOTES "Sourced from our 30-year-old vines, produced only in stainless steel tanks. This 'Queen' of German wines offers oodles of fruit and acidity in perfect balance. It features a scintillating fruity lemon nose and ripe apples on the palate. A Riesling that will surprise and convince at the same time, as it is *not sweet at all* and for that reason a matchmaker when it comes to food pairing." Drink by 2020.

Riesling Classic 2014

Alcohol 13.7%. Residual sugar 8.5 grams per litre. Production 500 cases.

WINERY TASTING NOTES "Sourced from our 29-year-old vines, produced only in stainless steel tanks. This 'Queen' of German wines offers oodles of fruit and acidity in perfect balance. It features a scintillating fruity lemon nose and ripe apples on the palate. A Riesling that will surprise and convince at the same time, as it is not sweet at all." Drink now to 2019.

Riesling Classic 2013

Alcohol 12.3%. Residual sugar 9 grams per litre. Production 500 cases.

AUTHOR'S TASTING NOTES "The wine begins with aromas of citrus and a hint of developing petrol, leading to zesty flavours of citrus. This is an exceptionally well-balanced dry Riesling." Drink now to 2018.

Riesling Classic 2012

Alcohol 13.2%. Residual sugar 9 grams per litre.

WINERY TASTING NOTES "Made from our 25+-year-old vines, produced only in stainless steel tanks. This 'Queen' of German wines offers oodles of fruit and characteristic acidity in perfect balance. It features a scintillating fruity lemon nose and a whisper of ripe apples on the palate. Zesty, refreshing, layered with apples and citrus and more finesse. Good notes of mineral." Drink now.

Elephant Island Orchard Wines

NAYSAYER

This winery, which Del and Miranda Halladay opened in 2001, has *orchard* in its name because at one time they produced just fruit wines. The wines earned considerable acclaim; in spite of that, there was one niggling irritant. "We were constantly hearing that we didn't make real wine," Del remembers. So they bought a small apple orchard and in 2005 replaced most of the fruit trees with about a hectare of vines, primarily Cabernet Franc and Viognier.

Their first two grape wines were made in the superb 2009 vintage. "The motivation was to demonstrate to other people, and maybe a little bit to ourselves, that in fact we could make real wine," Del says. And they made sure others noticed they had put down a marker by assigning provocative names to the wines. Naysayer is the red blend. Told You So is the Viognier. When a Chardonnay joined the portfolio in 2014, Del and Miranda called it the Other Way. Fruit wines, however, still account for 10 of the 13 wines in the portfolio. "We can't see ourselves getting rid of any," Del says. In fact, the couple launched the Naramata Cider Company in 2015, and Del now makes at least four hard ciders.

Miranda, born in Powell River in 1973, is a geologist. Del, born in Victoria in 1972, earned a marketing degree at Loyola College in Maryland, which he attended on a lacrosse scholarship. Until he retired from the game in 2007, he played lacrosse professionally, and the income supplemented the development of Elephant Island.

The winery's singular name memorializes a family legend. When Catherine Chard Wisnicki, an architect and Miranda's grandmother (who died at 97 in 2014), designed the house still on the winery property today, her husband, Paul (an engineer), scoffed that it was designed purely "for the eye." Having already been told the property would be a white elephant, she responded by calling the house "Elephant Eye-land."

Unlike many Okanagan red blends, Naysayer is built on Cabernet Franc supported by Merlot and a dash of Cabernet Sauvignon. Del ages the individual varieties in French oak barrels (50% new) for 14 months. "I think having a fairly aggressive new oak program aids in the addition of barrel tannins and helps the longevity of these wines," Del says. "They are made to age; they are made to be put down. They should improve over time."

2013 ($25.29)

Cabernet Franc 80%. Alcohol 13.2%. Harvest October 30. Production 263 cases.

AUTHOR'S TASTING NOTES "The wine begins with aromas of blackberry and cherry, leading to flavours of cherry, boysenberry, mulberry, and cherry cola. The texture is supple and full, and the finish lingers." Drink by 2023.

2012

Cabernet Franc 74%, Merlot 21%, Cabernet Sauvignon 5%. Alcohol 14.5%. Harvest November 3. Production 512 cases.

AUTHOR'S TASTING NOTES "Production doubled in 2012, when excellent Cabernet Franc was available from another Naramata grower. The wine has spicy cherry and blackberry aromas and flavours of black cherry, blackcurrant, and vanilla. Supple oak tannins and minerality give this wine backbone." Drink by 2023.

2011

Cabernet Franc 58%. Alcohol 12.9%. Harvest November 2. Production 201 cases.

AUTHOR'S TASTING NOTES "This is an excellent wine from a notoriously cool vintage. A higher percentage of Merlot in the blend accounts for jammy aromas of vanilla and cherry, and a juicy texture. On the palate, there are flavours of plum, cherry, and chocolate." Drink by 2020.

2010

Cabernet Franc 80%. Alcohol 14.5%. Harvest November 3. Production 199 cases.

AUTHOR'S TASTING NOTES "Made in another cool vintage, this wine is reminiscent of Chianti because of the lean texture, the bright aromas and flavours of cherry and cranberry, and the spine of minerals." Drink by 2020.

2009

Cabernet Franc 80%. Alcohol 15%. Harvest September 29. Production 205 cases.

AUTHOR'S TASTING NOTES "The debut Naysayer is from a hot, early vintage with a harvest a month earlier than usual. The wine has appealing spicy red fruit aromas. On the palate, there are flavours of spice, vanilla, black cherry, and mocha. The long, ripe tannins contribute to a polished, elegant texture." Drink by 2020.

Ex Nihilo Vineyards

PINOT NOIR

It was mad cow disease that propelled Jay Paulson into winemaking. It is a long story.

Jay is one of the partners in Ex Nihilo Vineyards, along with his wife, Twila, and Jeff and Decoa Harder, all of them former Albertans. Jay, Twila, and Jeff have been friends since high school.

Decoa, a former skiing instructor with a marketing education, was the first of the four in the wine business, as a wine salesperson for Quails' Gate and Mt. Boucherie. She says, "I woke up one morning [in 2003] and said 'Jeff, we have to find land.'" The following year, they bought a property in the municipality of Lake Country and built a house. After enlisting the Paulsons as partners, they planted two hectares of Pinot Noir, Pinot Gris, and Riesling vines in 2007. The vineyard doubled in size in 2013 after the Paulsons moved from Edmonton to the Okanagan.

Jeff and Decoa were instrumental in sparking Jay's interest in wine in 2002, after they invited the Paulsons to join them for a vacation in the Napa Valley, where Jeff's brother, James, owns a winery. When he returned to Edmonton, Jay immersed himself in wine appreciation courses. At the time, the Paulsons were in the cattle industry, with Jay operating a cattle brokerage business (buying and selling livestock for feeder lots and slaughterhouses). The incidence of mad cow disease in some Alberta herds devastated the industry, triggering Jay's decision to partner with his friend in Ex Nihilo.

The early vintages of Ex Nihilo, which opened in 2008, were made by Jim Faulkner and Dr. Alan Marks, both of whom were associated with Mt. Boucherie. After being mentored by them in the cellar, Jay emerged as assistant winemaker in 2012 and took full charge two years later.

Most of the wines in the Ex Nihilo portfolio are collectible, including a notable Riesling, a Bordeaux blend called Night, and intense Merlots. However, Pinot Noir has emerged as the signature varietal because it is planted in the estate vineyard.

The incidence of mad cow disease in some Alberta herds . . . trigger[ed] Jay's decision to partner with his friend in Ex Nihilo.

2014 ($55)

Clone 115. Alcohol 13%. Aged 9 months in French oak barrels (30% new). Production 1,156 cases.

WINERY TASTING NOTES "Lovely ripe cherry aromas are sprinkled with strawberry, violets, and coffee. The satin palate is well balanced with dark spice on the finish. After whole berry fermentation, the wine was aged nine months in a combination of French and American oak. The result is a wine with a gorgeous texture that will please the Pinot Noir enthusiast." Drink by 2020.

2013

Clone 115. Alcohol 13%. Aged 9 months in French oak barrels (30% new). Production 1,156 cases.

WINERY TASTING NOTES "Lovely ripe cherry aromas are sprinkled with strawberry, violets, and coffee. The satin palate is well balanced with dark spice on the finish." Drink by 2019.

2012

Clone 115. Alcohol 13.4%. Aged 9 months in French oak barrels. Production 504 cases.

WINERY TASTING NOTES "A seductive Pinot Noir showing notes of dried cherries, plums, and ripe strawberries. Complexities of star anise, allspice, and black tea balance the wine and give it a smooth, lingering finish." Drink by 2018.

2011

Clone 115. Alcohol 13.5%. Aged 10 months in French oak barrels. Production 840 cases.

WINERY TASTING NOTES "Our 2011 Pinot Noir displays notes of wild raspberries, dried cherries, plums, and ripe rhubarb. Complexities of allspice, anise, and black teas highlighted by French Oak, give way to silky tannins and a beautiful structure. The finish is rich and elegant." Drink now.

2010

Clone 115. Alcohol 13.2%. Aged 10 months in French oak barrels.

WINERY TASTING NOTES "Aromas of dried cherries, plums, and ripe strawberries give way to the complexities of star anise, allspice, and black teas." Drink now.

Fairview Cellars
ICONOCLAST

The familiar cliché about wine being made in the vineyard is amply demonstrated by the wines of Fairview Cellars. Most are grown in the 2.4-hectare (6-acre) vineyard that proprietor Bill Eggert planted in 1993, almost entirely with Bordeaux red varieties. "I have some of the best land for supporting reds and I honestly didn't want to waste any on whites," he says—before finding room for a little Sauvignon Blanc. The largest block is Cabernet Sauvignon, a challenging variety to ripen in the Okanagan—but one that Bill has mastered. It anchors his Bear (a Meritage) and wholly comprises Iconoclast, the limited-volume $120 red he has made since 2008.

"It boils down to the site," he says. "We're in the hottest area in Canada where they grow grapes. When you compare the heat units to Bordeaux, we're 50 to 100 more heat units higher." His vineyard is on the brow of an alluvial fan with ideal southern exposure and complex, mineral-laden soils. "It's not just the soils. It is the morning sun. We get that sun exposure early in the morning on the grapes, and there is more time for the vine to develop flavours."

Bill, who was born in Ottawa in 1957, has an agriculture degree from the University of Guelph. He learned viticulture in a vineyard his uncle owned near Beamsville, Ontario. The uncle rejected Bill's suggestion that he replace hybrid varieties with vinifera, and Bill moved to the Okanagan in 1983. He did vineyard work and construction over the next decade until he could afford to buy his vineyard property.

He thinks of himself as a grape grower, not a winemaker. Although he taught viticulture at Okanagan College for several years, he regarded his own viticulture practices as proprietary. "It is not so much a secret anymore," he says now. "The boys have done the science, and it is not anecdotal anymore. What I am doing is what more and more people are doing. You can see it in the wines."

In an ideal world, he would make one premium Bordeaux blend from his estate. He lost that option when, after barrel tastings with customers, he gave in to pleas to keep this or that barrel separate. Soon he had a following for Cabernet Franc, Merlot, and Bear, his Meritage, also sought by collectors.

In 2008, he bought two new barrels from the French barrel-maker Berthomieu and aged some estate Cabernet Sauvignon for 26 months rather than 14 months. "I had a pyramid of barrels with my Cabernet Sauvignon," Bill recalls. "To a man, people that tasted those two barrels said you have to keep them separate." He did the same in 2009.

And he decided this would be Fairview's icon wine. One customer familiar with Bill's outspoken personality said: "Bill, if you are going to have an icon wine, it has to be called Iconoclast."

"For me, it is not about having small lots that are ridiculously expensive," Bill says. "My goal is to have it all there, especially off my own property. Pretty well everything off my own property goes for $35 or more."

2012 (Price not available)

Alcohol 13.7%. Aged 26 months in barrel. Production 140 cases.

WINERY TASTING NOTES "A rich violet colour with floral notes of tobacco, spice, and leather. The generous mouthfeel is layered with hints of blueberries, hazelnuts, chocolate, vanilla, and stewed cherries that round the supple tannins into an age-worthy, lengthy, and opulent finish." Drink by 2027.

2011 (Price not available)

Alcohol 13.9%. Aged 26 months in barrel. Production 95 cases.

WINERY TASTING NOTES "Vibrant ruby in colour with a nose of focused white pepper, eucalyptus, and spice. Followed by flavours of juicy red fruit, red licorice, plums, and lapin cherries. Mineral notes combine with raspberries to round out soft, restrained tannins for the finish." Drink by 2026.

2010 ($119.90)

Alcohol 13.8%. Aged 26 months in barrel. Production 95 cases.

AUTHOR'S TASTING NOTES "This is a cool-vintage Cabernet Sauvignon with bright fruit flavours (blackcurrant, black cherry) and a touch of mint. The firm Bordelaise texture promises a life of 10 to 15 years." Drink by 2025.

2009

Alcohol 14.7%. Production 95 cases.

AUTHOR'S TASTING NOTES "This is a powerful wine from a vintage so warm that the grapes were picked before the end of September, two to three weeks earlier than usual. The wine has aromas of cassis, mint, and vanilla. The flavours of this wine present layers of blackcurrant, black cherry, and dark chocolate. Long, ripe tannins give the wine a svelte but concentrated texture." Drink by 2022.

2008

Alcohol 13.4%. Production 95 cases.

AUTHOR'S TASTING NOTES (in 2015): "This is an elegant wine with silky tannins. It begins with aromas of cassis lightly kissed by vanilla. On the palate, there are flavours of cassis, boysenberry, and cherry with a delicate hint of bell pepper, adding up to an appealing basket of fruit flavours with a lingering finish. Good acidity adds freshness and vitality." Drink now to 2020.

50th Parallel Estate
PINOT NOIRS

50th Parallel's focus on Pinot Noir arises from both the northerly location of the vineyard and the sensibilities of the partners. Grant Stanley, the winemaker and a partner since 2013, once remarked that he thinks about Pinot Noir 80 percent of the time.

The vineyard is at Carr's Landing in the North Okanagan. Since 2009, when planting began, at least six clones of Pinot Noir have been planted, taking up 68 percent of the 16.6 hectares (41 acres). The remainder is Pinot Gris, Riesling, Gewürztraminer, and Chardonnay.

The winery's founders, Albertans Curtis Krouzel and Sheri-Lee Turner-Krouzel, spent almost a decade looking for Okanagan vineyard property before they found these sunbathed slopes above the eastern shore of Okanagan Lake. There is a history of grape growing here. Jordan & Ste-Michelle Cellars, a winery then based in Victoria, bought grapes—mostly French hybrids but also Riesling and Bacchus—from the vineyard in the 1970s. Frank Whitehead, then a viticultural manager for the winery, remembers it as "good dirt." Ste-Michelle closed after being acquired by Brights Winery in 1981, and the vines were pulled out in 1988. Curtis and Sheri-Lee spotted the slopes when they were staying at a resort on the other side of the lake.

"It was about three times the size of the project I intended," Curtis says. "But I had always wanted to do something fairly world-class. So we set out on this mission to create a winery focused on Pinot Noir." His initial vineyard manager and winemaker was New Zealander Adrian Baker, who has a master's degree in oenology from the University of Adelaide and more than a decade's experience making Pinot Noir. When Adrian left 50th Parallel to develop another major Pinot Noir vineyard nearby, Grant Stanley took over as winemaker.

Born in Vancouver in 1967, Grant trained in New Zealand, where he made six vintages with legendary Pinot Noir producer Ata Rangi. In Canada, he made 10 vintages at Quails' Gate Winery.

The 50th Parallel Pinot Noirs display a "feminine" style—perfumed aromas, bright berry flavours, and silky textures. To a degree, that reflects the youthfulness of the vines, which can be expected to deliver darker and bolder flavours as the vineyard matures. The style also reflects Grant's winemaking. The grapes, handled with utmost gentleness, are fermented in small batches, naturally with wild yeast. The wines are aged in French oak, with barrels bought primarily from four coopers, including François Frères—"a go-to barrel for Pinot Noir for 100 years," Grant says. The wines, with no racking, are aged on the lees for about 10 months: "I prefer to go to bottle at 10 months and keep the wines fresh." The wines are all under screw cap because Grant believes that makes them retain vibrant flavours longer than they would under cork.

2014 Unparalleled ($50)

A special release comprising the 14 best barriques. From three vineyard blocks and four clones (115, 144, 667, 828). Alcohol 13.5%. Production 350 cases.

WINERY TASTING NOTES "Aroma: Savoury herbs and warm earth, hint of rose petal, toasted walnut, and anise. Palate: An intense entry showcasing the Okanagan spirit of Pinot Noir—ripe black staccato cherry, blackcurrant, baked blueberries, and a breath of roasted red pepper. Layers of structured tannin promise years of drinkability but still with the silky presence to drink now. The finish presents the impression of freshly toasted cashews, black pepper, and slatey minerality." Drink by 2024.

2014 ($32)

Pinot Noir (Dijon clones 115, 114, 777, 667, 828, 943). Alcohol 13.5%. Fermented with natural yeast; aged 13 months in French oak; unfiltered. Production 3,194 cases and 190 magnums.

WINERY TASTING NOTES "A rich and fruitful entry that immediately fills the mouth with concentrated dark fruit flavours. Ripe black raspberry, truffle, toasted nuts, and peppery chocolate prevail and then blend seamlessly with beautiful mineral undertones. The sipper is rewarded with the characteristic silky, long finish we have come to expect from our estate Pinot Noir." Drink by 2024.

2013

Pinot Noir (eight Dijon clones). Alcohol 14.5%. Fermented with natural yeast; aged 12 months in French oak; unfiltered. Production 2,145 cases and 195 magnums.

WINERY TASTING NOTES "Bright red, purple hue. [Aromas of] wild blackberry, dusty cocoa, exotic spice, violets, and truffle. Palate: A youthful, supple entry unfolds into silky, satiny textures unwinding with firm, fine tannins and exceptional concentration and length. Dark berry flavours with undertones of truffle and chocolate." Drink by 2023.

2012

Pinot Noir. Alcohol 14%. Fermented with natural yeast; aged 12 months in French oak; unfiltered. Production 1,286 cases.

WINERY TASTING NOTES "Bright red purple hue. [Aromas of] dark cherry, chocolate, rose petal, vanilla, spice. Palate: rich, plus entry with silky textures and balanced attack, leading to a long and smooth finish." Drink by 2019.

2011

Pinot Noir. Alcohol 14%. Aged in French oak. Production 100 cases.

AUTHOR'S TASTING NOTES "Made from the estate's first Pinot Noir harvest, this wine has lovely aromas of cherry and strawberry, with layers of flavour—strawberry, cherry, mocha, spice, and subtle oak. It also has a rich and silky texture that one expects in fine Pinot Noir." Drink now.

Fort Berens Estate Winery
MERITAGE

An entirely new British Columbia viticultural area was pioneered when Fort Berens Estate Winery planted its first 8 hectares (20 acres) of vineyard in 2009 on the Fraser River Bench near Lillooet. When the vineyard achieved full production in 2014, the winery owners began developing another 8 hectares. The winery's Meritage, originally made with grapes purchased from the Okanagan, has attracted collector interest because it now reflects this distinctive terroir.

The winery's founders, management consultant Rolf de Bruin and banker Heleen Pannekoek, left their native country, the Netherlands, for the wine grower's lifestyle in BC. "One of the primary reasons why we chose to start a vineyard was that we could not foresee ourselves working in a corporate environment and having kids," Rolf explains. "We are both very, very ambitious. If we embark on something, we go all for it." They arrived in Kelowna in 2008—it had taken two years to get a visa to come to Canada—and began looking for vineyard properties. Deterred by the high cost of Okanagan property, they turned to sunburnt Lillooet on the advice of Richard Cleave, a veteran vineyard manager in the Okanagan.

There is a modest history of grape growing on the Fraser River Bench. The Fort Berens property was once part of a BC Electric Co. farm that, in the 1960s, included trial blocks of Maréchal Foch and other grapes. Robert Roshard, who managed

the farm until it closed, continued growing grapes on a nearby property that was later taken over by his daughter, Christ'l Roshard. That led to a seven-year-long study, the Lillooet Grape Project, which began in 2005, when Christ'l was Lillooet's mayor. At least 22 different varietals were evaluated. The study left no doubt that the Lillooet area's growing conditions are comparable to those of the South Okanagan. The surrounding Coast Mountains give Lillooet, 325 kilometres north of Vancouver, hot, dry summers. The winters are cold but usually not vine-killing. Fort Berens has succeeded with Pinot Gris, Chardonnay, Riesling, Pinot Noir, Merlot, and Cabernet Franc. The vineyard also has small plots of Petit Verdot and Grüner Veltliner.

The area's history is rich and colourful. The winery is named for the Hudson's Bay Company trading post that operated there between 1859 and 1861. During the Cariboo gold rush, which began in 1858, Lillooet briefly boomed to a population of 15,000 and was the second-largest settlement on the west coast north of San Francisco. In 1862, a businessman brought 23 camels as pack animals. That proved to be a fiasco; besides the terrain being too rocky for camel feet to navigate, the animals panicked the pack horses and mules. Fort Berens references the history with two wines—a red blend and a white blend under the 23 Camels label.

Fort Berens has met the challenge of being off the beaten path of the BC wine industry by building a 12,000-case winery in 2013. The modernistic structure is dramatically perched on a hilltop overlooking the vineyard and the Fraser River. The vineyards here are expected to fulfill most of the winery's needs, which are supplemented with grapes from the Okanagan and the Similkameen.

Until 2011, the Meritage, which is generally anchored by Merlot, was made entirely with Okanagan fruit, with the first one, in 2007, blended from finished wine. The winery has established a style for this wine, as well as for the other reds, that the Lillooet terroir will sustain. The reds are ready to drink on release but are capable of cellaring an additional four to eight years.

2014 ($28)

Merlot 65%, Cabernet Franc 20%, Cabernet Sauvignon 15%. Alcohol 13.3%. Aged 10 to 12 months primarily in French oak barrels (20% new) and one year in bottle before release. Production 1,170 cases.
WINERY TASTING NOTES "This primarily estate-grown wine is a juicy, big red blend that is lush with flavours of ripe red fruit, smoky bacon, and roasted red peppers." Drink by 2024.

2013

Merlot 60%, Cabernet Franc 20%, Cabernet Sauvignon 20%. Alcohol 14.5%. Estate and Sundial vineyards. Aged 9 months in French and American oak. Production 1,246 cases.
WINERY TASTING NOTES "It features rich aromas of blackcurrant and grilled red peppers with a silky texture, firm tannins, and a lengthy finish." Drink by 2023.

2012

Merlot 72%, Cabernet Sauvignon 18%, Cabernet Franc 10%. Alcohol 14%. Sundial Vineyard 60%, Estate Vineyard 40%. Aged 12 months in French and American oak barrels. Production 844 cases.
WINERY TASTING NOTES "Aromas of dark roses, chocolate, and sage, with hints of summer cherries and blackcurrants." Drink by 2020.

2011

Merlot 47%, Cabernet Sauvignon 34%, Cabernet Franc 19%. Alcohol 13.4%. Sundial and Estate vineyards. Aged 12 months in French and American oak barrels. Production 743 cases.
AUTHOR'S TASTING NOTES "Dark in colour, it begins with an appealing aroma of black cherry, blackcurrant, and vanilla. On the palate, the wine's long, ripe tannins give it a generous richness. The flavours echo the aroma with added touches of chocolate and spice." Drink by 2020.

2010

Merlot 65%, Cabernet Sauvignon 30%, Cabernet Franc 5%. Alcohol 14.5%. Sundial Vineyard. Aged 12 months in French and American oak. Production 475 cases.
WINERY TASTING NOTES "Features aromas of blackcurrant, cherry, and spices. Well-structured with elegant tannins and a long, lingering finish." Drink by 2020.

2009

Merlot 70%, Cabernet Sauvignon 25%, Cabernet Franc 5%. Alcohol 14%. Sundial Vineyard. Production 445 cases.

AUTHOR'S TASTING NOTES "It has the soft, ripe texture of Merlot, with attractive aromas of blueberry and blackberry. The berry flavours echo these aromas. The rich, ripe tannins give the wine an early accessibility and appeal." Drink by 2019.

2008

Merlot 80%, Cabernet Sauvignon 15%, Cabernet Franc 5%. Alcohol 14.2%. Aged 18 months in French oak barrels. Production 112 cases.

WINERY TASTING NOTES "Chocolate cherries, succulent berries, fruitcake spices, and coffee liqueur with faint chalky minerality . . . supple and fresh . . . blueberry and cherry flavours dominate with a seam of sweet liquorice; appealing texture, approachable fruit." Drink by 2018.

2007

Merlot 80%, Cabernet Sauvignon 15%, Cabernet Franc 5%. Sundial Vineyard. Aged 18 months in French and American oak.

AUTHOR'S TASTING NOTES "The debut Meritage, this wine was blended by a Naramata Bench winery in the approximate style of future Meritages at Fort Berens." Drink now.

Foxtrot Vineyards
PINOT NOIR

Foxtrot Vineyards' proprietor Torsten Allander was apprehensive when a friend he was dining with in 2015 produced a 1999 Kettle Valley Pinot Noir made with Foxtrot Vineyards grapes. He expected a wine that old would be over the hill. "They cracked it and it was fantastic," recounts Torsten's son, Gustav. "It was not past its peak." This confirms the age-worthiness of the legendary Burgundy-style wines that the Allander family, including Kicki, Torsten's wife, began producing in 2004 from this Naramata Bench property.

The 1.4-hectare (3.5-acre) vineyard was planted in 1994 and 1995 by Don and Carol Munro, academics from Vancouver who had retired to the Okanagan. They chose just Clone 115 Pinot Noir, one of the best all-around clones. The vineyard got its name when a bear ambled among the vines in a manner that recalled the foxtrot dance.

"The entire vineyard is own-rooted," Gustav said in 2015. "I think that is good. The vines are now 20 years old. We have not seen any struggle." The Allander family, which bought the vineyard in 2002, has since doubled its size by planting an adjacent property. Most of the vines are cuttings from the original Clone 115 plants, and all are self-rooted.

New to viticulture, Torsten, who is a retired pulp and paper engineer, sold the grapes for several years. In the 2004 vintage, he started a winemaking trial at the nearby Lake Breeze winery. He wanted to determine whether a world-class Pinot Noir could be produced on the Naramata Bench if one applied the resources (including premium French oak and a state-of-the-art press) to his fruit. When the answer was yes, Torsten built his own cellar in 2008 on the Foxtrot property. Gustav, who was studying engineering in Sweden when his parents bought the vineyard, returned home to become the winemaker. He was mentored by his wife, Nadine, a New Zealand-trained winemaker.

Foxtrot Pinot Noir quickly became the most coveted and collectible of Okanagan Pinot Noirs. The wine invariably has richly seductive fruit and a sultry texture with refreshing acidity. "I want to make a wine that you are going to be able to lay down and let it evolve over time," Gustav says. "You can drink the wine now, but I prefer that people hold on to it for a bit."

The wine is aged 18 to 20 months in barrel, two to four months longer than most Okanagan Pinot Noirs. "We are exclusively using François Frères barrels," Gustav says. "We have worked with them since day one. It is one of the cooperages of choice for top Pinot Noir producers around the world." Until 2012, the wine was aged entirely in new barrels. Gustav now ages 40 percent of each vintage in second-fill barrels, moderating the oak to better reveal the fruit flavours.

Foxtrot is tightly focused. Intending to cap production at 3,000 cases a year, the winery makes vineyard-designated Pinot Noir from the Foxtrot vineyard. Waltz Pinot Noir is made from purchased grapes or from the fruit of young vines. The portfolio is rounded out with Chardonnay and Pinot Noir rosé.

2013 ($55)

Dijon clone 115. Alcohol 13.6%. Aged 20 months in François Frères barrels (80% new, 20% second fill).

WINERY TASTING NOTES "In the glass, the [wine] shows a beautiful ruby red colour. The aroma is of red and black cherries, fresh spice, and classic Pinot Noir earthiness. On the palate, the [wine] shows both power and elegance with great minerality and balanced acidity. Dark red fruit flavours complemented by a light spiciness and minerality continue onto the long, supple finish framed by the lush, ripe tannins." Drink by 2026.

2012

Dijon clone 115. Alcohol 13.7%. Aged 20 months in François Frères barrels (80% new, 20% second fill).

WINEMAKER'S TASTING NOTES "[The wine has] a stunning nose of red and black fruits, oriental spice, and earthy notes. The intensity of the fruit and earthiness continues on the palate and is wonderfully framed by the vibrant acidity and bold, silky-smooth tannins." Drink by 2025.

2011

Dijon clone 115. Alcohol 13.7%. Aged 18 months in new François Frères barrels.

WINEMAKER'S TASTING NOTES "The wine [has] a bright ruby hue . . . with an array of red fruits, spice, and earthy aromas. On the palate the wine strikes a perfect harmony between power and elegance with silky tannins and beautiful red fruit characteristics and more of the classic Pinot Noir earthiness." Drink by 2021.

2010

Dijon clone 115. Alcohol 13.6%. Aged 20 months in new François Frères barrels (medium and medium plus toast).

AUTHOR'S TASTING NOTES "This wine begins with spicy cherry aromas. The flavours have a core of cherry and raspberry framed by the spice of the oak barrels. The wine has the rich, silky texture that is the hallmark of Foxtrot." Drink by 2020.

2009

Dijon clone 115. Alcohol 13.5%. Aged 18 months in new François Frères barrels.

AUTHOR'S TASTING NOTES "The wine announces itself with dramatic aromas of cherry, spice, mocha, and French oak. It is rich and fleshy on the palate, delivering flavours of cherry, strawberry, and spice with a sultry elegance. If ever there was a wine to elope with, this is it." Drink by 2019.

2008

Dijon clone 115. Alcohol 13.6%. Aged 16 months in new François Frères barrels.

WINEMAKER'S TASTING NOTES "The wine with a bright ruby hue has fresh aromas of blackberry, raspberry, hints of plum, and floral and spicy notes on the finish. On the palate the wine strikes a perfect harmony between power and elegance with silky tannins, beautiful red fruit characteristics, and classic Pinot Noir earthiness." Drink by 2018.

2007

Dijon clone 115. Alcohol 13.7%. Aged 16 months in new François Frères barrels.

WINEMAKER'S TASTING NOTES "The wine with a ruby hue has aromas of ripe cherry, raspberry, floral and spicy notes with a hint of earthy forest floor . . . The fantastic richness of this wine centres on succulent dark berry flavours, earthy and spicy notes, framed by subtle oak elements, which will continue to integrate with aging, and good acidity." Drink now.

2006

Dijon clone 115. Alcohol 13.9%. Aged 16 months in new François Frères barrels (medium and medium plus toast).

WINEMAKER'S TASTING NOTES "The wine with a lovely light hue has aromas of ripe cherry and spicy notes. The fantastic richness of the wine centres on succulent dark berry flavours enhanced by subtle oak elements . . . a marvellous texture and silky, lengthy finish." Drink now.

2005

Dijon clone 115. Alcohol 13.7%. Aged 16 months in new François Frères barrels.

WINEMAKER'S TASTING NOTES "The wine has intense aromas of ripe cherry, dark plum, and floral and spicy notes. The fantastic richness of the wine centres on succulent dark berry flavours enhanced by subtle oak elements [and] a marvellous mid-palate and silky, lengthy finish." Drink now.

2004

Dijon clone 115. Alcohol 14%. Aged 16 months in new François Frères barrels.

WINEMAKER'S TASTING NOTES "Intense aromas of ripe cherry, raspberry, and strawberry fruit. The fantastic richness of the wine centres on succulent dark berry flavours enhanced by subtle oak elements. This deeply coloured Pinot Noir has evolving layers of complexity, with a marvellous mid-palate and a silky, lengthy finish." Drink now.

Garry Oaks Winery

PINOT NOIR

Elaine Kozak and Marcel Mercier, who opened this Salt Spring Island winery in 2003, gently make the case for collecting Zweigelt because theirs ages so well. However, few wineries grow this red Austrian variety—even if it should be collected, there is a negligible following for a varietal rarely planted in British Columbia. It is far easier to make the case for Pinot Noir. "We really, really like it," Elaine says of theirs.

They have two clones of Pinot Noir: 115 and 375. Two blocks comprising about 1 hectare (2.5 acres) were planted in 2000 on a steep south-facing slope, formerly an apple orchard cultivated by the Lee family, pioneers of Salt Spring Island. To find a suitable location, Marcel, an environmental engineer, prepared an extensive topographical map of the island. That led him to the property on Lee's Hill, which they were able to buy from retiring owner Evelyn Lee. Marcel took it as a good omen that the slope overlooks Burgoyne Bay, even though the bay is named for a British naval officer and not Bourgogne in France.

He likens the terroir to that of Oregon's Pinot Noir country. "We are on the northern edge of the climate zone for Pinot Noir," he claims. "The French always say you get the best expression of fruit at the northern edge of the range." Pinot Noir ripens here with slightly lower levels of sugar than in hotter climates and delivers flavour and elegance even in tough vintages.

Elaine, a former economist, makes wines that are bright and fresh, with a silky texture. "Our temperate growing environment produces grapes that retain their acidity, making the wines bright and vibrant in their youth and giving them the structure to age well, with our older vintages showing that ethereal Pinot character that we love," she says. "When I am making the wine, I really focus on texture because if it is rough, it is not true to Pinot Noir."

However, she has also blended Zweigelt with Pinot Noir when such an iconoclastic decision made a better wine. That was done in the difficult 2011 vintage, when yields were too small to make varietals from each. It was done again in 2013 when a spur-of-the-moment blend yielded what, to her palate, was a superior wine. Perhaps it is not surprising that the blend succeeded. Pinot Noir is believed to be a grandparent of Blaufränkisch, one of the varieties in the cross that produced Zweigelt in 1922.

In 2016, Elaine and Marcel sold the winery to a Texas businesswoman. Future direction of the winemaking remains to be determined.

Pinot Noir 2014 ($25)

Alcohol 13%. Production 380 cases.

WINERY TASTING NOTES "This is shaping up to be a beautiful wine. It's medium-bodied with an intense nose of dark fruit, tea, and a hint of celery seed. The palate is showing cassis and more tea with notes of cherry skin, vanilla, and clove on the finish." Drink by 2024.

Pinot Noir + Zweigelt 2013

Pinot Noir 60%, Zweigelt 40%. Alcohol 13%. Production 500 cases.

WINERY TASTING NOTES "Medium-bodied with fine tannins. Smoky, black toffee nose and bright fruit flavours of cherry and cassis with spicy caramel notes." Drink by 2023.

Pinot Noir 2012

Alcohol 13%. Production 230 cases.

WINERY TASTING NOTES "Medium-bodied, velvet-textured wine with aromas of cherry, violets, and vanillin leading to flavours of cassis and cherry with notes of mint, tea, and black pepper." Drink by 2022.

Labyrinth 2011

Pinot Noir 65%, Zweigelt 35%. Alcohol 12%. Production 310 cases.

WINERY TASTING NOTES "Delicate wine reflecting the vintage with aromas of red berry and toffee leading to brambly flavours with notes of caramel, brown spice, and pepper." Drink by 2020.

Pinot Noir 2010

Alcohol 12%. Production 429 cases.

WINERY TASTING NOTES "Garnet in colour with aromas of red fruit, cedar, mushroom and sous-bois [forest floor], and raspberry and black pepper. Balanced and complex with moderate tannins." Drink by 2020.

Pinot Noir 2009

Alcohol 13%. Production 266 cases.

WINERY TASTING NOTES "Medium-bodied, satin-textured wine. Cranberry and cherry flavours, delicate yet firm tannins and good acidity." Drink by 2019.

Pinot Noir 2008

Alcohol 12%. Production 300 cases.

WINERY TASTING NOTES "Aromas of fresh raspberry and rose petal with vibrant flavours of raspberry and cherry, and hints of black pepper and vanilla." Drink by 2018.

Pinot Noir 2007

Alcohol 12%. Production 363 cases.

WINERY TASTING NOTES "Delicate wine reflecting the vintage. Fruit-punch nose with cherries, blueberries, leather, and cedar leads to bright fruit on the palate with cherry, more blueberry, and a touch of cranberry on the finish." Drink now.

Pinot Noir 2006

Alcohol 12.5%. Production 319 cases.

WINERY TASTING NOTES "Medium-bodied with cherry-berry nose. Canned raspberry dominates the palate with earthy, smoky, meaty, spicy notes." Drink now.

Pinot Noir 2005

Alcohol 12.5%. Production 192 cases.

AUTHOR'S TASTING NOTES "This wine was tasted at its 10th year. It still showed a dark, lively colour, with aromas and flavours of plum. The fruit is concentrated and sweet. The savoury notes of forest floor contribute to the wine's complexity." Drink now.

Gold Hill Winery
MERITAGE FAMILY RESERVE

Sant and Gurbachan Gill got invaluable advice from a relative when they first bought land for fruit trees: stay away from Black Sage Road because fruit trees don't do well on sand. So in 1995 they bought orchards on the west side of the South Okanagan, on the slopes of the Golden Mile Bench. It was a good, frost-free, sunbathed site for tree fruits. After they switched to grapes in 2007, they discovered the property was even better for vineyards.

Sant Gill emigrated from India in 1984, followed five years later by Gurbachan, his younger brother. They had an ironic first exposure to viticulture: they were among the farm labourers employed to rip out hybrid varietals on Black Sage Road, which were deemed too mediocre to compete under free trade. A few years later, they were being employed to plant new vineyards with the European varietals that could make premium wine.

The home vineyard on the mountain slope above the winery is one of four vineyards now operated by the Gill brothers, who opened Gold Hill Winery in 2011. The Meritage, which the winery began making in 2012, is always made with home vineyard grapes because the site is so reliable. Freezing air cascades down the slope into a low-lying marsh across the road. The hard winter of 2008 showed just how reliable the site is. One of the other Gill vineyards is at Haynes Point, near Osoyoos. The winter killed 1.2 hectares (3 acres) of Syrah there, while all the vines on the home vineyard, including Syrah, survived.

The home vineyard has enabled Gold Hill to produce exceptionally bold red wines. The steep slope affords good sun exposure for the vines. The rock-laden soil at the top also serves as a heat sink, warming the vines into the evening. The Gills ensure optimal ripeness by limiting the size of the crop and stressing the plants with sparse watering, so that the vines produce small, intensely flavoured grapes. Gold Hill red grapes are usually so ripe that consulting winemaker Philip Soo can make robust, even jammy wines with 15-percent alcohol.

Much to the chagrin of the Gill brothers, Gold Hill and the home vineyard are not included in the Golden Mile appellation that was proclaimed in 2014, with boundaries defined by soil analysis. The Gills contend that the Golden Mile designation was coined in the 1960s by tree-fruit growers whose orchards extended a mile south from Testalinden Creek. Their trees were spared damage during one hard winter that devastated surrounding orchards. They began to call their fortunate area the Golden Mile, and a fruit stand with the same name opened beside the highway, popularizing the term.

2013 ($34.90)

Merlot 40%, Cabernet Franc 30%, Malbec 30%. Alcohol 15.4%. Production 250 cases.

AUTHOR'S TASTING NOTES "This is a bold wine. The concentrated richness is signalled by its dark colour. It has aromas of black cherry and blueberry that are echoed on the palate, along with flavours of cassis and mocha. The long, ripe tannins and the mouth-filling volume of this intense wine completely integrate the alcohol." Drink by 2023.

2012

Merlot 33.3%, Cabernet Franc 22.2%, Cabernet Sauvignon 22.2%, Malbec 22.2%. Alcohol 14.3%. Production 250 cases.

AUTHOR'S TASTING NOTES "Bold and ripe, the wine's aroma has the appealing floral note attributable to the Malbec, along with cassis and blueberry. On the palate, there are flavours of black cherry and blackcurrant in a pool of sweet fruit. There is a lingering finish of blueberry and blackcurrant." Drink by 2022.

Gray Monk Estate Winery

ODYSSEY MERITAGE

The founders of Gray Monk Estate Winery, George and Trudy Heiss, once famously said there would be no barrels in the winery they opened in the North Okanagan in 1982. Their vineyard was planted almost exclusively to white varieties, and their son, George Jr., trained in Germany to make whites. The focus initially was on whites that would not benefit from barrel-aging. In 1976, the Heiss family imported Auxerrois, Gewürztraminer, and Pinot Gris (a mere 50 vines) from Alsace, and the winery succeeded with white wines, notably Pinot Gris. It is now the most widely planted white variety in BC and the flagship wine for Gray Monk, at 26,000 cases a year. The old vintages in the Gray Monk wine library show that Pinot Gris and the other whites can be aged. Most consumers, however, drink the whites within their first two years.

Seventy percent of Gray Monk's production is white wine. But the winery began making red wines in the 1990s. It acknowledged the demand for these wines by building a dedicated barrel cellar in 2006 (it houses more than 700 barrels). Two years later, the winery, which already owned 34 hectares (85 acres) of vineyard, planted its 6-hectare (15-acre) Paydirt Vineyard near Osoyoos. The five major Bordeaux varietals were planted to support the winery's new red Odyssey Meritage program. "We started that property with the intention to do a single-vineyard Bordeaux blend, with all five varietals on-site," Gray Monk general manager Robert Heiss said in 2014. "We haven't quite got there yet."

The grapes for the Meritage are sourced from several premium vineyards in the South Okanagan that grow for Gray Monk under contract, in part because Paydirt had a difficult start, with some young plants being damaged or killed by cold winters in 2008 and 2009. The lost vines were replaced, but the resulting mix of younger and older vines has made it hard to assess the quality of the fruit. Judging from successful older vineyards nearby, Paydirt will prove to be a solid producer.

Gray Monk had the good fortune of launching Odyssey Meritage in the outstanding 2009 vintage, with fruit from Harry McWatters's Sundial Vineyard on Black Sage Road and John and Lynn Bremmer's Dry Creek Vineyard on the west side of the Okanagan Valley. Both vineyards have well-managed mature vines that delivered a rich palate of flavours. In 2014 and 2015 tastings of the first four vintages, the 2009 was Robert's favourite.

2013 ($34.99)

Merlot 59.4%, Cabernet Sauvignon 25%, Cabernet Franc 12.5%, Malbec 3.1%. Alcohol 13.7%. Production 800 cases.

AUTHOR'S TASTING NOTES "The wine begins with aromas of cassis, cherries, and spice, leading to bright and vibrant flavours of cherries and currants. The texture is full, with long ripe tannins promising good aging potential." Drink by 2023.

2012

Merlot 48.5%, Cabernet Sauvignon 28.6%, Cabernet Franc 17.1%, Malbec 2.9%, Petit Verdot 2.9%. Alcohol 13.7%. Aged in new French oak barrels. Production 860 cases.

AUTHOR'S TASTING NOTES "This is a lush and generous red, beginning with aromas of black cherry and vanilla. On the palate, there are flavours of black cherry, blackcurrant, and leather with a hint of minerality on the long finish." Drink by 2022.

2011

Cabernet Franc 36.4%, Merlot 34.6%, Cabernet Sauvignon 23.6%, Malbec 3.6%, Petit Verdot 1.8%. Alcohol 13.2%. Aged 12 months in new French oak barrels. Production 1,365 cases.

AUTHOR'S TASTING NOTES "Firm in structure, this wine has aromas and flavours of blackcurrant and blackberry; the brambleberry flavours reflect the bold use of Cabernet Franc." Drink by 2021.

2010

Merlot 46.1%, Cabernet Sauvignon 45.4%, Cabernet Franc 5.7%, Malbec 2.8%. Alcohol 14.7%. Production 850 cases.

AUTHOR'S TASTING NOTES "Reflecting the cooler vintage, this wine has vibrant aromas and flavours of cassis, blackcurrant, and blueberry. The lingering flavours on the finish show a refreshing brightness." Drink by 2020.

2009

Merlot 58.6%, Cabernet Franc 34.5%, Cabernet Franc 6.9%. Alcohol 14.4%. Production 780 cases.

AUTHOR'S TASTING NOTES "Rich and generous on the palate, this wine begins with aromas of cassis. There is a core of black cherry flavours, with chocolate and strawberry on the long finish." Drink by 2019.

Hester Creek Estate Winery

THE JUDGE

The Judge was born from winemaker Rob Summers's determination to make an estate blend. Before joining Hester Creek in 2006, he had spent the better part of two decades making single varietals in the Niagara region for Andrew Peller Ltd. He envied J-L Groux, then a colleague, who made the storied Trius blend at Peller-owned Hillebrand.

"I said, 'We can do better, more complex wines if we do a blend,'" Rob argued. "But I was the varietal winemaker, and you don't have a lot of choice when you are at a large winery. I always loved Cabernet Franc, anyways."

Hester Creek, with its old vines, gave him the opportunity to make estate blends. "As an estate, you have to have your iconic wine," Rob believes. "Just because you have to have one." A prototype blend for the Judge, made in the 2006 vintage, was never released because, in Rob's judgment, more vineyard improvements were needed. Under the new ownership of businessman Curt Garland, Hester Creek was still recovering from its 2004 bankruptcy.

The 28-hectare (70-acre) Hester Creek vineyard dates from 1968, when Italian immigrant Joe Busnardo planted vinifera grapes exclusively. The so-called "Italian Merlot" he planted is now part of another of the winery's red blends. Subsequent owners added French clones of the Bordeaux red varieties to the vineyard after Joe sold the winery in 1996.

Rob had recognized this as one of the best vineyards in the South Okanagan when he visited the Valley in 2002 as Peller's national winemaker. By 2007, significant upgrades in the vineyard and the winery enabled Rob to make the first vintage of the Judge. It remains a blend of almost equal parts Merlot, Cabernet Sauvignon, and Cabernet Franc.

The Judge is notable for its rich flavours and silky tannins. This reflects both the old vines and the winemaking technology in Hester Creek's new winery, built in 2010. The winery's Italian-made Ganimede fermenters extract flavour but not hard tannins by stirring the crushed skins with recirculated fermentation gas rather than with mechanical devices. "It is a very thorough mixing, but it is also very gentle," Rob explains.

The Judge is crafted from select blocks of vines that are 15 or more years old. The winery's award-winning Cabernet Franc and Merlot reserve wines come from the same blocks, but the best barrels are set aside for the Judge. The three varietals in the Judge age separately in barrels (75% French, 25% American) for 12 to 14 months before being blended and aged together for another year. For consistency of flavour and style, up to 15 percent of the previous vintage is added to each blend.

"I am trying to make a fairly big-style red that is approachable and yet complex enough to be interesting," Rob says. "The fruit concentration and ripeness we get is pretty exciting."

2012 ($45)

Cabernet Franc, Cabernet Sauvignon, Merlot. Alcohol 14.3%. Aged 26 months in oak barrels. Production 900 cases.

AUTHOR'S TASTING NOTES "This is a dark, concentrated wine beginning with aromas of black cherry, plum, and vanilla. On the palate, there are flavours of black cherry, dark chocolate, vanilla, and cedar. The texture is rich and elegant with a long, long finish." Drink by 2020.

2011

Cabernet Franc, Cabernet Sauvignon, Merlot. Alcohol 14.3%. Aged 26 months in oak barrels. Production 800 cases.

WINERY TASTING NOTES "This big, ripe wine offers smoky aromas of fig, plum, and leather followed by generous flavours of coffee, chocolate, and blackberry in the mid-palate, all finishing with long, silky tannins." Drink by 2019.

2010

Cabernet Franc, Cabernet Sauvignon, Merlot. Alcohol 14.3%. Aged 26 months in oak barrels. Production 500 cases.

WINERY TASTING NOTES "Heady aromas of leather, cassis, blackberry, vanilla, and hints of tarragon lead to a palate filled with vibrant cherry, allspice, caramel, and cigar box combining to create a soft, round mid-palate. The wine finishes with long, supple tannins, making it approachable in its youth and at the same time showcasing its ability to age." Drink by 2018.

2009

Cabernet Franc, Cabernet Sauvignon, Merlot. Alcohol 14.1%. Aged 26 months in oak barrels. Production 500 cases.

WINERY TASTING NOTES "Heady aromas of warm spice, mocha, and chocolate lead to a palate filled with vibrant cherry, allspice, caramel, and cigar box combining to create a soft, round mid-palate." Drink by 2018.

2008

Cabernet Franc, Cabernet Sauvignon, Merlot. Alcohol 14.1%. Aged 26 months in oak barrels. Production 285 cases.

WINERY TASTING NOTES "Full mouth-feel and notes of rich dark fruit are well integrated with tannin structure that shows the depth of the wine through the fruit. Notes of spice, berries, herbs, caramel, black pepper, and cherry combine with a long finish of plum and cassis for a wine that is meant to age." Drink now.

2007

Cabernet Franc, Cabernet Sauvignon, Merlot. Alcohol 14.1%. Aged 26 months in oak barrels. Production 285 cases.

WINERY TASTING NOTES "Full mouth-feel and notes of rich dark fruit are well integrated with tannin structure that shows the depth of the wine through the fruit. Notes of spice, berries, herbs, caramel, black pepper and cherry combine with a long finish of plum and cassis for a wine that is meant to age." Drink now.

Hillside Winery

MOSAIC

Hillside's Mosaic was conceived when an ambition and a need intersected in 2003. Eric von Krosigk, Hillside's winemaker at the time, wanted to make a premium wine that blended all five of the major Bordeaux red varietals. Hillside's management needed a wine that made a statement. "Hillside wasn't necessarily famous for making good statements," says Ken Lauzon, who was the winery's general manager back then.

Hillside was one of the first two wineries (Lang Vineyards was the other) to open on the Naramata Bench; both opened in 1990. Founders Vera and Bohumir Klokocka were among the earliest to plant Cabernet Sauvignon, a precursor, perhaps, of Mosaic. After Bohumir's death, the winery was sold in 1996 to a group of Albertans. The cost of building a new Robert Mackenzie–designed facility nearly bankrupted the winery three years later. New investors hired Ken in 1999 to engineer the turnaround that led, ultimately, to a portfolio crowned by Mosaic.

The first three vintages were primarily blended with grapes from the South Okanagan. Hillside only began planting its Hidden Valley Vineyard, now an important source for Merlot, in 2002 in the hills above the winery. Since 2006, however, Mosaic has been made entirely with Naramata Bench grapes.

"Before I came here, I would not have thought that was wise," says winemaker Kathy Malone. She came to Hillside in 2008 from Mission Hill, where she had worked primarily with South Okanagan fruit, not Naramata grapes. She is now one of the strongest advocates of the Naramata terroir. "I love the type of ripeness we get on the Naramata Bench," she says. In the 2010 and 2011 vintages, Hillside lost one source of Naramata Bench Cabernet Franc. Rather than compromise on the winery's commitment to terroir, Kathy made those two vintages with no Cabernet Franc in the blend. That varietal returned to the wine in 2012 when Hillside secured a new source.

The 2006 vintage was the first Mosaic to win a gold medal (at the Northwest Wine Challenge). While fermenting just Naramata fruit brought the first upgrade to Mosaic, subsequent advances also reflected winemaking changes. Early vintages spent only nine months aging in French and American oak barrels. By 2008, barrel-aging had been extended to 13 months. Now the wine spends at least 14 months in barrel, all in French oak, and more than a quarter of the barrels are new.

Looming over the road, the big Hillside winery is still not big enough to contain all the fermentation tanks required. When temperature controls were added to those tanks in 2008, the winemaker was able to extend maceration as long as 28 days. The additional flavour extraction produced another step forward.

While Mosaic has evolved, it has always been structured to age. Current vintages are expected to improve in the cellar for at least 10 years.

2012 ($40)

Merlot 48%, Malbec 20%, Cabernet Sauvignon 18%, Cabernet Franc 12%, Petit Verdot 2%. Alcohol 13%. All Naramata fruit. Aged 16 months in small French barrels (36% new). Production 395 cases.

AUTHOR'S TASTING NOTES "This is an elegant wine. There are aromas and flavours of cassis and black cherry, with a hint of chocolate and cedar on the finish." Drink by 2022.

2011

Merlot 66%, Cabernet Sauvignon 26%, Malbec 6%, Petit Verdot 2%. Alcohol 13%. All Naramata fruit. Aged 16 months in small French oak barrels (46% new). Production 349 cases.

WINERY TASTING NOTES "Mosaic is small pieces coming together to create a work of art. Vineyard skill, careful barrel selection, and cellar craftsmanship come together to realize a wine of great depth and finesse." Drink by 2021.

2010

Merlot 68%, Cabernet Sauvignon 25%, Malbec 4%, Petit Verdot 3%. Alcohol 13.6%. All Naramata fruit. Aged 14 months in French oak barrels (31% new). Production 337 cases.

AUTHOR'S TASTING NOTES "This bright, cheerful medium-bodied wine reflects cool-vintage vibrancy, with aromas and flavours of cassis and cherry." Drink by 2020.

2009

Merlot 55%, Cabernet Sauvignon 22%, Cabernet Franc 9%, Malbec 9%, Petit Verdot 5%. Alcohol 13.6%. All Naramata fruit. Aged 13 months in French oak barrels (22% new). Production 499 cases.

AUTHOR'S TASTING NOTES "This wine has aromas of blackcurrant, which is echoed on the palate, along with notes of dark chocolate and coffee. The texture is firm and dense, signalling the wine's ability to age." Drink by 2020.

2008

Merlot 71%, Cabernet Sauvignon 18%, Cabernet Franc 6%, Malbec 3%, Petit Verdot 2%. Alcohol 13.8%. All Naramata fruit. Aged 13 months in French oak barrels (13% new). Production 840 cases.

AUTHOR'S TASTING NOTES "Big and bold, this wine begins with aromas of cassis, plum, and vanilla, echoed by the core of sweet fruit on the palate. The structure is polished and the finish lingers." Drink by 2019.

2007

Merlot 34%, Cabernet Sauvignon 27%, Cabernet Franc 23%, Malbec 13%, Petit Verdot 3%. All Naramata fruit. Production 753 cases.

AUTHOR'S TASTING NOTES "A wine with a generous body, this has red fruit aromas. The flavours are savoury, with notes of black cherry, blackcurrant, chocolate, and coffee. The minerality expresses itself with hints of graphite." Drink by 2018.

2006

Merlot 57%, Cabernet Sauvignon 22%, Cabernet Franc 11%, Malbec 5%, Petit Verdot 5%. All Naramata fruit. Production 220 cases.

AUTHOR'S TASTING NOTES "This wine has aged to beautiful elegance, with aromas of cassis and flavours of cherry and plum. The fruit is sweet and juicy on the palate and the finish lingers. This is a Mosaic at its peak." Drink now.

2005

Merlot 46%, Cabernet Franc 24%, Cabernet Sauvignon 20%, Malbec 5%, Petit Verdot 5%. Production 720 cases.

AUTHOR'S TASTING NOTES "This wine has aromas of spicy fruit and cassis, with blackcurrant flavours. The texture has become lean, and the dusty hints on the finish indicate a wine that is past its peak when tasted in 2014." Drink now.

2004

Merlot 53%, Cabernet Franc 24%, Cabernet Sauvignon 17%, Malbec 3%, Petit Verdot 3%. Production 703 cases. Tasting notes unavailable.

2003

Merlot 72%, Cabernet Franc 9%, Cabernet Sauvignon 9%, Malbec 5%, Petit Verdot 5%. Alcohol 13.3%. Aged 9 months in French and American oak. Production 500 cases. Tasting notes unavailable.

Howling Bluff Estate Winery
SUMMA QUIES PINOT NOIR

This Naramata Bench vineyard has evolved dramatically since proprietor Luke Smith planted primarily Bordeaux varietals in 2004. Today, Pinot Noir has taken over as the lead varietal, with three blocks totalling 2.6 hectares (6.5 acres).

Luke, whose mother, Lynda Smith, was secretary of the International Wine and Food Society's Vancouver chapter, became a stockbroker after getting a degree in economics. Success in business enabled him to collect wines and visit favourite wine regions. He bought this Okanagan property in 2003, intending to produce great Bordeaux-style wines. He planted a small block of Pinot Noir because he had been told it was a difficult variety; that appealed because he likes being challenged. "There was never meant to be a Pinot here," he says. To his surprise, Howling Bluff's first major award was earned by his 2006 Pinot Noir. "Mother Nature is telling me that my vineyard makes a good Pinot Noir," he admits.

As painfully expensive as it was to replant much of what he named the Summa Quies Vineyard, Luke believed he had to do it to produce superior wines. "I have come to the conclusion that one out of four years on the Naramata Bench, you have the possibility of making a world-class Bordeaux blend with just Bench grapes," he says. "But three out of four years, you have a chance of making a world-class Burgundy, or Pinot Noir, on the Bench because of the weather. So why would I fight that?"

The experience turned him into a Pinot Noir champion. "Pinot Noir is one of the best wine [grapes] in the world," he says with a convert's conviction. "The most memorable wines I have ever had have been Pinot. What an incredible grape! You can make Champagne, table wine, and rosé. There is the magic and the versatility of the heartbreak grape."

Luke made Howling Bluff's first Pinot Noir rosé in 2014. It was made by bleeding 10 percent of the juice from each of his Pinot Noir tanks before fermentation, a practice that also concentrates the flavours and texture of the Pinot Noir. "The vineyard gives all that I need to make a world-class Pinot Noir," Luke believes.

The most memorable wines I have ever had have been Pinot. What an incredible grape!

2013 ($35)
Clones 114, 115, 667, 777. Alcohol 13.9%. Aged 11 months in French oak (33% new). Production 211 cases.

AUTHOR'S TASTING NOTES "This bold Pinot Noir begins with aromas of ripe plums mingled with hints of forest floor. On the palate, the flavours are dramatic and profound, showing notes of cherry and plum with a savoury and earthy note on the finish." Drink by 2023.

2012
Clones 115, 667, 777. Alcohol 12.9%. Aged 12 months in French oak (30% new) and 8 months after blending in stainless steel. Production 500 cases.

WINERY TASTING NOTES "A nose of berry fruit; strawberry, plum, raspberry with floral undertones of potpourri . . . hints of allspice, fennel, lavender, and cedar. There are earthy notes with a hint of minerality and a smoky nose. Earthy, cherry, coffee, compost flavours mark the finish." Drink by 2025.

2011
Clones 114, 667, 777. Aged in French oak (60% new). Production 411 cases.

WINERY TASTING NOTES "The nose is reminiscent of tart red fruit—cherry, cranberry, red currants, and rhubarb with violets, fine spice, leather, and rain forest floor—notably cedar. It's smooth on the tongue with similar wild, tart red fruit and leather. It is an Old World style with restraint." Drink by 2021.

2010
Clones 114, 667, 777. Aged in French oak (30% new). Production 311 cases.

WINERY TASTING NOTES "The wine's lovely colour would flatter a jewel case. There is a dramatic explosion of cherries in the aroma, carrying through to spicy, cherry flavours and a silky but concentrated texture." Drink by 2020.

2009
Clones 667, 777. Aged in French oak (30% new). Production 111 cases.

WINERY TASTING NOTES "This wine begins with glorious aromas of strawberries. Big and fleshy on the palate, yet with the classic silky texture emerging, this seductive wine has flavours of cherry and strawberry that linger and linger." Drink by 2020.

2008
Clones 667, 777. Aged in French oak (30% new). Production 250 cases.

WINERY TASTING NOTES "Expect a cool nose of celery, carrot top, rhubarb, Worcestershire, and raspberry/floral aromas. Soft, round, dry, light palate with strawberry, rhubarb, cola, carrot, tobacco leaf, and light compost flavours." Drink by 2018.

2007
Clones 667, 777. Aged in French oak (50% new). Production 161 cases.

WINERY TASTING NOTES "Spicy, sour cherry, rhubarb notes with bits of minerals, cola, and cool compost/forest floor aromas. The entry is dry, round, and supple with cherry/cola, coffee, spicy, herbal, tobacco, beef, and rhubarb flavours." Drink now.

2006
Clones 667, 777. Aged 12 months in new French oak. Production 141 cases.

WINERY TASTING NOTES "The nose is a beautiful combination of ripe strawberry and cherry with notes of sweet spice, chocolate, coffee, vanilla, orange zest, and hints of burlap. The palate is seductively silky in texture and shows vanilla, cherry, raspberry, orange zest, and more sweet baking spice." Drink now.

Inniskillin Okanagan
DARK HORSE VINEYARD MERITAGE

Inniskillin's Dark Horse Vineyard is one of the best terroirs in the South Okanagan for big red wines. "Cabernet Sauvignon loves this place," says Sandor Mayer, the winemaker who unlocked the potential of the site.

The 9.3-hectare (23-acre) vineyard was first planted with hybrid varieties in the 1970s for a winery called Vinitera, which opened in 1979. It failed twice before it was taken over in 1987 by Alan Tyabji, who promptly uprooted the hybrids in the 1988 grape pullout and then hired Sandor to replant with vinifera varieties.

Born in Hungary in 1958, Sandor had grown up on a farm with a modest vineyard. That led him to study horticulture and ultimately earn a degree in oenology and viticulture from a leading Hungarian university. He immigrated to Canada and the Okanagan in 1988 (he had relatives there), superbly equipped for the nascent wine industry, which had few jobs because two-thirds of the vineyards had just been pulled out.

Reviving the Dark Horse Vineyard was one of the few jobs available. Sandor arrived in 1989 to find that he first had to clean up a tangle of dead vines, trellis posts, and wire. He accelerated the work by setting fire to the dead vines. The blaze was only prevented from incinerating nearby hillsides by the arrival of the Oliver fire department. Sandor feared he would be fired. He was retained to replant the vineyard. He made his first vintage there in 1992

and spent almost all of his Canadian winemaking career at Inniskillin Okanagan, as the winery has been known since 1996. When Sandor returned to his native Hungary in 2014, he was succeeded by Derek Kontkanen, a Brock University graduate whose career had focused on making white wines at Jackson-Triggs, a sister winery to Inniskillin Okanagan. (Inniskillin also has an Ontario winery in the Niagara region.) He is also an authority on icewine (his university thesis was on that topic). Inniskillin Okanagan's icewine is as renowned as the reds from Dark Horse Vineyard.

Several factors make Dark Horse Vineyard special. The soils are complex and laden with volcanic minerals. The vineyard is nestled slightly in a bowl, with sunbathed slopes facing south and southeast. In the early years, Sandor discovered the vineyard was too hot for a few of the varieties planted there, notably Gewürztraminer. But the heat units are ideal for the Bordeaux red varietals now dominating the vineyard. The wines invariably have ripe flavours of dark fruit, with an earthy structure and firm tannins that make them ideal for aging. The technical notes indicate a shift in style, with more robust alcohol levels since 2002 that suggest riper, fuller flavours. "The lower alcohol level in early vintages was due to above-average crop [yields] and a vineyard that was still young," Sandor explains. With the exception of 1995 and perhaps one other vintage, he made every wine through the 2013 vintage.

2014 ($25)

Merlot 60%, Cabernet Sauvignon 30%, Cabernet Franc 10%. Alcohol 14%. Aged 16 months in French and American oak.

WINERY TASTING NOTES "[The wine] is deep red in colour and boasts a complex bouquet with notes of blackcurrant, blackberry, and cherry and other ripe dark fruits. The very well-integrated oak creates layers of toasty oak, vanilla, chocolate, and spice, all supported by soft, round tannins." Drink by 2021.

2013

Merlot 60%, Cabernet Sauvignon 30%, Cabernet Franc 10%.

WINERY TASTING NOTES "This wine shows a complex bouquet with hints of currant and blackberry. The palate of this beautiful blend is layered with toasty oak and soft tannins." Drink by 2020.

2012

Merlot 60%, Cabernet Sauvignon 30%, Cabernet Franc 10%. Alcohol 14%. The component wines are aged separately for 12 months in French and American oak before being blended. Production 932 cases.

WINERY TASTING NOTES "The 2012 Dark Horse Meritage is deep red in colour and boasts a complex bouquet, with notes of blackcurrant, blackberry, and other ripe, dark fruits. The very well-integrated oak creates layers of toasty oak, vanilla, and spice, all supported by soft, round tannins." Drink by 2019.

2011

Merlot, Cabernet Franc, Cabernet Sauvignon. Alcohol 14.3%. Aged 12 months in French and American oak.

WINERY TASTING NOTES "Our 2011 Meritage displays a deep red colour and a complex bouquet with aromas of ripe cherry, plum, and a hint of chocolate layered in with spicy oak character and smooth tannins." Drink by 2018.

2009

Merlot, Cabernet Franc, Cabernet Sauvignon. Alcohol 14.3%. Aged 12 months in French and American oak.

WINERY TASTING NOTES "Our 2009 Meritage displays a deep red colour and a complex bouquet, with hints of currant and blackberry and layered with toasty oak and soft tannins. The aromas carry through to the palate with a rich mouth feel and a lasting finish." Drink by 2018.

2006

Merlot 78%, Cabernet Franc 19%, Cabernet Sauvignon 3%. Alcohol 14%. Aged 12 months in French and American oak.

WINERY TASTING NOTES "A deep-purple-toned wine with ripe cherry and chocolate aromas, firm tannins and rich flavours of vanilla-infused oak and plums." Drink now.

2002

Merlot 50%, Cabernet Franc 30%, Cabernet Sauvignon 20%. Alcohol 14.4%. Aged 18 months in French and American oak. Production 1,200 cases.

WINERY TASTING NOTES "Our 2002 vintage has black cherry aromas, soft tannins, and a toasty, long, smooth finish." Mature.

2000

Merlot 50%, Cabernet Franc 30%, Cabernet Sauvignon 20%. Alcohol 12.8%. Production 1,000 cases.

WINERY TASTING NOTES "Black cherry aromas, soft tannins, and a toasty, long finish." Fully mature.

1998

Merlot 70%, Cabernet Sauvignon 20%, Cabernet Franc 10%. Alcohol 12.5%. Production 2,500 cases.

WINERY TASTING NOTES The wine "displays a deep ruby colour; a complex nose of ripe cherry, vanilla, and chocolate aromas. The mouth reveals dry plum, hazelnut flavours with fruit standing up to dry tannins and oak spice." Fully mature.

1995

Cabernet Sauvignon 60%, Cabernet Franc 25%, Merlot 15%. Alcohol 12.5%. Aged 18 months in American (75%) and French oak. Production 450 cases.

WINERY TASTING NOTES "Full-bodied with a range of blackberry, cocoa flavours married with delicate, well-integrated oak." Fully mature.

Intersection Winery

ALLUVIA

Two-thirds of Intersection Winery's 4-hectare (10-acre) vineyard was dedicated to Merlot when the vineyard was planted between 2007 and 2009. There was no segregation of blocks within the vineyard until 2012, when French-trained winemaker Dylan Roche brought his sensibility of terroir to bear.

Born in Vancouver in 1976, Dylan became passionate about wine while working in Beaune, France, as a bicycle mechanic and guide. "Beaune is a place where everyday life is inseparably linked with wine," he says. Already trained as an urban geographer, he earned a diploma in viticulture and oenology from a Dijon wine school in 2004. That led to employment with producers in Burgundy and Bordeaux, including prestigious Château Lynch-Bages, where he directed a wine education program. He returned to Canada in 2012 to take over from Intersection's consulting winemaker and to manage the vineyard. He had left his mark on Intersection by the time he left in mid-2016 to focus, with his wife Pénélope, on their own label, Roche Wines.

Dylan noticed there were distinctly different soils side by side in the vineyard. In the French tradition, he decided to farm each block differently and to produce block-specific wines. The northeastern block is underlain with alluvial soil, while the northwestern block is sandy. That led to the production of two unfiltered Merlots—one now called Alluvia, the other Silica. "You can actually walk from one zone to another," winery owner Bruce Schmidt says. "It is the same vineyard. The irrigation line segments the blocks. It is fascinating. What is ironic is that we always felt this northeast block wasn't very good. Yet the Alluvia turned out to be brilliant."

He recommends Alluvia to collectors (even though Silica is $4 more a bottle). Alluvia is the more concentrated and textured of the two. Both, however, are excellent examples of what a French-inspired winemaker can achieve with Okanagan Merlot.

Dylan became passionate about wine while working in Beaune, France, as a bicycle mechanic and guide.

Alluvia Merlot 2013

($28.90)

Merlot. Unfiltered. Alcohol 14.8%. Aged 12 months in French oak (30% new). Production 455 cases.

WINERY TASTING NOTES "The 2013 Alluvia opens with mineral and flint notes and toasty caramel oak. Bold fruit and sturdy tannins promise richness and balance as this wine develops in the bottle." Drink now to 2025.

Alluvia Merlot 2012

Alluvia-block Merlot only. Unfiltered. Alcohol 14.8%. Aged 12 months in French oak (15% new). Production 325 cases.

WINERY TASTING NOTES "A beautifully warm year with a long ripening season that provided excellent fruit expression. This was also the first year the oldest block of Merlot was divided to produce two distinct wines: Alluvia and Silica. The Alluvia, grown on alluvial fan soils, is well balanced, with slightly floral blackberry and tobacco on the nose. The palate integrates dense and pure fruit, balanced tannins, length, and finesse." Drink now to 2025.

Unfiltered Merlot 2011

Alluvia and Silica Merlot blocks. Alcohol 14.8%. Production 370 cases.

WINERY TASTING NOTES "Cooler than average again until mid-July. Great autumn weather drove well-managed tannin levels and excellent fruit expression. Crop loads somewhat better but bunch-thinning was needed to assure ripening. The 2011 shows delicate violet, raspberry, and cracked pepper on the nose, with a hint of smoke. The palate is clean and fresh, with huckleberry, raspberry, and tobacco." Drink now to 2018.

Unfiltered Merlot 2010

Alluvia and Silica Merlot blocks. Alcohol 14.1%. Production 265 cases.

WINERY TASTING NOTES "A late start along with lighter crop load as a result of the 2009 early freeze. Great weather from mid-July to mid-August. Delayed ripening was saved with a burst of heat in late September that carried into October. Still, extended hang time was needed into late October to provide decent ripening. The 2010 developed beautifully into a cleaner, lighter wine than its predecessor. Vanilla and raspberry patch on the nose lead to refreshing herbal notes and juicy fruit elements on the palate." Drink now to 2018.

Unfiltered Merlot 2009

Alluvia and Silica Merlot blocks. Alcohol 14.8%. Production 205 cases.

WINERY TASTING NOTES "Summer was extremely hot and dry leading to a relatively early crush. The South Okanagan was essentially ripe before the Thanksgiving weekend. The wines were rich and intense with smooth tannins even though most vines only in their third leaf. With substantial oak maturation and several years to develop in the bottle, the 2009 is open, dark, and smooth. Toasty oak notes present as cacao and vanilla on the nose and on the fore palate, developing into plush plum and black forest cake." Drink now to 2019.

Jackson-Triggs Okanagan Estate Winery

SUNROCK RED MERITAGE

In the late 1990s, the parent company of Jackson-Triggs at the time (Vincor International) planted five vineyards in the South Okanagan totalling 300.6 hectares (745 acres). Arguably, the jewel was the 40-hectare (100-acre) SunRock Vineyard, planted in 1999.

"The SunRock Vineyard is our top-tier vineyard," Brooke Blair said in 2013 (Brooke was the winemaker at Jackson-Triggs from 2004 to 2015, when she returned to Australia). "It gets the most amount of attention. It is not surprising that the grapes coming from that vineyard were able to ripen, even in a difficult year. The crop levels are a lot lower. We hand-pick these grapes as well, so there is better selection in the field as to what you want to bring into the winery."

This vineyard, a gentle slope on the northern shore of Osoyoos Lake, is one of the Okanagan's warmest. "Its northernmost section is bordered by a wide, rocky ledge jutting out from the mountain," according to the company. "This reflects considerable radiant heat and shelters the vineyard from daily breezes, making it even hotter."

The vineyard now grows red varietals only: Shiraz, Merlot, Cabernet Sauvignon, and Cabernet Franc. A block of Chardonnay was planted as well in 1999 but was subsequently grafted over to Shiraz and Zinfandel. Brooke called it a "wasted opportunity" to grow Chardonnay in this sun-drenched vineyard.

Brooke and her predecessor at Jackson-Triggs, winemaker Bruce Nicholson, were consistently able to make award winners from SunRock grapes. Some examples: double gold for the 2012 SunRock Cabernet Sauvignon at the San Francisco International Wine Competition; gold for the 2008 SunRock Shiraz at the All Canadian Wine Championship; and best red Meritage for the 2010 SunRock Meritage at the Okanagan Wine Awards. All of the SunRock red wines are collectible, including Illumina 2012, a full-bodied blend of 51% Zinfandel and 49% Shiraz.

SunRock Red Meritage has always aged in barrel at least 18 months. However, Brooke fine-tuned the style by reducing the proportion of new oak to 35 percent, compared with 60 percent in the early vintages. The aim is to let the fruit flavours express themselves better. The bar is set high for this wine. None was made in 2008, 2009, and 2012, when the winemakers decided the grape quality was not high enough.

2011 ($35)

Cabernet Franc 46%, Merlot 44%, Cabernet Sauvignon 10%. Alcohol 13.4%. SunRock Vineyard. Aged 20 months in French and American oak (35% new). Production 506 cases.

WINERY TASTING NOTES "The Jackson-Triggs SunRock Red Meritage has intense [flavours] with aromas of blueberry, raspberry, mocha, and spice. All flavours follow through to the palate; this wine is rich and smooth with silky tannins and a prolonged finish." Drink by 2020.

2010

Merlot 47%, Cabernet Franc 36%, Cabernet Sauvignon 17%. Alcohol 14%. SunRock Vineyard. Aged 18 months in French and American oak (40% new). Production 500 cases.

AUTHOR'S TASTING NOTES "The wine begins with appealing aromas of black-berry, blueberry, raspberry, and mocha. On the palate, there are flavours of plum and blackcurrant. The tannins are ripe but still firm." Drink by 2022.

2007

Merlot 50%, Cabernet Franc 40%, Cabernet Sauvignon 10%. Alcohol 14.7%. SunRock Vineyard. Aged 18 months in French and American oak (50% new). Production 300 cases.

Tasting notes unavailable. Drink now.

2006

Merlot 50%, Cabernet Sauvignon 30%, Cabernet Franc 20%. Alcohol 13.6%. SunRock Vineyard. Aged 18 months in French and American oak (50% new). Production 500 cases.

Tasting notes unavailable. Drink now.

2005

Merlot 50%, Cabernet Sauvignon 30%, Cabernet Franc 20%. Alcohol 14.2%. SunRock Vineyard. Aged 18 months in French and American oak (60% new). Production 250 cases.

Tasting notes unavailable. Drink now.

2004

Merlot 50%, Cabernet Sauvignon 30%, Cabernet Franc 20%. Alcohol 14.4%. SunRock Vineyard. Aged 18 months in French and American oak (60% new). Production 250 cases.

Tasting notes unavailable. Drink now.

JoieFarm

EN FAMILLE RESERVE PINOT NOIR

JoieFarm began releasing reserve wines with 100 cases of Chardonnay from the 2005 vintage, one of the young winery's earliest vintages. JoieFarm was then relying entirely on purchased grapes and benefited from quality fruit in an excellent year. The 2007 Reserve Chardonnay, from another superb vintage, won the winery its first Lieutenant Governor's Award of Excellence.

Since then, JoieFarm has come to control the sources of its grapes. "We own 12 acres; we lease 35 and the other 30 acres are under well-managed contracts," winery owner Heidi Noble said in 2015. "They have been growers for a long time. The improvements in the wines in the last seven years are directly due to the amount of time we have spent in the vineyards."

While the winery's reserve wines now include Gewürztraminer, the focus is on the Burgundy varieties the founders enjoy. Heidi, a former chef and cookbook author, believes that Pinot Noir, Gamay, and Chardonnay grow well in the Okanagan and pair well with the cuisines of the West Coast.

"For our West Coast cuisine, Gamay and Pinot are complete no-brainers," Heidi said. "I think the wines are very much influencing what is happening in Vancouver [restaurants], and West Coast cuisine is influencing our wines at JoieFarm."

While not called a reserve, the winery always releases a red called PTG with its reserves. *PTG* is an abbreviation for "Passe-Tout-Grains," which is what winemakers in Burgundy call blends of Gamay and Pinot Noir. Over the centuries, Gamay has been overshadowed by Pinot Noir. In 1395, Philippe the Bold, the Duke of Burgundy, ordered Gamay banned because he believed the wine was inferior to Pinot Noir. Almost certainly, his mind would have been changed by a bottle of PTG from JoieFarm. (The duke's intervention is recounted in *Wine Grapes*, the comprehensive 2012 book by Jancis Robinson, Julia Harding, and José Vouillamoz.)

The reality, however, is that Pinot Noir gets the glory. JoieFarm released its first reserve Pinot Noir in the 2010 vintage. It was, and continues to be, a selection of the best barrels in the cellar in the best years. (No reserve was made in 2013.) Grapes are sourced from vineyards in Summerland, on Skaha Bench, and on Naramata Bench. The winemaking involves Burgundian techniques: the hand-sorted grapes are fermented in 500-litre, open-top fermenters, with gentle punch-downs. The wines are aged just eight to 10 months in French oak; only one-quarter to one-fifth is new, ensuring that aromas and flavours of fruit remain dominant. At a time when screw caps have become ubiquitous, JoieFarm remains committed to natural cork. "We feel that the gradual exchange of oxygen that natural cork allows will enable the wine to improve for another five to seven years and hold for at least 10," the winery has asserted.

En Famille Reserve Pinot Noir 2014 ($39.90)

Multiple clones. Alcohol 13.2%. Aged 8 months in Burgundian barriques and 18 months in bottle before release. Production 299 cases.

WINERY TASTING NOTES "This powerful pinot noir is intensely perfumed with rose petal and almost incense-like jasmine and cedar. It has a bright core of cherry fruit and a subtle white pepper spice. Fine tannins give a graphite lead pencil backbone that will allow it to age gracefully for at least 5-7 years." Drink by 2024.

En Famille Reserve Pinot Noir 2012

Dijon clones 113, 114, 115, 667, 777 plus heritage clone. Alcohol 14%. Aged 8 months in Burgundian barriques and 18 months in bottle before release. Production 215 cases.

WINERY TASTING NOTES "Earthy, wild aromas give way to a robust palate of wild blackcurrant fruit balanced with savoury flavours of truffle, bacon, and coffee. Firm tannins give this wine depth and longevity." Drink by 2022.

En Famille Reserve Pinot Noir 2011

Dijon clones 113, 114, 115, 667, 777 plus heritage clone. Alcohol 13.5%. Aged 10 months in Burgundian barriques and 1 year in bottle before release. Production 204 cases.

AUTHOR'S TASTING NOTES "The winery says this is the most masculine Pinot Noir it has yet made. It begins with earthy cherry aromas. On the palate, the cherry flavours mingle with coffee and cola." Drink by 2021.

Reserve Pinot Noir 2010

Dijon clones 113, 114, 115, 667 plus heritage clone. Alcohol 13.6%. Aged 10 months in French oak (25% new) and 1 year in bottle before release. Production 189 cases.

WINERY TASTING NOTES "Aromas of plums, white pepper, spice, and violets. On the palate, flavours of bright cherry and spice with a structure highlighted by vibrant acidity and fine tannins." Drink by 2020.

Kanazawa Wines

RONIN

Collectors of Ronin join winemaker Richard Kanazawa on his quest to produce a wine that is better and more interesting with each vintage. "I have told consumers that this wine will change every year," he says. "You will never see this blend being the exact same components every single time." The only certainty is that it will be a blend of some or all of the five major Bordeaux red varieties.

In feudal Japan, ronin were samurai warriors who had no master. Richard, who was born in Langley in 1972, honours his Japanese heritage in the names of his wines and the elegance of their labels. The Diamond Flower on each label appeared on his mother's kimonos.

Richard's interest in making wine began when he was delivering wine for Langley's Chaberton Estate Winery. After studying food technology, he went to Australia in 2002, where he took courses at Charles Sturt University and worked at Simon Gilbert Wines. He returned to Canada in 2004 to make wine at several wineries, including Red Rooster Winery and Blasted Church Vineyards.

A modern definition of *ronin* is someone wandering between jobs. Richard's determination to create his own wines turned him into a ronin when several of his employers objected. It is not uncommon for wineries to forbid winemakers to work on private projects. In Richard's case, the concern that he might shortchange an employer was unfounded; he made award-winning wines wherever he worked.

Since 2015, Kanazawa Wines has been based on Naramata Road, and Richard has had a stable and consistent group of growers. He has begun to establish a style with his red wines that includes moderate alcohol, moderate oak aging, and a generous texture. The grapes, handled gently, are fermented with natural yeast, and the blends are assembled soon after the wine is pressed from the skins. "They are the easiest but also the most stressful wines to make," he says about wild yeast fermentations. "I am tired of throwing buckets of yeast into juice and watching it go. I think this is far more exciting."

The blends of Ronin, with a large portion of Petit Verdot, depart somewhat from the mainstream of Okanagan Meritages. "I don't want to have that much control over how this is going to turn out," Richard says. "When I press them off and put them into wood, I am just there to shepherd them. I don't need to micromanage these wines."

2012 ($29.90)

Merlot 37%, Cabernet Sauvignon 31%, Petit Verdot 26%, Malbec 6%. Alcohol 12.6%. Aged 10 months in French oak. Production 311 cases.

AUTHOR'S TASTING NOTES "The wine has an appealing fruity aroma that includes cherry and blueberry accented with vanilla. On the palate, there are flavours of blackcurrant, blackberry, cherry, cola, and coffee. The texture is firm, with long, ripe tannins. The finish persists." Drink by 2020.

2011

Merlot 50%, Petit Verdot 38%, Cabernet Franc 6%, Cabernet Sauvignon 6%. Alcohol 12.9%. Aged 10 months in French oak. Production 217 cases.

WINERY TASTING NOTES "Bouquet: cherries, plums, hints of cranberry, blackcurrant, vanilla. Palate: ripe, bright flavours of red and black berries, leading to a toasty finish with soft tannins." Drink by 2019.

2010

Merlot 88%, Cabernet Sauvignon 6%, Petit Verdot 6%. Alcohol 13%. Aged 10 months in French oak. Production 110 cases.

WINERY TASTING NOTES "Bouquet: meaty, black cherry, plums, currants, leather, pencil shavings, and violets. Palate: medium-bodied red with layers of ripe dark fruits, with firm tannins on the finish." Drink by 2018.

Kettle Valley Winery

OLD MAIN RED

Kettle Valley's owners, Bob Ferguson and Tim Watts, build every one of their red wines to age at least 10 years. "During our 20th anniversary, we tasted wines back to 1994," Bob says. "They were certainly showing the signs of age, but they were quite nice." The longevity, which Kettle Valley's peers might envy, is a result of the winery's well-chosen vineyards. These are farmed to grow grapes with robust tannins and dark flavours, which are captured in the winemaking.

Old Main Red, the winery's flagship Bordeaux red, is named for one of the first vineyards the partners bought when they were leaving professional business careers in 1990 to grow wine. The vineyard, 1.6 hectares (4 acres) in size, is on Old Main Road, a thoroughfare near Naramata Village. It slopes to the west close to Okanagan Lake; it is sunbathed all summer, but the lake effect tempers the summer heat and keeps the vineyard free of frost very late in autumn.

The vineyard was planted in 1990 and 1991 with the intent of making a Bordeaux blend. "We have three varietals in that one vineyard," Tim says, "and we have a third each—Cabernet Sauvignon, Cabernet Franc, and Merlot." Malbec and Petit Verdot, the other members of the Bordeaux five, were subsequently planted in a nearby Kettle Valley vineyard.

"We were told we were stupid to plant Cabernet Sauvignon," Tim remembers. "We were told it would never grow. Then we were told after it grew that it would never ripen. Then we were told maybe it will ripen but it will never be any good." Such was the pessimism in the Okanagan Valley in the early 1990s when the pioneering vintners took a chance on premium varieties.

The three varieties in Old Main Red usually ripen evenly enough that the winery picks them at the same time. The grapes for the Old Main Red blend are co-fermented rather than blended later. "We usually pick them together, crush them together," Tim says. "There have been a couple of times when we have separated out the Merlot because acids were falling and it was not going to be ideal by the time the Cabernet Sauvignon was ready. For the most part, we pick them all together. It makes a difference. If you wait a couple of years and then blend things, it will taste like a Cabernet and a Merlot blended together. If you start right from the beginning, it becomes much more harmonious and develops its own set of flavours, rather than [tasting like] combinations of the components."

The crushed grapes get a cold soak on the skins for about six days—which extracts fresh, fruity flavours—but little maceration after fermentation, when the alcohol can extract bitter tannins from the seeds. The wine is taken through malolactic fermentation and then put in barrel after Christmas. Old Main Red then ages an average of 20 months in French oak barrels (mostly used ones) before being bottled.

"We started off with one year of barrel-aging," Tim recalls. "We did that for a while, until we discovered that it made a huge difference when the wine aged in oak for a second year. There is so much concentration that goes on in that barrel. We don't do any humidifying in the barrel room; we are actually looking to have some of that evaporation and concentration."

2013 ($38)

Cabernet Franc, Cabernet Sauvignon, Merlot from Old Main Vineyard with 5% Malbec and Petit Verdot from King Drive Vineyard, both located in Naramata. Alcohol 14.3%. Aged in French oak for 21 months. Production 502 cases.

AUTHOR'S TASTING NOTES "The wine begins with aromas of cassis, cherry, and vanilla, leading to flavours of cherry, blackcurrant spice, and cedar. On being decanted, the wine reveals an appealing core of sweet fruit flavours, with a hint of chocolate and tobacco on the finish." Drink by 2024.

2012

Cabernet Franc, Cabernet Sauvignon, Merlot from Old Main Vineyard with 5% Malbec and Petit Verdot from King Drive Vineyard, both located in Naramata. Alcohol 13.5%. Aged in French oak for 20 months. Production 430 cases.

AUTHOR'S TASTING NOTES "This wine begins with appealing aromas of spice, cassis, lingonberry, and vanilla. On the palate, the vibrant fruit flavours of black cherry, blackberry, and plum are framed with notes of vanilla and oak. The tannins are firm but not harsh. It has the structure and concentration to continue to improve for the next decade before it plateaus." Drink by 2023.

2011

Cabernet Franc, Cabernet Sauvignon, Merlot from Old Main Vineyard with 5% Malbec and Petit Verdot from King Drive Vineyard, both located in Naramata. Aged in French oak for 21 months. Production 263 cases.

AUTHOR'S TASTING NOTES "This is an intense, even brooding, red with aromas of black cherry, blackcurrant, and vanilla. This is echoed on the palate, along with flavours of dark chocolate and coffee." Drink by 2022.

2010

Cabernet Franc, Cabernet Sauvignon, Merlot from Old Main Vineyard with 5% Malbec and Petit Verdot from King Drive Vineyard, both located in Naramata. Alcohol 15.2%. Aged in French oak for 21 months. Production 334 cases.

WINERY TASTING NOTES "The deep garnet-coloured charmer is elegant on the nose and palate and has a long, balanced finish." Drink by 2020.

2009

Cabernet Franc, Cabernet Sauvignon, Merlot from Old Main Vineyard with 5% Malbec and Petit Verdot from King Drive Vineyard, both located in Naramata. Alcohol 14.5%. Aged in French oak for 22 months. Production 715 cases.

Tasting notes unavailable. Drink by 2020.

2008

Cabernet Franc, Cabernet Sauvignon, Merlot from Old Main Vineyard with 5% and Malbec Petit Verdot from King Drive Vineyard, both located in Naramata. Alcohol 14.5%. Aged in French oak for 21 months. Production 547 cases.

Tasting notes unavailable. Drink by 2019.

2007

Cabernet Franc, Cabernet Sauvignon, Merlot from Old Main Vineyard with 5% Malbec and Petit Verdot from King Drive Vineyard, both located in Naramata. Alcohol 14.5%. Aged in French oak for 21 months. Production 790 cases.

Tasting notes unavailable. Drink by 2018.

2006

Cabernet Franc, Cabernet Sauvignon, Merlot from Old Main Vineyard with 5% Malbec and Petit Verdot from King Drive Vineyard, both located in Naramata.

AUTHOR'S TASTING NOTES "This is the winery's flagship red Bordeaux blend—a big, earthy red with flavours of plum and fig and chocolate, with licorice on the finish. The structure is firm, and the wine has just begun to open up." Drink now through 2018.

1999

Cabernet Franc, Cabernet Sauvignon, Merlot. Aged in American oak for 21 months. Production 264 cases.

WINERY TASTING NOTES "Dark red colour. Full, rounded blackberry bouquet with aromatic cedar and lots of depth. Smooth, rich, outgoing berry flavours are complemented by full body and depth." Fully mature.

Krāzē Legz Vineyard and Winery
SKAHA VINEYARD RESERVE IMPULSION

When Gerry and Sue Thygesen opened the winery in 2010, they built its brand around a Prohibition theme. The 1920s was the golden era of the Charleston, a provocative dance whose high-kicking steps inspired the winery's name, Krāzē Legz, pronounced "crazy legs." Gerry and Sue calculated, correctly as it turned out, that using the Roaring Twenties theme would make their tasting room and their wines memorable. They named the wines after popular dances of the period, and their first reserve-quality wine from the 2009 vintage was called Black Bottom Stomp.

The idea worked in the tasting room, where the prize-winning wines sold well. It did not have quite the same traction elsewhere. When consumers and collectors were slow to wrap their heads around the theme, Sue and Gerry created a more contemporary brand, Skaha Vineyard. The name of the winery remains Krāzē Legz. Recordings by Jelly Roll Morton and other musical legends of the time still provide the lively soundtrack in the tasting room, but the wines once bearing those dance names have largely been rechristened. In the 2012 vintage, Black Bottom Stomp became Skaha Vineyard Reserve Impulsion.

This flexibility on branding reflects Gerry Thygesen's previous career as a marketer of consumer food products. That marketing career began in 1980 with Okanagan Dried Fruits, a Penticton company that became a national success with Gerry as its vice-president of marketing and sales. He joined a similar company in Seattle in 1996 and worked as a marketing vice-president for several American food companies before returning to the Okanagan in 2007 to plant the Krāzē Legz vineyard at Kaleden, on a former orchard he and Sue had purchased in 1995.

The winery has been winning awards since its very first vintage. "There is nothing magical," Gerry says modestly. "It is the vineyard. We have shale and sandstone. I don't know anybody else who has that substrate, and it is providing minerality to all of the varietals we grow here. If we don't intervene too much, the vineyard will produce lovely wines all on its own."

Merlot and Cabernet Franc are especially happy in this terroir. Gerry has begun making collectible estate-grown wines from these, as both varietals and blends. Grapes from the choice locations in the vineyard are fermented and aged separately in barrel for 18 to 20 months. The best barrels of each varietal are selected for the final blend of Reserve Impulsion, seldom more than 100 cases. Some collectors may prefer the winery's Cabernet Franc, a pure varietal, or the tawny-style fortified Merlot called Rogue.

Skaha Vineyard Reserve Impulsion 2012 ($29)

Merlot 60%, Cabernet Franc 40%. Alcohol 14.1%. Aged 20 months in French oak barrels (26% new). Production 200 cases.

AUTHOR'S TASTING NOTES "Dark in colour, the wine begins with aromas of plum, cherry, and vanilla. The fruit flavours on the palate are vibrant and sweet, with hints of blueberry, blackberry, and cherry. The concentrated texture suggests good ageability." Drink by 2022.

Black Bottom Stomp Merlot/Cabernet Franc 2011

Merlot 66%, Cabernet Franc 34%. Alcohol 14%. Aged 18 months in French oak.

WINERY TASTING NOTES "Our estate-grown blend is rich and balanced with rhythmic layers of black cherry, raspberry, and ripe plum. Sultry notes of crème brûlée, espresso, and dark chocolate dance on the finish." Drink by 2020.

Black Bottom Stomp Merlot/Cabernet Franc 2009

Merlot 72%, Cabernet Franc 28%.

AUTHOR'S TASTING NOTES "This wine, with a good, concentrated texture, begins with berry and vanilla aromas. On the palate, there are the brambly flavours of the Cabernet Franc, along with blackcurrants and minerality. The finish includes hints of coffee and chocolate." Drink by 2020.

La Frenz Winery
GRAND TOTAL RESERVE

The precursor to this wine was called Grand Reserve when the first vintage was made in 2001. Jeff and Niva Martin had launched La Frenz the year before. Until their first vineyard came into production in 2003, they relied entirely on purchased grapes.

Born in Australia, where he made wine for 20 years with McWilliam's, Jeff was recruited in 1994 as the senior winemaker for Quails' Gate Winery in West Kelowna. By the time he left to start his own winery, Jeff had come to know many growers in the Okanagan. One of the best was Robert Forshaw. His 5.6-hectare (14-acre) vineyard on Black Sage Road had some of the oldest Cabernet Sauvignon and Merlot vines in the Okanagan. This top-quality fruit was the backbone of Grand Reserve for five or six vintages, until Forshaw died and the vineyard was sold.

By that time, Jeff had acquired a rugged vineyard on the Golden Mile that he christened Rockyfella, which he began to plant in 2005. "The only true way [to make great wine] is to get that piece of dirt, own it, and farm it exactly as you want to do it," Jeff says. The Cabernet Franc, Petit Verdot, and Malbec from this vineyard were blended with the two other Bordeaux varietals. This was also the occasion for promoting the wine to Grand Total Reserve.

A decade of reliable, ripe Okanagan vintages allowed Jeff to build the wine around the structure of Cabernet Sauvignon overlaid with softer Merlot. Rockyfella Cabernet Franc was brought into the blends in 2008. Then the cool and challenging 2010 and 2011 vintages came along. "They were tougher years, and that convinced me that a Merlot/Cabernet Franc blend, with possibly some Cabernet Sauvignon, is the way to go," Jeff explains.

The shift in style was not dramatic; collectors might not even have noticed. "All we want is a Bordeaux-style wine," Jeff says. "You can't see where one variety finishes and another variety starts. The palate should be seamless. Concentration and power is pretty much a given."

Making the wine involves rigorous selection. "Our best parcels of fruit go into our best selection of barrels," says Jeff, who prefers barrels from the French cooper Alain Fouquet. The wine spends about 18 months in oak. At that point, an extensive tasting identifies the best barrels, from which the varietals are blended for that year's Grand Total Reserve. The blend then marries for several months in barrel before being bottled unfined and unfiltered. The winery ages the Grand Total Reserve in bottle for another year before release.

"It is very drinkable and approachable, but it is still a wine you want to put away for a while," says Jeff, acknowledging that restaurants are unlikely to cellar the wine. "We make the wines to be big and opulent. Restaurants are going to be pouring them now, but I think between five and 10 years is the best time to drink these."

Recent vintages of Grand Total Reserve have

been labelled "one hundred series." The reason: the label replicates the view over the Naramata Bench that appeared on the Canadian $100 banknote from 1954 to 1975. La Frenz updated the view by adding the vineyards, which had not yet been planted in the 1950s.

2013 ($45)

Merlot 58%, Cabernet Sauvignon 25%, Cabernet Franc 17%. Alcohol 14.7%. Each varietal was aged 22 months in French oak (50% new) before blending.

WINERY TASTING NOTES "This wine is concentrated and inky, with aromatics of dried dark berries and leather on the nose. These notes follow through on the velvety palate with further layers of chocolate-covered nuts, vanilla rooibos, cassis, and espresso beans." Drink by 2023.

2012

Merlot 60%, Cabernet Franc 27%, Cabernet Sauvignon 13%. Alcohol 15%.

WINERY TASTING NOTES "This Grand Total is, we believe, the absolute best we have ever produced: dense, dark, concentrated, and superb. All the parcels of fruit used in the 2012 were cropped at one bunch per shoot, resulting in under 3 tons per acre, offering incredible flavour intensity across all varieties. At almost 15% alcohol, the ripeness and concentration achieved in this release is beyond compare in Canada." Drink by 2022.

2011

Merlot 45%, Cabernet Sauvignon 31%, Malbec 13%, Cabernet Franc 11%. Alcohol 14%. Production 400 cases.

WINERY TASTING NOTES "The apex wine of our red wine program, the Grand Total Reserve can be summed up in three words: dark, saturated, and gorgeous. The 2011 vintage leans toward being more Pomerol in style with Merlot as the dominant proportion of the blend. Wrapped in a silky and lingering mouth-feel are the vivid dark fruit aromatics of black cherry pie, and crème de cassis sprinkled with notes of cacao nibs, cedar shavings, and tobacco." Drink by 2021.

2010

Alcohol 14%. Production 400 cases.

AUTHOR'S TASTING NOTES "The wine begins with aromas of plum, vanilla, and chocolate, leading to flavours of plum, blackcurrant, and spice mingled with oak, tobacco, and chocolate." Drink by 2020.

2009

Alcohol 14%. Production 400 cases.

AUTHOR'S TASTING NOTES "This intense and complex wine begins with brooding aromas of black cherry, blackcurrant, and vanilla. The aromas open to display notes of spice and almost perfumed berries. On the palate, there are flavours of cassis and red and black cherries. The finish is lingering, with a classic touch of cigar box." Drink by 2020.

2008

AUTHOR'S TASTING NOTES "The warm 2008 vintage delivered optimally ripe grapes. This wine shows a ripe, juicy but concentrated texture with generous aromas and flavours of black cherries and spiced plums." Drink by 2018.

Lake Breeze Vineyards

TEMPEST

Lake Breeze Vineyards was 10 years old in 2005 when it began producing Tempest, a Pomerol-inspired red wine built around Merlot. The production has typically been 200 cases a year. While the winery plans to increase production, this is unlikely to grow beyond 300 cases a year.

"With us, this is not our bread and butter," says Garron Elmes, the winemaker and president at Lake Breeze. "Pinot Blanc, Pinot Gris, and Sauvignon Blanc pay the bills. Our reputation is predominantly for whites." The success of the white wines—Lake Breeze's annual production is 14,000 cases—has given him the resources to buy the best barrels and source premium grapes, and the ability to take his time to craft Tempest.

The winery was established by a Swiss-born South African businessman, Paul Moser, who came to the Okanagan in 1994 with his wife, Vereena, and bought a 10-year-old vineyard on the Naramata Bench. A restless entrepreneur, he sold the winery in 1998 and opened a bison ranch in Saskatchewan. His winemaker, Garron, then a recent graduate of Elsenburg College of Agriculture in Cape Town, arrived in time to make the very first vintage. Born in 1972, Garron has remained at Lake Breeze through three subsequent ownership changes. The current owners are Calgary investment banker Drew MacIntyre and his wife, Barbara.

"In 2005, we decided we wanted to do something to showcase the fact that we can make big premium reds just as well as everybody else," Garron says. "We had this vision in our mind where we wanted to use four, if not all five, Bordeaux varieties." The first vintage was a blend of estate-grown Merlot and Cabernet Franc. Cabernet Sauvignon and Malbec were added when Garron sourced the grapes. He had Petit Verdot for two vintages until he stopped sourcing this variety that is difficult to ripen in the Okanagan. Beginning with the 2014 vintage, all of the grapes are grown on the Naramata Bench. "Going forward it will be Merlot-based, more often than not," Garron says. "That was always the idea. I still think it is one of the varieties, especially around here, that we grow better than anything else."

The individual varietal wines are aged in new French oak for a year before the Tempest blend is assembled. It then spends six months in older barrels. It is also aged in bottle until Garron decides it is ready for release. While Tempest can be appreciated on release, the wine is structured to age.

"It wasn't too long ago that we opened up a 2007," Garron recounted in 2015. "We looked for 2005 and 2006, but I have a suspicion that somebody drank them. The 2007 was fantastic and still had legs. The idea in my mind when I am making it is somewhere between 15 and 20 years. But based on the earlier ones we have opened, I think it would go much longer than that."

Tempest 2012 ($45)

Merlot 45%, Malbec 30%, Cabernet Franc 10%, Cabernet Sauvignon 10%, Petit Verdot 5%. Alcohol 15%. Aged in new French oak for 15 months.
Tasting notes unavailable.

20th Anniversary Tempest 2011

Merlot 45%, Malbec 30%, Cabernet Franc 10%, Cabernet Sauvignon 10%, Petit Verdot 5%.

WINERY TASTING NOTES "The sum is greater than its parts in this classic Bordeaux blend. Aged in new French oak for 15 months, this wine is full and rich." Drink by 2021.

Tempest 2010

Cabernet Sauvignon 55%, Merlot 35%, Cabernet Franc 5%, Malbec 5%.

WINERY TASTING NOTES "The sum is greater than its parts in this classic Bordeaux blend. Aged in new French oak for 15 months, this wine is full and rich." Drink by 2020.

Tempest 2009

Merlot 50%, Cabernet Franc 25%, Cabernet Sauvignon 25%.

WINERY TASTING NOTES "The wine was aged in new French oak barriques for 15 months and is rich and full-bodied. Full of flavours and aromas of plum and cassis followed by hints of spice and chocolate." Drink by 2019.

Tempest 2008

Merlot 60%, Cabernet Franc 35%, Cabernet Sauvignon 5%.

AUTHOR'S TASTING NOTES "The wine begins with an attractive perfume of blueberries and cassis. Rich on the palate, it tastes of plum, blackcurrant, and red licorice. The wine is elegant and balanced." Drink by 2018.

Tempest 2007

Merlot 60%, Cabernet Franc 35%, Cabernet Sauvignon 5%.
Tasting notes unavailable. Drink now.

Tempest 2006

Merlot 60%, Cabernet Franc 35%, Cabernet Sauvignon 5%. Production 220 cases.
Tasting notes unavailable. Drink now.

Tempest 2005

Merlot 60%, Cabernet Franc 40%. Production 220 cases.
Tasting notes unavailable. Drink now.

Lariana Cellars

NUMBERED SERIES

Carol Scott's interest in wine-growing began when, as a teenager, she spent several summers working in the Shannon Pacific Vineyard on Black Sage Road. Her father, Larry Franklin, was one of the vineyard's owners. Until the hybrid grapes were pulled out of the Okanagan in 1988, Larry and Carol used some for home winemaking in the family's Burnaby home. New owners bought the vineyard in the early 1990s and planted Bordeaux varietals.

In the late 1960s, not long after Shannon Pacific was planted the first time, Larry bought a 4-hectare (10-acre) Osoyoos orchard property that included the Shady Lagoon Campsite on Osoyoos Lake. Carol, a travel agent, and her husband, Dan, a machinist, took over the property in 1989. They still operate the lakeside recreational vehicle camp. Growing cherries and apples became unprofitable and the trees were pulled out in 2006. "It was my dream to plant grapes," Carol says.

Since 2007, they have planted 1.8 hectares (4.5 acres) of vines. The largest block is Cabernet Sauvignon, followed by Carmenère and Viognier. Accordingly, the winery's red blend is anchored by Cabernet Sauvignon. The Merlot and Syrah fleshing out the debut blend are purchased from nearby growers because Dan and Carol's vineyard is fully planted. They have no current plans to double production by turning the campground into vineyard.

The modest winery, which was built in 2012, is very well-equipped. Lariana was one of the earliest small wineries in the Okanagan to install a concrete egg for fermenting and aging wine. The 1,800-litre vessel, made in California, is used to ferment Lariana's exceptional Viognier. The reds are fermented in small stainless-steel tanks and aged in oak barrels.

Lariana's winemaking consultant is Senka Tennant, the founding winemaker with Black Hills Estate Winery. Currently, Senka is the co-proprietor and winemaker at Terravista Vineyards. Lariana's decision to launch its red portfolio just with Twelve, a premium red wine named for the vintage, echoes Senka's strategy at Black Hills. That winery opened in 2001 with a Bordeaux blend called Nota Bene, which quickly became and remains to this day an Okanagan icon.

The winery's name, Lariana, pays homage to Carol's parents, Larry and Anna, who nurtured her love of wine in the Shannon Pacific Vineyard.

Thirteen 2013 ($45)

Cabernet Sauvignon 68%, Syrah 20%, Carmenère 12%. Alcohol 14.5%. Fermented and aged separately until blending at 8 months. Total aging 20 months, predominantly in French oak. Production 555 cases.

AUTHOR'S TASTING NOTES "The wine begins with aromas of cassis lightly touched with mint. On the palate, the flavours are savoury and earthy, with notes of black cherry, blackcurrant, and black coffee mingling with peppery dark chocolate and polished tannins on the finish." Drink by 2023.

Twelve 2012

Cabernet Sauvignon 53%, Syrah 25%, Merlot 21%, Carmenère 1%. Alcohol 14%. Aged 18 months in 90% French oak (45% new). Production 480 cases.

WINERY TASTING NOTES "Dominated by aromas of black fruits with a slight hint of black olives and licorice. The palate is further substantiated with a concentrated yet broad profile of Italian plums and black cherries [with] gentle, supple tannins." Drink by 2022.

LaStella

FORTISSIMO

Both the architecture and the portfolio of the LaStella winery evoke Tuscany. This is particularly so with Fortissimo, a Super Tuscan-inspired blend that takes some of its personality from the Sangiovese grapes in the blend.

Sangiovese vines are rare in the Okanagan. The vines at the LaStella vineyard date from a decision in 2006, when Daniel Bontorin was the winemaker, to graft them onto Pinot Gris. A dual Canadian-Italian citizen, Daniel had worked at several Okanagan wineries after completing the winery assistant course at Okanagan University College in 2000. He gained international experience by spending the 2005 crush at a winery in northern Italy. He returned to the Okanagan and joined LaStella for the 2005 harvest.

The LaStella vineyard included a north-facing slope with Pinot Gris that retained too much acidity. Therefore, it was decided in the spring of 2006 to convert the vines to Sangiovese, a variety with lower acidity. "We harvested a small crop of Sangiovese in 2007," Daniel recalls. "I have never had a wine so delicious, so seductive, yet elegant and feminine." It was added to the first Fortissimo.

Since then, an additional block of Sangiovese has been planted at a LaStella-owned vineyard nearby.

Severine Pinte, a French-trained winemaker, took over making Fortissimo in the 2012 vintage. The basic blend has been maintained: Merlot and Cabernet Sauvignon are the foundation, while Cabernet Franc and Sangiovese provide the spine and the aromatics. The proportion of Sangiovese has grown with increased production from those vines. Severine anticipates a maximum of 20 percent Sangiovese in the blend.

"The whole idea of the Super Tuscan red is using the grapes that we have here in the Okanagan and trying to achieve a balance," she says. "People ask me all the time, 'How long will Fortissimo age?' It is a hard question to answer. We will be able to show, I think, wines that will be drinkable 10, 20 years from now because we have that natural acidity." The acidity is preserved by the hot days and cool nights during the growing season. "It is something you cannot reproduce in any other wine region," Severine maintains. "That is what will put us on the map."

2014 ($34.90)

Merlot 57%, Sangiovese 21%, Cabernet Franc 11%, Cabernet Sauvignon 11%. Alcohol 14.5%. Aged 15 months in French and Slavonian oak (15% new). Production 1,495 cases, 120 magnums, 24 double magnums, 60 cases of 375 mL bottles. **WINERY TASTING NOTES** "The wine has fantastic layers of flavour and nuances. Bing cherry mingles with red and black cherry fruit. Herbal underbrush notes meet tobacco notes and damp earth." Drink by 2029.

2013

Merlot 49%, Cabernet Sauvignon 21%, Sangiovese 16%, Cabernet Franc 14%. Alcohol 14.3%. Aged 15 months in French and Slavonian oak (14% new). Production 1,148 cases.

WINERY TASTING NOTES "The highest percentage of Sangiovese to date has lent the wine those telltale aromas of Bing cherries, new saddle leather, and dark floral notes that Sangiovese is admired for." Drink by 2028.

2012

Merlot 39%, Cabernet Franc 38%, Cabernet Sauvignon 17%, Sangiovese 6%. Alcohol 14.9%. Aged 19 months in French and Slavonian barrels and puncheons (new and used). Production 833 cases plus 113 cases of 375 mL bottles, 96 magnums, and 12 double magnums.

AUTHOR'S TASTING NOTES "The model for this wine, which includes 6 percent Sangiovese in the blend, is a Super Tuscan blend. The Sangiovese adds the dusty tannins one finds in Tuscan reds (aging the wine 19 months in French and Slavonian oak also plays a role). The wine has aromas and flavours of blackcurrant and cherry." Drink by 2025.

2011

Merlot 67%, Cabernet Sauvignon 22%, Cabernet Franc 6%, Sangiovese 5%. Alcohol 14.2%. Aged 18 months in French and Slavonian oak barrels (70%) and puncheons (30%). Some 17.5% of the oak was new. Production 857 cases.

AUTHOR'S TASTING NOTES "The wine has the 'dusty' aroma and dry finish that recalls good Chianti. It has aromas and flavours of cherry, cranberry, and red currant. Aged in Slavonian oak, this wine has been finished with a rustic elegance that really does echo Tuscany." Drink by 2024.

2010

Merlot 41%, Cabernet Franc 28%, Cabernet Sauvignon 23%, Sangiovese 8%. Alcohol 14.4%. Aged 18 months in French and Hungarian oak barrels (11% new) and puncheons. Twenty percent of the blend spent six months in 1,000-litre casks. Production 370 cases.

WINERY TASTING NOTES "The wine is medium-full bodied, dry, dusty earthy, and quite refined. The length is very good to excellent. The nose shows more lift and elegance than its more expensive stablemates, a prime example of a 'lesser' wine delivering more of what makes wine pleasurable: balance, freshness, florality, drinkability." Drink by 2022.

2009

Merlot 67%, Cabernet Sauvignon 20%, Sangiovese 8%, Cabernet Franc 5%. Alcohol 14.9%. Aged in French and Slavonian barrels and puncheons. Production 367 cases.

AUTHOR'S TASTING NOTES "This is a bold red with an appealing aroma of blackcurrants, with brambly flavours of currants, plums, and blackberries. There is a lovely core of sweet fruit on the palate, supported by ripe tannins." Drink by 2024.

2008

Equal parts Merlot and Cabernet Sauvignon with 8 % each of Cabernet Franc and Sangiovese. Alcohol 14.2%. Aged 16 months in French and Slavonian barrels and puncheons. Production 512 cases.

AUTHOR'S TASTING NOTES "This is a juicy red with sweet berries in the aroma and flavours of cherries enhanced with savoury spice." Drink by 2020.

2007

Merlot 52%, Cabernet Sauvignon 43%, Cabernet Franc 5%. Alcohol 13.9%. Aged 17 months in French and Slavonian oak. Production 245 cases.

WINERY TASTING NOTES "It's a forceful, powerhouse of a wine. Pronounced nose of mocha, black forest cake, scorched earth, and grilled herbs." Drink by 2018.

Laughing Stock Vineyards

PORTFOLIO

Before David Enns blended the 2003 debut vintage of Portfolio, he made what he calls "the pilgrimage" to Bordeaux. In two weeks, he tasted about 1,000 red wines to determine the style that would serve, to some degree, as the model for Portfolio. "When you start out, you have got to have a style," David maintains. "You have to stick to it for a number of years." That discipline worked for him, making Portfolio a widely collected Okanagan red blend.

David and his wife, Cynthia, were successful investment consultants in Vancouver when, in 2002, they bought a newly planted 2-hectare (5-acre) vineyard on Naramata Road for a future winery. They called it Laughing Stock, because they would embarrass themselves with their clients if it flopped. After all, David's winemaking was limited to two vintages in his basement with Washington state grapes when he processed one ton of Cabernet Sauvignon in 2001 and two tons of Syrah in 2002.

David and Cynthia made the debut 500 cases of Portfolio in 2003, after their viticulture consultant told them there might never be a better vintage with which to launch. It had been the hottest season in a decade. "The grapes were crazy ripe, which translated into quite high alcohol in the wines," recalls Cynthia. The Portfolio 2003 had 15.1 percent alcohol, although due to a printing error, the label read 13.8 percent.

Because the Laughing Stock winery was not built until 2005, David crushed his grapes at the nearby Poplar Grove winery for two vintages. That enabled him to mentor under Poplar Grove's Ian Sutherland. The skill transfer was invaluable even though the original Poplar Grove winery had rudimentary equipment. Soon, the well-equipped Laughing Stock winery enabled David to improve Portfolio.

The greatest improvements have come with Laughing Stock farming its own vineyards. "Our original business plan was that we were going to buy a lot of our fruit so we don't have to become farmers," David says. "Well, we quickly realized that if you want good wine, you need good fruit—and you have to grow it." In 2007, the year after they sold their investment business, David and Cynthia, who now manages the vineyards, bought their Perfect Hedge Vineyard: 9 hectares (22 acres) on the Osoyoos East Bench. About half of Laughing Stock's grapes are now from Osoyoos, while the other half are from Naramata. Perfect Hedge grapes—Cabernet Sauvignon, Merlot, and Malbec—have added flesh and rich flavours to Portfolio since the 2008 vintage.

Laughing Stock's total production is limited to about 6,000 cases a year, so that David can practise detailed, hands-on winemaking. "When I am making Portfolio, I have four or five Merlot vineyards, two or three Cabernet Sauvignon vineyards, a couple of Cabernet Francs, a couple of Malbecs, and one source of Petit Verdot," he says. Fermented as individual lots, these come together during the blending trials about 15 months after vintage. When the premium Portfolio blend has been decided, it spends at least three more months in barrel, all of it French oak. Wines that do not make it into Portfolio are blended for an early-drinking wine called Blind Trust Red.

Portfolio has seen continual improvement through more sources of grapes, better winemaking equipment, and refined selection of barrels. Vintage variations are less dramatic than might be expected, given growing conditions. In 2011, when the degree days (days warm enough to mature grapes) were the lowest in Laughing Stock's history, David made a wine good enough to win a Lieutenant Governor's Award of Excellence. "My goal is to make better wine every year, based on what Mother Nature gives us," he says.

2014 ($45)

Merlot 49%, Cabernet Sauvignon 28%, Cabernet Franc 20%, Malbec 2%, Petit Verdot 1%. Alcohol 14.9%. Aged 19 months in French oak (40% new, 60% second fill). Production 2,450 cases. **WINERY TASTING NOTES** "The 2014 . . . has a luscious nose with flavour notes of sun-soaked strawberry, rich plum, dried thyme and a powerful and somewhat savoury body. The tannins are muscular and are highlighted by refreshing acid, which will ensure the ageability of this wine. The finish is smooth and velvety." Drink by 2026.

2013

Merlot 41%, Cabernet Sauvignon 30%, Cabernet Franc 18%, Malbec 8%, Petit Verdot 3%. Alcohol 14.4%. Aged 19 months in French oak (55% new). Production 2,500 cases. **WINERY TASTING NOTES** The wine "is a complex layering of blackberry compote and clove spice aromas that jump from the glass. Solid notes of black fruit and dark chocolate, with tannins that are already soft and plush, thanks to a warm growing season. The end result is a smooth, long finish and a wine built to age." Drink by 2025.

2012

Merlot 45%, Cabernet Sauvignon 25%, Cabernet Franc 22%, Malbec 7%, Petit Verdot 1%. Alcohol 14.7%. Production 2,087 cases. **WINERY TASTING NOTES** "This wine is a complex layering of dark berries, herbs, and oak aromas. Strong notes of mint, cassis, and thyme are in harmony with the jammy fruit, dark chocolate, and vanilla undertones. On the palate, the tannins are supple and the fruit is prominent, proudly showcasing the warm growing season. The end result is a smooth, long finish and a wine built to age." Drink by 2024.

2011

Merlot 42%, Cabernet Sauvignon 32%, Cabernet Franc 17%, Malbec 7%, Petit Verdot 2%. Alcohol 13.9%. Production 2,040 cases. **WINERY TASTING NOTES** "The resulting wine has a nose of dark dried berries, cedar, and a hint of clove. On the palate, black cherry and bramble with anise and thyme notes. More elegant in body from the cooler vintage, it has a great structure and long finish." Drink by 2022.

2010

Cabernet Sauvignon 42%, Merlot 32%, Malbec 18%, Cabernet Franc 6%, Petit Verdot 2%. Alcohol 14.9%. Production 1,675 cases.

WINERY TASTING NOTES "The wine has a nose of dark berries, tobacco, and a hint of clove. On the palate, black cherry compote with toasted nuts . . . More classic Bordeaux than New World." Drink by 2021.

2009

Merlot 36%, Cabernet Sauvignon 27%, Cabernet Franc 22%, Malbec 14%, Petit Verdot 1%. Alcohol 14.4%. Production 1,990 cases.

WINERY TASTING NOTES "The wine has a nose of dark berries, tobacco, clove, and a hint of dark chocolate. The extra Cab Sauv brings a deeper earthiness with concentrated blackcurrant and dried cherry flavours." Drink by 2020.

2008

Merlot 53%, Cabernet Sauvignon 24%, Cabernet Franc 12%, Malbec 9%, Petit Verdot 2%. Alcohol 14.6%. Production 2,050 cases.

WINERY TASTING NOTES "The wine has a nose of blackberry jam and caramelized pecans. Full-bodied, the flavours of black cherry and concentrated berries have a velvety mid-palate and lengthy finish." Drink by 2019.

2007

Merlot 56%, Cabernet Sauvignon 25%, Cabernet Franc 12%, Malbec 6%, Petit Verdot 1%. Alcohol 14.3%. Production 2,750 cases.

WINERY TASTING NOTES "The wine is densely packed with candied cherry, black berries, and dark chocolate tones." Drink by 2018.

2006

Merlot 61%, Cabernet Franc 16%, Cabernet Sauvignon 16%, Malbec 5%, Petit Verdot 2%. Alcohol 14.5%. Production 2,900 cases.

AUTHOR'S TASTING NOTES "The 2006 vintage was warm and consistent. Beginning with aromas of plum and blueberries, the wine has a concentrated texture with flavours of plum, blackcurrant, chocolate, and espresso." Drink now.

2005

Merlot 59%, Cabernet Sauvignon 33%, Malbec 4%, Cabernet Franc 3%, Petit Verdot 1%. Alcohol 14.5%. Production 1,890 cases, 50 magnums. This was the first Portfolio made in the new gravity-flow winery, and the first that incorporated five varietals.

WINERY TASTING NOTES "A classic wine that begins with cocoa, almond, and cassis on the nose. Velvety raspberry and dark chocolate flavours integrate with dry tannins on the palate and complete with a full-bodied finish. The new varietals included in the blend bring some spice and complexity." Drink now.

2004

Merlot 55%, Cabernet Sauvignon 35%, Cabernet Franc 10%. Alcohol 14.1%. Production 1,180 cases, 50 magnums.

WINERY TASTING NOTES "The 2004 . . . is a Bordeaux-style that shows elegance in balance, refinement in tannin structure, and fruit that tastes throughout the palate. [The wine has] a rich and spicy nose of clove and coffee [, and] black cherry and chocolate flavours mixed with a hazelnut finish." This wine is now past its prime.

2003

Merlot 64%, Cabernet Sauvignon 33%, Cabernet Franc 3%. Alcohol 15.1%. Production 500 cases.

AUTHOR'S TASTING NOTES "The debut Portfolio was produced during the hottest growing season in the Okanagan in a decade, with degree days of 1,494. That was 15 to 20 percent above an average season. The wine was super ripe (with 15.1 percent alcohol) and packed with almost porty fruit flavours." This wine is now past its prime.

Le Vieux Pin
ÉQUINOXE SYRAH

The Le Vieux Pin winery, which opened in 2006, has made an unusual journey: it debuted with premium Pinot Noir and Bordeaux varietals, but has now become a superb Syrah producer.

The winery was intended to be a Syrah specialist from the start. It occupies 4 hectares (10 acres) on Black Sage Road that were planted in 2005 with Syrah and Rhône white varietals. But its portfolio included other varietals until the winery vineyard and other South Okanagan Syrah vineyards were in full production. "I have five different blocks of Syrah across the South Okanagan," says winemaker Severine Pinte. With a master's degree in viticulture and oenology from a university in Montpellier, she practised winemaking in Languedoc, Bordeaux, and Australia before coming to the Okanagan in 2010.

Severine now makes the wines for both Le Vieux Pin and its sister winery near Osoyoos, LaStella, which has an Italian-themed portfolio. "I like the challenge of having the two wineries," she says. "I do have to think outside of the hat, and really change my way to approaching the grapes and the final product. I joke that I turn my hat the other way when I switch wineries."

Équinoxe Syrah crowns the three tiers of Syrah made at Le Vieux Pin. Cuvée Violette Syrah is made in a floral, feminine style, while Cuvée Classique Syrah is a darker, masculine wine. Équinoxe combines the best features of both. "*Equinox* means equal day, equal night," the winemaker explains. "What we are trying to do is achieve a balance of the feminine and masculine sides. We want to make something that is perfect. I don't think I have reached perfection yet."

The grapes from the five vineyards in the South Okanagan are picked by hand into 30-pound bins and are crushed, fermented, and aged separately in French oak. When the wines have aged 13 or 14 months, the winemaker begins assessing each of the barrels. She identifies the distinct flavours of each block and the best barrels from which to blend each Syrah tier. "I feel like a painter with different colours," Severine says. "When I am blending, I am trying to mix the colours. I have so much to choose from." The Équinoxe Syrah blend spends several more months in barrel before bottling.

Severine prefers barrels from the Berthomieu cooperage (which are also favoured by top Rhône producers). "Those barrels are always helping the Syrah to express some elegant notes," she says. "For me, the oak is there to bring complexity and not to overwhelm the wine. The oak should almost be invisible . . . but there."

2013 ($92)

Syrah 100%. Alcohol 14.4%. Aged 18 months in French oak (none new). Production 267 cases.

TASTING NOTES by Rhys Pender MW: "The nose is intense and complex and ticks so many boxes of what you are looking for in moderate climate Syrah. Blueberry, floral, baking spices, and so much more that due to its complexity is hard to describe. The palate is silky, smooth, round, and ripe with a lovely balance of crisp acidity, ripe, round tannins, and a fantastic complex palate of spices, blueberry, blackberry, black olive, and some minerality. The finish is long and the complexity keeps evolving." Drink by 2023.

2012

Syrah 96.5%, Viognier 3.5% (co-fermented). Alcohol 13.9%. Aged 19 months in French oak barrels (34% new). Production 334 cases, 36 magnums, 6 double magnums.

WINERY TASTING NOTES "A very complex wine with medium+ garnet colour . . . This monumental wine is at the same time feminine and masculine. It has grace and power, spice and florals, game and savoury notes." Drink by 2022.

2011

Syrah 99%, Viognier 1% (co-fermented). Alcohol 12.9%. Aged 18 months in French oak barrels and puncheons (36% new). Production 298 cases.

WINERY TASTING NOTES "[The wine has] an intensely aromatic nose that has spices, black and white pepper, and floral notes."

AUTHOR'S TASTING NOTES "It has gamy, rare meat flavours, along with notes of cherry, raspberry, and blackberry and white pepper and spice on the finish." Drink by 2021.

2010

Syrah co-fermented with Viognier. Alcohol 14.2%. Aged 19 months in French oak (23% new). Production 153 cases, 24 magnums, 6 double magnums.

WINERY TASTING NOTES "The heat of the desert days gives us lushness, exuberance, and comfort; the cool desert nights give us balanced natural acidity and elegance. The combination lays the groundwork for a balanced, perfumed, and aromatic wine. The . . . explosive aromatics present a melange of white, pink, and black peppercorn aromas and unmistakeable floral notes of roses and violets." Drink by 2020.

2009

Syrah, Viognier. Alcohol 14.8%. Aged 18 months in French oak (72% new). Production 160 cases.

AUTHOR'S TASTING NOTES "It starts with an intriguing aroma of red licorice, pepper, and raw steak. On the palate, there are generous flavours of plums, black cherries, and red licorice. The texture is full, rich, and elegant." Drink by 2019.

2008

Syrah, Viognier. Alcohol 14.1%. Aged 18 months in French oak (50% new). Production 70 cases.

WINERY TASTING NOTES "Pink and white peppercorns, lilacs, red liquorice, and game greet you on the nose. On the palate it is slightly spicy and crescendos to an astounding, harmonious finish." Drink now.

Liquidity Wines

PINOT NOIR

It is telling that when Matt Holmes, Liquidity's founding winemaker, returned to Australia in 2015, the winery recruited a winemaker who was passionate about Pinot Noir. "Pinot Noir is where my heart is," says Alison Moyes. An Ontario native, Alison put herself through a microbiology program in Halifax by working in a wine bar. That triggered a change in her career path to winemaking studies at Brock University. In 2008 she joined Stoneboat in the south Okanagan, where, among other wines, she made award-winning Pinot Noir.

Liquidity is at least as committed to Pinot Noir as Alison is, with a vineyard that shares a fence line with Blue Mountain Vineyard, one of the Okanagan's legendary Pinot Noir producers. (Blue Mountain co-founder Ian Mavety once farmed this slope as well.) The property was acquired in 2009 by a group of business people, most of them Calgarians and all of them wine lovers.

The Liquidity vineyard has 10 acres of mature vines, notably Pinot Noir; another 10 acres on the prime south-facing slope has been replanted. In typical Okanagan fashion, this second block extends the winemaking options with Viognier, Chardonnay, Pinot Gris, Merlot, Cabernet Franc, and a little Cabernet Sauvignon. An adjoining vineyard purchased in 2014 includes many of the same varieties but, crucially, more Pinot Noir. "Our goal is not to be a big operation," says winery manager Ian MacDonald. "It is more about the quality, long-term, than about the quantity."

The owners of Liquidity have underlined their ambitions by adding facilities that have turned this into a destination winery. The tasting room includes displays of art and sculpture, and adjoins an elegant restaurant with panoramic vineyard views.

 Pinot Noir is where my heart is.

Pinot Noir Estate 2014

($26)

Pinot Noir clones 91, 115, 667, 777, 828. Alcohol 13.4%. Aged 11 months in French oak (25% new). Production 910 cases.

WINERY TASTING NOTES "Fresh aromas of raspberry, cocoa, tobacco leaf, and bergamot tea entice the nose. Medium-bodied with bright acidity and smooth tannins, this wine features flavours of ripe dark berries, pomegranate, red currant jelly, baking spice, and vanilla, with elegance and a long finish." Drink by 2021.

Pinot Noir 2013

Pinot Noir clones 91, 115, 667, 777, 828. Alcohol 13%. Aged 11 months in French oak (16% new). Production 500 cases.

WINERY TASTING NOTES "Fresh aromas of raspberry, kirsch, strawberry, violets, cinnamon, and hints of earthiness . . . Bright acidity runs through this wine with flavours of raspberry, cherry, red plum, pomegranate, and notes of vanilla, caramel, and spice with a dusty finish." Drink by 2020.

Pinot Noir 2012

Pinot Noir clones 91, 115, 667, 777, 828. Alcohol 13%. Aged in French oak (very little new). Production 405 cases.

WINERY TASTING NOTES "Apparent black and red fruits with hints of dried mushroom and cocoa; notes of nuts, caramel, and espresso along with some subtle spice make this a very confident and complex Pinot Noir."

Pinot Noir Reserve 2012

Pinot Noir clone 115. Alcohol 13.3%. Aged 14 months in French oak (33% new). Production 55 cases.

WINERY TASTING NOTES "Dark cherry, red plum, and raspberry aromas go along with hints of dark chocolate, caramel, and spice. The palate is dominated by red fruit, currant, vanilla, and hints of spicy liquorice to make this a smooth, classic, medium-bodied Burgundian-style Pinot Noir."

Little Engine Wines

GOLD CHARDONNAY
GOLD PINOT NOIR

The labels on bottles of Little Engine wines show a ladder reaching to a stylized moon. "The ladder is what it takes to reach for the moon," says Steven French, who owns the winery with his wife, Nicole. "Our family motto is 'Dreams don't come true; dreams are made true.' If it takes a ladder to get there, don't give up. It is just like the little engine that could." This refers to the well-known 1930s children's book about a little locomotive pulling a train over a mountain when more powerful engines could not. During the planning of this winery, which opened in 2016, a friend suggested keeping that book in the tasting room as a symbol of the French family's tenacity. "The name Little Engine was born," Steven laughs.

Previously, Nicole and Steven, both born in 1969, were energy industry professionals in Calgary with a serious consumer interest in wine. "We started becoming wine collectors more than a decade ago," Steven says. "And we started doing wine tastings with groups." They came to the Okanagan in 2011 so that their sons could attend hockey school in Penticton. They built a home on an orchard property. Replacing the fruit trees with vines propelled them into wine-growing.

"I wanted to create something that is tangible, and I wanted to make a mark," Steven says. To help them shoot for the moon, the Frenches recruited winemaker Scott Robinson, someone they both describe as a perfectionist.

Scott managed a wine and beer store while getting a degree in kinesiology from Simon Fraser University. A trip he and his wife, Danielle, took to the southern hemisphere, including Australia, in 2003 led him to winemaking. "It was very rewarding work, but I didn't see myself doing it forever," he says of kinesiology. "We spent two weeks in Perth and drove through the Margaret River wine region," Scott recalls. "I thought I could park it there and never leave. It is quite a magical place. I went to some wineries there, and I thought this is something I might come back to."

When they returned to Vancouver in 2004, Scott went back to kinesiology but began working part-time with Langley's Township 7 Vineyards. The following year, he moved to the Okanagan, dividing his time between kinesiology, winery work, and winery assistant courses at Okanagan College. He did several harvests at Township 7 before returning to Australia in 2008 to do a master's degree in winemaking at the University of Adelaide.

Scott returned to the Okanagan in 2009 and was the winemaker at La Frenz until 2012. He almost went back to Australia for a doctorate in oenology but chose instead to become the winemaking partner in Stable Door Cellars, a winery that operated near the home Steven and Nicole were building. When the Stable Door partnership was dissolved after less than two years, Scott joined Little Engine.

The plan is to grow Little Engine to producing about 5,000 to 6,000 cases of boldly flavoured wines a year, with Chardonnay accounting for about a third of the volume. "When Scott, Nicole, and I started talking," Steven says, "we said when it comes to reds, we want something that is big. There are a lot of Pinot Noirs in the Okanagan that, in my opinion, are very subdued. We said to Scott, if we are going to make a Pinot Noir, we want big. And we will reflect that in our Merlots and Cabernets and blends."

Little Engine's gold-label wines are its reserve tier. The silver-label wines should prove equally collectible.

Gold Chardonnay 2014 ($55)

Alcohol 13.5%. Barrel-fermented in French oak (three different cooperages) and aged *sur lie* for 15 months, with barrel stirring biweekly for that duration. Production 200 cases.

WINERY TASTING NOTES "A golden hue, our Reserve Chardonnay has a complex bouquet of fruit and spices. White peach, citrus, and tropical fruits mingle with toasted oak and butterscotch. Lively on the palate, there are flavours of stone fruits and lemon coupled with a creamy, weighted texture." Drink by 2020.

Gold Pinot Noir 2014 ($55)

Clones 115, 777; 15% of the berries were left whole in the fermenter, and the wine was fermented spontaneously. Alcohol 14.1%. Aged 15 months in French oak (40% new). Unfiltered. Production 132 cases.

WINERY TASTING NOTES "This deeply coloured and brooding Pinot Noir is composed of the best barrels from our 2014 vintage. Complex aromas of red and dark fruits, particularly cherry and raspberry. Spicy notes of cloves and star anise give it an underlying earthy character. The palate is full and the tannins are supple enough to drink now. However, the structure and acidity will support significant aging." Drink by 2024.

Marichel Vineyard

ESTATE SYRAH

Airplane pilots go through checklists on every flight in order to achieve a consistent result. Richard Roskell was an Air Canada pilot until he retired in 2005 to launch Marichel Vineyard with his wife, Elisabeth. He never abandoned the pilot's habit of disciplined routine, however.

"I use the same simple techniques every year for our Estate Syrah," Richard says. "The idea I have is simplicity and consistency. I wanted our wines to be very terroir-driven. If you are going to taste the terroir through a vertical, if the winemaker is always dicking around with the way he made it, it just muddies the waters. I try to keep it as simple as possible and as consistent as possible from year to year. So when people taste the different vintages, they taste the evolution of the vineyard, and of course the weather, without Richard being in there, waving his wand."

In 2000, Richard and Elisabeth planted just two varieties, Syrah and Viognier, on their scenic Naramata Bench vineyard. These two were wines they liked to drink. "We did not want to plant what everybody else was planting," Richard adds. "That ruled out Merlot and some of the other Bordeaux varieties. I also was not that sanguine about the Bordeaux varieties here. When you think about where Bordeaux varieties are grown and you think about the climate we have here, they are not similar. I like the match between the Rhône Valley and the

Okanagan much more than I like the match between Bordeaux and the Okanagan."

Richard's philosophy of keeping things simple starts with keeping yields moderate and, when the grapes come into the winery, using straightforward winemaking techniques. "I use the same yeast," he says. "I use the same tank. It usually gets about a 24-hour cold soak. Extended maceration is strictly a matter of taste. I will extend the macerations as necessary or if it is propitious to enhance the wine. But there is no formula for it."

His approach to barrel-aging—he prefers American oak for Syrah—is also uncomplicated. "There again, there is no formula," Richard says. "I taste the wine as it is aging in barrel and I call it when it is ready. The longest I have gone is two years [in barrel]. I think that was for the 2009. The shortest has been 16 months."

Marichel's 2 hectares (5 acres) of Syrah grapes produce between 400 and 700 cases a year of Estate Syrah. None of the production in 2011 or 2012 was labelled Estate because, in Richard's judgment, the vintages were not strong enough. The wines were released as Syrah/Viognier and, beginning with 2013, as Lone Wolf Syrah. Richard says, "It's a very nice wine, too." He will release Estate Syrah from grapes grown in 2014, 2015, and 2016.

2013 ($48)

Alcohol 14.5%. Aged 18 months in French and American oak. Production 85 cases.

WINERY TASTING NOTES "Full-bodied and smoky with leather, earth, plum, and berry flavours. Refined tannins and structure." Drink by 2023.

2010

Alcohol 13.5%.

WINERY TASTING NOTES "The extended 2-year barrel maturation enhanced the character imparted by the custom-made French oak barrels used for this vintage. Each barrel was unique: hand-made by a master cooper from wood harvested in different French forests, then aged and toasted to separate specifications. (In the world of barrel-aged reds, it doesn't get any better than that.) The aromas coming from this wine are stunning—a potpourri of spices and floral notes. The barrel toast was moderated to respect fruit flavours, which come through accurately and in abundance. The tannins are silky." Drink by 2020.

2009

WINERY TASTING NOTES "I describe 2009 as a Jekyll-and-Hyde vintage, in that it began as the warmest on record and ended abruptly with a hard frost in early October. Fortunately our Syrah was already very ripe, and we let it hang for ten days after the frost to desiccate and concentrate flavours. The result is potent and bold, solidly in the Marichel legacy. We included some American oak barrels in this vintage, which lends a hint of Aussie Shiraz character to it." Drink by 2020.

2008

WINERY TASTING NOTES "Smooth with a fruity tang, even at an early age the 2008 was always one of our most approachable Syrahs. It begged to be drunk from the moment it went into bottle, as opposed to, say, the 2007 vintage, which benefited from a little time in bottle before drinking. Time hasn't changed the early appeal of the 2008, and yet years later it's holding up perfectly in every way. Slightly lower tannin content suggests that this wine's longevity may be a little shorter than some of our vintages." Drink now.

2007

WINERY TASTING NOTES "From the weather perspective, 2006 and 2007 were the last great vintages in BC. (While still fine, somewhat cooler and wetter growing seasons have prevailed since.) The 2007 Syrah matches the previous vintage in many ways, yet is unmistakably a wine all its own. Shows exceptional balance with flavours, intensity, tannins, acids, and alcohol creating a harmonious whole. Soft and silky on the palate without a hint of flabbiness, this wine will satisfy the most discriminating palate." Drink now.

2006

WINERY TASTING NOTES "2006 was an excellent vintage. Depth, lushness, intensity, varietal character, and structure—the 2006 has them all in abundance. Slightly diminished from the behemoth it was in youth, this wine is now showing wonderful balance along with all its other fine qualities." Drink now.

2005

WINERY TASTING NOTES "This was our first Syrah release. A good vintage year, the 2005 Syrah has held up very well. A little to the leaner-than-lush side compared to later releases, there is abundant flavour, structure, and tannin, all in good measure and pleasing balance." Drink now.

Maverick Estate Winery

RUBEUS

It is not by chance that Maverick Estate Winery's tasting room, which opened in 2014, echoes the design of wineries in South Africa's Cape wine region: most of the principals of Maverick are from South Africa. Winemaker Bertus Albertyn, who was born in 1978, studied oenology at Stellenbosch University. He then worked at a large wine cooperative and Avondale Estate, a family-owned winery, before coming to the Okanagan in 2009 with his wife, Elzaan de Witt, who was a physician then establishing her practice in Osoyoos.

Elzaan's father, another Maverick owner, is Schalk de Witt, also a doctor who immigrated to Canada in 1990. While he spent most of his Canadian career working in Edmonton, he was drawn to the Okanagan, where the geography reminded him of South Africa. In 2006, he purchased 19.4 hectares (48 acres) of raw land adjacent to the Osoyoos Larose vineyard. Three years later, he purchased a former organic farm beside the highway and tapped his son-in-law's expertise to plant 3 hectares (7.5 acres) of vines in 2011 and to develop the winery. "When Bertus came into the picture, obviously, that was the way to go," Schalk said.

The estate vineyard is planted with Pinot Noir, Shiraz, Sauvignon Blanc, and a little Chardonnay. The other property, which has just enough water to support 6 hectares (15 acres) of vines, will be planted in coming years with similar varieties.

"Personally, I prefer the Burgundian and Rhône varieties," says Bertus.

Rubeus/Rubicon, with Syrah as the anchoring varietal, is a generous, full-bodied red. "Date of picking [is] of the utmost importance to ensure that we get grapes with the highest possible level of phenolic and flavour maturity," Bertus explains in the technical notes for the wine. The grapes are fermented with indigenous yeasts in an open-top wooden fermenter, given extended maceration after fermentation, and aged in a large oak vat before bottling. The name changed in 2013 to resolve a trademark conflict with Meerlust Estate in South Africa, which already had a red called Rubicon.

Schalk de Witt . . . was drawn to the Okanagan, where the geography reminded him of **South Africa.**

Rubeus 2014 ($25)

Syrah 50%, Merlot 35%, Cabernet Franc 7%, Cabernet Sauvignon 7%. Alcohol 14.5%. Aged 18 months in 3- and 4-year-old French oak. Production 650 cases.

WINERY TASTING NOTES "This truly multi-dimensional wine offers up a bouquet of plum, cherry, and blueberry. A captivating palate is alluring and voluptuous, yet poised and restrained. Intense red fruit, balanced with mineral undertones and an elegant lingering finish." Drink by 2021.

Rubeus 2013

Syrah 35%, Cabernet Franc 25%, Cabernet Sauvignon 25%, Merlot 15%. Alcohol 14%. Aged 18 months in 3- and 4-year-old French oak. Production 500 cases.

WINERY TASTING NOTES "The 2013 vintage starts out with a beautiful combination of mulberry, tobacco, plum, and dark chocolate, then develops into a more elegant red fruit and cassis. Fruit comes beautifully to the palate and integrates with mineral undertones that present in a very elegant finish. Unrestrained fruit with reined-in power, textured, composed, and seamless in style." Drink by 2020.

Rubicon 2012

Syrah 65%, Cabernet Franc 20%, Cabernet Sauvignon 15%. Alcohol 14.1%. Aged in a 3,500-litre oak vat. Production 360 cases.

WINERY TASTING NOTES "Deep, dark red colour with dense, powerful, and assertive aromas. Racy red fruit in combination with white pepper and spice. Hint of anise and tobacco leaf adds to the layers of enticing flavours." Drink by 2018.

Rubicon 2011

Syrah 65%, Cabernet Sauvignon 35%. Aged in a 3,500-litre oak vat.

AUTHOR'S TASTING NOTES "It is a bold wine, with pepper on the aroma and the palate, along with flavours of black cherry and chocolate." Drink now.

Meyer Family Vineyards

MICRO CUVÉE PINOT NOIR
MICRO CUVÉE CHARDONNAY

The 2006 vintage in the Okanagan, the first for Meyer Family Vineyards, was outstanding: the dry and sunny summer and the long, warm autumn produced grapes that were well balanced and perfectly ripe. They were just the type of grapes from which a super-premium wine could be made. Meyer seized the opportunity.

The winery was launched by JAK Meyer and his partner, Janice Stevens-Meyer. It was a hobby initially. Born in Alberta in 1958, JAK had succeeded as an investment dealer and real-estate developer while becoming passionate about wine. With help from James Cluer, MW, then a Vancouver wine educator, JAK bought a 1.5-hectare (3.5-acre) Chardonnay vineyard that had been planted in 1994 on Old Main Road near Naramata. He engaged an architect to design a winery while arranging to have both the 2006 and 2007 vintages made by Michael Bartier, whose mastery of barrel-fermented Chardonnay is legendary.

"During blending [the 2006 Chardonnay]," recounts the notes on the vintage, "five French oak barrels stood out as being superior quality. Blended together, the five barrels created a truly special wine that demanded to be bottled on its own as a small batch or Micro Cuvée." Ever since, the flagship Chardonnay from Meyer has always emerged from the best barrels, while also being a single-vineyard wine. Virtually all the Chardonnay from the Old Main Road vineyard is treated the same way: fermented in French oak and aged on the lees for seven or eight months before being bottled. Those barrels that do not rise to the Micro Cuvée standard are usually blended and bottled for the winery's Tribute Series Chardonnay—also a fine wine that some collectors even prefer.

The winery was still something of a hobby, producing 600 cases of wine a year, when JAK began marketing the wines in February 2008. He discovered "how much work it is to sell the wine," he recalls. "We realized that we will never make money at 600 cases. So we made the commitment to expand in the spring of 2008." Before the year was over, JAK had taken over an incomplete winery and vineyard in Okanagan Falls. The 6.5-hectare (16-acre) McLean Creek Road Vineyard, as it is called now, has been replanted largely with Pinot Noir and Chardonnay.

Chris Carson, the New Zealand-trained Canadian winemaker who joined Meyer in 2008, has a special passion for those varieties. The 2012 vintage was another stellar year in the Okanagan, producing the best Pinot Noir Chris had ever worked with, either in the Okanagan or New Zealand. The best barrels in the cellar were selected for the winery's first Micro Cuvée Pinot Noir.

Going forward, collectors will be offered both Chardonnay and Pinot Noir under the Micro Cuvée label, but only if the wine is judged to be outstanding. Meyer made neither in 2013, when an inopportune September rain caused sporadic mould in the vineyard. Micro Cuvée production resumed in the splendid 2014 vintage.

"We only do it in years where we feel the vintage is exceptional," JAK says. "You have to stay true to the philosophy of making Micro Cuvée only in vintages where something really stands out."

In other vintages, you might look to Meyer McLean Creek Pinot Noir and McLean Creek Chardonnay. They are always well-made and in greater quantities. Both wines have the potential to age.

Micro Cuvée Pinot Noir
2014 ($65)

Pommard clone 91, with some clones 115, 667, 777. Alcohol 13.5%. McLean Creek Road Vineyard. Selected from wine that was aged in two 500-litre French oak puncheons (one new) and one French oak barrel. Production 110 cases.

WINERY TASTING NOTES "With fruit for this special blend coming predominantly from the Pommard Clone 91 block on the south-facing slope in Okanagan Falls, the pedigree of the grape comes through. It's a bit of an 'iron fist in a velvet glove' whereby the use of 50% new French oak (one puncheon) gives the wine structure and dark fruit flavours, yet at the same time the wine is elegant and silky. Crafted in a fresh, modern style, the wine is more New Zealand than Burgundy, yet the mix of both commercial and indigenous yeasts combined with organic farming practices preserve the terroir of the land, and the result is a deliciously savoury, deep-fruited, age-worthy wine." Drink by 2029.

Micro Cuvée Pinot Noir
2012

Pommard clone 91, with some clones 667, 777. Alcohol 13.5%. McLean Creek Road Vineyard. Aged in 2 new French oak barrels and a year-old 500-litre French oak puncheon. Production 110 cases.

TASTING NOTES by Steven Spurrier: "Good medium-deep colour, more elegant, spicy, and more lifted than the McLean [Pinot Noir] and less lush than the Reimer [Vineyard Pinot Noir, also from Meyer], good natural vigour on the palate and good length." Drink by 2022.

Micro Cuvée Chardonnay
2015 ($65)

Alcohol 14%. McLean Creek Vineyard. Aged 11 months in French oak (50% new). Production 105 cases.

AUTHOR'S TASTING NOTES "This is a wine with intensity but also with elegance. It has aromas of citrus with a hint of brioche. There are flavours of lemon and apple well integrated with the oak. The texture is generous, with enough acidity to support development over the years." Drink by 2023.

Micro Cuvée Chardonnay 2012

Alcohol 13.5%. Old Main Road Vineyard, Naramata. A blend of wine from two new French oak puncheons, one of Tronçais oak, one of Vosges oak. Production 110 cases.

WINERY TASTING NOTES "A shining example of age-worthy Chardonnay, this wine is just coming into its own in 2016 and will hold in the bottle for a few years more. The vintage was outstanding on the Naramata Bench, and this particular vineyard's north-facing aspect kept acid levels naturally bright while at the same time harvesting grapes with optimal ripeness and sugar levels. The wine has a rich, round mouthfeel yet is not at all cloying, thanks to the bright acidity. Tropical fruit flavours are balanced with a slightly savoury component." Drink by 2020.

Micro Cuvée Chardonnay 2011

Alcohol 13.5%. Old Main Road Vineyard, Naramata. Production 105 cases.

WINERY TASTING NOTES "Each year the vintages we believe to be worthy, we individually taste and select barrels that we feel stand out. During blending we tasted 2 new French oak puncheon barrels that stood out as exceptional. These 2 new French oak puncheons were made up of one barrel from the Vosges forest and one from the Tronçais forest. Blended together the two barrels created a truly special wine that demanded to be bottled on its own as a small batch, or Micro Cuvée." Drink by 2019.

Micro Cuvée Chardonnay 2009

Old Main Road Vineyard, Naramata.

WINERY TASTING NOTES "Clear and bright with a pale to medium lemon colour. The nose has a high level of intensity and shows complex notes of citrus, white peach, cedar, and toast. The palate is dry, with perfect weight in a medium to full-bodied style. The acidity is fresh and crisp providing refreshment to the palate and counterbalancing the richness of the fruit. The mineral, citrus, vanilla, and peach flavours return on the palate and persist through an exceptionally long finish." Drink by 2018.

Micro Cuvée Chardonnay 2008

Old Main Road Vineyard, Naramata. Production 150 magnums, 50 jeroboams.

AUTHOR'S TASTING NOTES "A devastating spring frost so reduced the yields in 2008 that the winery released the limited production of the Micro Cuvée Chardonnay only in large-format bottles. Quality, however, was high and the wine had good longevity, especially in the large bottles." Drink by 2018.

Micro Cuvée Chardonnay 2007

Old Main Road Vineyard. Production 141 cases.

WINERY TASTING NOTES "Clear and bright with a pale to medium lemon colour. The nose has a high level of intensity [with] notes of citrus, white peach, cedar, and toast. The acidity is fresh and crisp, counter-balancing the richness of the fruit. The mineral, citrus, vanilla, and peach flavours . . . persist through an exceptionally long finish." Mature.

Micro Cuvée Chardonnay 2006

Alcohol 13.4%. Old Main Road Vineyard, Naramata. Production 111 cases.

WINERY TASTING NOTES "A medium lemon colour and intense on the nose, the wine shows a complex range of aromas. Classic Chardonnay character of lemon and stone fruit mingles with the complex spice, nut, and toast aromas of the French oak . . . The oak- and lees-derived savoury flavours combine with nuts, peaches, nectarines, and lemon . . . with a backbone of minerality." Mature.

Mission Hill Family Estate

OCULUS

Launched in the 1997 vintage, Oculus was the first icon wine to come out of the Okanagan. (Sumac Ridge's discontinued Pinnacle was also first made in that vintage.) The price of Oculus has nearly quadrupled since its debut, but that can be justified by Mission Hill's ongoing investment in making a wine of international quality. John Simes, the now-retired winemaker, told me in 2013: "Every year we continue to learn new methods and techniques as we strive to elevate the quality of every vintage."

Now one of the largest vineyard owners in the Okanagan, Mission Hill had just begun developing its estate vineyards when Oculus was created. The first vintage was made with grapes purchased from a Black Sage Road vineyard that was acquired the following year by Mission Hill. The Osoyoos Lake East Bench vineyards that Mission Hill began planting in 1997 were soon producing the best Bordeaux varietals in most years. Oculus was made entirely with Osoyoos grapes in 1998. Osoyoos grapes have predominated in every vintage since, except for 2005.

The first four vintages of Oculus were aged in both French and American oak. The decision in 2001 to use French oak exclusively and age the wines more than 12 months in barrel took the quality of Oculus up a notch.

In 2004, Michel Rolland, the legendary Bordeaux winemaking consultant, was asked for his advice. Mission Hill had already built an underground cellar ideally suited to aging wine in barrels. The consultant recommended major upgrades to the winemaking technology. "Starting in 2005 and 2006, we effectively built a small winery inside the big winery," John Simes said. "There was significant investment in equipment that allowed us to really elevate what we could do, as winemakers, with those premium red grapes."

The small winery was equipped with sophisticated sorting tables, allowing only the best individual grapes to go into the fermenting tanks. Michel also recommended using oak fermentation tanks able to handle the fermenting grapes gently. And he recommended using a basket press—gentler than a bladder press—to squeeze the liquid from the skins at the end of fermentation. This careful handling avoids extracting harsh tannins. The consultant's impact was immediately evident in the elegance of the 2005 Oculus.

Further gains in the quality of Oculus have come from the vineyards. Aside from the five strong vintages between 2005 and 2009, vineyard practices have improved. Drip irrigation, which replaced overhead sprinklers, enables precise delivery of water to the vines. Compost now nourishes the soils. Aerial photography (with aircraft or drones) guides the detailed management of vineyard blocks. The vines, which are now mature, produce deeply flavoured grapes. In the challenging cool vintages of

2010 and 2011, the vineyards still delivered Oculus-quality grapes to the winery.

"I think the future is tremendous," John Simes said in 2013. "We are just starting, really. Our oldest vines that go into Oculus were planted in 1997 in Osoyoos. That is like 12 or 13 harvests that have come off that vineyard. That is nothing. In terms of what we can do in the vineyard and how we turn it into wine here, there are tremendous opportunities ahead of us. We don't even know what they are yet."

2013 ($125)

Merlot 51%, Cabernet Sauvignon 23%, Cabernet Franc 22%, Petit Verdot 4%. Alcohol 14.5%. Fermented in small French oak fermenters and aged 14 months in French oak barrels (56% new). Production 79 barrels.

WINERY TASTING NOTES "Firm and graceful, this polished red delivers a core of blackcurrant, dark plum, and fig layered on top of black licorice and dusty earth details, all leading to the flavour's tension and traction. Despite the wine's dense, dark, and brooding personality, it is graceful and elegant with restrained oak influence and seamless integration of all the elements." Drink by 2026.

2012

Merlot 52%, Cabernet Sauvignon 30%, Cabernet Franc 18%. Aged 14 months in French oak.

AUTHOR'S TASTING NOTES "This is a ripe, juicy-textured wine with aromas of cassis, black cherry, spice, and red licorice, leading to generous flavours of currants, cherries, and figs." Drink by 2025.

2011

Merlot 71%, Cabernet Sauvignon 16%, Cabernet Franc 13%. Aged 13 months in French oak.

AUTHOR'S TASTING NOTES "The aromas display cassis, cherries, and a touch of cedar, followed by bright, vibrant flavours of red and black currants. The structure is firm. It finishes with spicy cigar box notes." Drink by 2021.

2010

Merlot 51%, Cabernet Sauvignon 26%, Cabernet Franc 23%. Alcohol 14%. Aged 14 months in French oak.

WINERY TASTING NOTES "Spicy oak aromas greet the nose, while concentrated flavours of blackcurrant, plum, and graphite are buried underneath." Drink by 2020.

2009

Merlot 50%, Cabernet Sauvignon 30%, Cabernet Franc 15%, Petit Verdot 5%. Alcohol 14%. Aged 14.5 months in French oak.

WINERY TASTING NOTES "Medium ruby red colour and ripe, intense fruit on the nose, with notes of plum and dark berries. The smooth, toasted character of cocoa beans and chocolate is given by the subtle use of French oak that accompanies this wine's aroma." Drink by 2022.

2008

Merlot 46%, Cabernet Sauvignon 29%, Cabernet Franc 22%, Petit Verdot 3%. Alcohol 14%. Aged 15 months in French oak.

WINERY TASTING NOTES "Aromas of blackcurrants, violets, figs, and cedar. The rich, full-bodied palate shows multiple layers of fruit, spice, and earth notes. Flavours of blackberry, anise, dried earth, forest floor, and mocha are all framed by ultra-fine tannins and vibrant acidity." Drink by 2020.

2007

Merlot 50%, Cabernet Sauvignon 24%, Cabernet Franc 21%, Petit Verdot 5%. Alcohol 14.5%. Aged 16.5 months in French oak.

WINERY TASTING NOTES "The 2007 Oculus is a triumph of power and purity with deep, haunting aromas of both red and dark fruits, fresh tobacco leaf, leather, maple, and hints of nutmeg. The immense palate shows black raspberry, milk chocolate, cassis, and allspice, all framed by ultra-fine tannins and balancing acidity." Drink by 2020.

2006

Merlot 51%, Cabernet Sauvignon 26%, Cabernet Franc 15%, Petit Verdot 8%. Alcohol 14%. Aged 14.5 months in French oak.

WINERY TASTING NOTES "Captivating aromas of black cherry fruit, dark chocolate, and shaved vanilla bean lead the way for densely packed flavours of blackberries, plum, and bittersweet ganache." Drink by 2020.

2005

Merlot 42%, Cabernet Sauvignon 28%, Cabernet Franc 20%, Petit Verdot 10%. Alcohol 13.5%. Aged 13 months in French oak.

WINERY TASTING NOTES "The wine begins with gorgeous aromas of blackberry, cherry, and mineral. These notes build on the palate with toasty spice and a dusting of chocolate and earthiness, adding textural depth and complexity." Drink by 2018.

2004

Merlot 74%, Cabernet Sauvignon 13%, Cabernet Franc 10%, Petit Verdot 3%. Alcohol 14%. Aged 15 months in French oak.

WINERY TASTING NOTES "The signature of this wine is the multiplicity of layers that unfold into decadent plum, blackberry, and chocolate notes. The distinguishing rich, loamy earthiness and fine ripe tannins provide structure and mingle with lush fruit." Drink now.

2003

Merlot 47%, Cabernet Sauvignon 25%, Cabernet Franc 20%, Petit Verdot 8%. Alcohol 14%. Aged 15 months in French oak. Production 2,822 cases.

WINERY TASTING NOTES "Intricate layers of raspberry and blackberry, hints of cedar, truffle, and chocolate linger in the long finish." Fully mature.

2002

Merlot 50%, Cabernet Sauvignon 30%, Cabernet Franc 15%, Petit Verdot 5%. Alcohol 13.5%. Aged 14 months in French oak.

WINERY TASTING NOTES "Fruit forward with refreshing acidity . . . A richly concentrated and powerful artisan wine." Fully mature.

2001

Merlot 45%, Cabernet Sauvignon 35%, Cabernet Franc 15%, Petit Verdot 5%. Alcohol 13.5%. Aged 16 months in French and American oak.

WINERY TASTING NOTES "A delightfully complex wine that offers layers of characteristic bell pepper, blackberry, currant, cedar, smoke, and truffle notes. The combination of sweet, bright fruit fills the mouth and a fine coating of tannin builds toward the medium-long finish." Fully mature.

2000

Cabernet Sauvignon 55%, Merlot 30%, Cabernet Franc 15%. Alcohol 13.6%. Aged 14 months in French and American oak. Production 1,330 cases.

WINERY TASTING NOTES "A very deep, dark wine with firm layers of earthy blackberry, cedar, and chocolate flavours framed by well-structured tannins and spicy, cedary oak notes." Fully mature.

1999

Cabernet Sauvignon 58%, Merlot 22%, Cabernet Franc 20%. Alcohol 13.2%. Aged 12 months in French and American oak. Production 1,000 cases.

WINERY TASTING NOTES "Rich burgundy in colour, the '99 Estate Oculus delivers distinct earthy overtones accompanied by sweet bell peppers and toasty oak." Past its prime.

1998

Merlot 36%, Cabernet Sauvignon 32%, Cabernet Franc 32%. Alcohol 13%. Aged 12 months in French and American oak. Production 660 cases.

WINERY TASTING NOTES "This is a full-bodied wine with rich cherry, cedar, and raspberry flavours, velvety tannins, and a long finish." Fully mature.

1997

Cabernet Sauvignon 50%, Merlot 45%, Cabernet Franc 5%. Alcohol 13%. Aged 11 months in French and American oak. Production 500 cases.

WINERY TASTING NOTES "Fig and cherry aromas and cooked plum flavours are balanced nicely with moderate tannins and good length." Past its prime.

Moon Curser Vineyards
DEAD OF NIGHT

Chris and Beata Tolley, the proprietors of Moon Curser, are often among the first to embrace varieties that fall outside the Okanagan's mainstream. They grow Arneis, Dolcetto, and Nero d'Avola and have tried to grow Corvina from Italy. They grow Carmenère, which flourishes in Chile; Touriga Nacional from Portugal; Tempranillo from Spain; and Tannat, a robust red found primarily in Madiran (in southwestern France) and Uruguay.

The decision to be different was formed by the wines Chris and Beata tasted during their winemaking studies at Lincoln University in New Zealand in 2003. "It was Sauvignon Blanc over and over," Chris remembers. When they toured wineries in Australia, most of the reds and red blends were Shiraz and Cabernet Sauvignon. "By the time Beata and I finished, we decided that when we planted our vineyard, our choices of varieties would be broader."

They have also grown or purchased the classic Bordeaux and Rhône varieties. The winery's best-known red, a blend called Border Vines, was initially called Six Vines because it incorporated the six major Bordeaux varieties. The wine, while eminently collectible, is crafted to be accessible when released. Dead of Night, a limited-production blend of Tannat and Syrah, is built for longer cellaring.

Moon Curser was the first winery in Canada to produce a Tannat wine. The first wines, from the 2007 and 2008 vintages, were released as single variety reds. In 2009, Chris did blending trials with Tannat combined with Cabernet Sauvignon or Cabernet Franc, as is done in Madiran. At Beata's suggestion, he also made several blends with various percentages of Syrah.

"We had this whole table of wines, and we both picked the same wine," Chris says. It contained equal parts Syrah and Tannat. "We liked it better than the Syrah on its own or Tannat by itself, or all the other blends. They [Syrah and Tannat] seem to partner well. It was something I did not see coming. The Tannat is this overly big wine, and the Syrah cuts it down. But the Tannat adds a new dimension to the Syrah." Each variety is fermented and aged separately. Moon Curser's flagship red is then created just before bottling.

Both Chris and Beata already had successful business careers before opening this Osoyoos winery in 2006. Chris, a software engineer, was born in Montreal in 1966 and acquired his initial interest in wine and Italian varietals from his father, who is from northern Italy. Polish-born Beata is a chartered accountant. Chris believes her wine palate is better than his. "She graduated from Lincoln University with first-class honours," Chris says. "She went through the post-graduate program at Lincoln without getting a single B."

2014

Syrah 50%, Tannat 50%. Alcohol 14.6%. Production 300 cases.

WINERY TASTING NOTES "This is a dry, medium- to full-bodied wine. The nose displays aromas of dark cherry, Italian plum, and violets. Notes of pepper and tobacco can be found as well. It has a well-balanced and integrated oak element that does not overpower other aspects of the wine. On the palate the wine is rich, with good acidity. The palate is consistent with the nose, with its cherry and plum notes." Drink by 2027.

2013 ($42.90)

Syrah 50%, Tannat 50%. Alcohol 14.6%. Aged 12 to 18 months in French and Hungarian oak. Production 198 cases.

WINERY TASTING NOTES "This is a dry, medium- to full-bodied wine. The nose displays aromas of dark cherry, Italian plum, and violets. Notes of pepper and tobacco can be found as well. On the palate, the wine is rich, with good acidity. The palate is consistent with the nose, with its cherry and plum notes. The finish is long and generous, with fine and soft tannins." Drink by 2026.

2012 ($42.90)

Syrah 50%, Tannat 50%. Alcohol 14.3%. Aged 12 to 18 months in French oak (35% new). Production 247 cases.

WINERY TASTING NOTES "This is a dry, medium-bodied wine. The nose displays aromas of dark cherry, prune plum, and violets [with] notes of black pepper and tobacco. On the palate, the wine is rich with good acidity. The palate is consistent with its plum and cherry notes, also displaying meaty and smoky characters. It also displays flavours reminiscent of red currants, blackberries, and cherry jam." Drink by 2025.

2011

Syrah 50%, Tannat 50%. Alcohol 14.3%. Aged 12 to 18 months in oak (20% new French oak, 20% new Hungarian oak). Production 206 cases.

AUTHOR'S TASTING NOTES "This is a firmly textured, medium-bodied wine with aromas and flavours of plum and leather." Drink by 2022.

2010

Syrah 53%, Tannat 47%. Alcohol 14%. Aged 12 to 18 months in oak (20% new French oak, 20% new Hungarian oak). Production 405 cases.

AUTHOR'S TASTING NOTES "The wine begins with aromas of black cherry, vanilla, and violets, leading to rich, meaty flavours of spiced plum and cherry. Delicate white pepper notes define the finish." Drink by 2022.

2009

Syrah 50%, Tannat 50%. Alcohol 14.2%. Aged 18 months in oak, with 65% of the Tannat in new French barriques and 25% of the Syrah in new Hungarian barriques. Production 340 cases.

WINERY TASTING NOTES "[This] is a rich, medium-bodied wine with a nose of violets, dark cherry, and blackberry complemented by cedar and plum. A nice spine of acidity and considerable, yet round and fine, tannins provide the structure for the dark red fruit, chocolate, and plum flavours of the palate." Drink by 2020.

Nagging Doubt Winery
THE PULL

When Rob and Abby Westbury launched this winery in 2010, they sought the advice of Vancouver wine-branding guru Bernie Hadley-Beauregard on naming the winery and developing the labels. "We kicked around a bunch of names," Rob recalls. "Finally he said, 'You know, Rob, this is really your nagging doubt. This is that dream you have wanted to fulfill all your life and it has been nagging at you.'"

A human resources professional who was born in Edmonton in 1969, Rob's passion for wine came alive during a posting in San Francisco. "I remember going to Napa and Sonoma almost every weekend. I just woke up one morning and thought, 'I could definitely do this for a living.'"

Before Nagging Doubt got its own licence in 2014, Rob made the winery's first four vintages at custom crush wineries in the Okanagan. This allowed him to mentor with experienced winemakers while pursuing studies at Washington State University. It also eased the cost of establishing a winery. "The hardest thing about the BC wine industry is how much it costs to get into the business," Rob says candidly. "I have had to be very creative in what I can accomplish."

His budget winery, a renovated stable, is on an East Kelowna farm. Since 2014, Rob has planted just over 2 hectares (5 acres) of vines. He has chosen cool-climate varieties suited to this terroir: Chardonnay, Pinot Noir, Siegerrebe, and Ortega. Other varieties he needs are secured from growers elsewhere in the Okanagan. The Bordeaux varietals for the Pull include Merlot from a leased Naramata vineyard and Cabernet Sauvignon, Cabernet Franc, Malbec, and Petit Verdot from growers in Osoyoos.

"It is thematically related to Nagging Doubt," Rob says about the name of the winery's Bordeaux blend. "Something is pulling at you to accomplish something. There is a double entendre referring to the cork and pulling it out." From a 106-case release in 2010, the Pull has grown to anchor Nagging Doubt's production, which totalled 1,600 cases in 2015 and will be capped at 2,000 cases for a while.

"I have always wanted to stay boutique," Rob says. "My dream was to have a small, family-owned, hands-on artisan winery." And that mirrors his approach to winemaking. "I am a big believer in terroir," he says. "Wines should taste like where they are grown. To me, the best way to achieve that is with minimal manipulation of the wine once it is picked."

2014 ($29.90)

Merlot 40%, Cabernet Sauvignon 28%, Petit Verdot 17%, Cabernet Franc 8%, Malbec 7%. Alcohol 12.6%. Aged 19 months in French oak (40% new). Production 394 cases.

WINERY TASTING NOTES "The 2014 vintage is a rich wine . . . It has an intense nose of black cherry, plum, blackberry, and baking spice with a hint of tobacco, all echoed in the palate." Drink by 2023.

2013

Merlot 45%, Cabernet Sauvignon 22%, Cabernet Franc 16%, Petit Verdot 11%, Malbec 6%. Alcohol 14.7%. Aged 18 months in French and American oak (33% new). Production 200 cases.

WINERY TASTING NOTES "Another warm vintage once again produced a rich wine. This vintage has an intense nose of plum, blackberry, black cherry, and spice, all echoed on the palate. We increased the percentage of Merlot in this vintage, which has created a wine with a very soft tannic structure, as always, balanced by nice acidity." Drink by 2022.

2012

Merlot 40%, Cabernet Sauvignon 25%, Malbec 14%, Petit Verdot 11%, Cabernet Franc 10%. Alcohol 13.5%. Aged 17 months in French and American oak (34% new). Production 200 cases.

WINERY TASTING NOTES "A warmer vintage added a beautiful richness to this wine, but with wonderful acidity to balance the fruit. This full-bodied, complex wine expresses intense notes of black cherry, plum, vanilla, and spice on the nose and palate. It is sophisticated but approachable and will improve with cellaring." Drink by 2022.

2011

Merlot 40%, Cabernet Sauvignon 25%, Malbec 15%, Cabernet Franc 10%, Petit Verdot 10%. Alcohol 14.2%. Aged 16 months in French and American oak (30% new). Production 193 cases.

WINERY TASTING NOTES "2011 was a colder grower season, adding finesse and elegance to this vintage. Intense notes of black cherry, plum, vanilla, and baking spice on the nose and palate, nicely balanced by higher acidity compared with other vintages. It is sophisticated but approachable." Drink by 2018.

2010

Merlot 44%, Cabernet Sauvignon 25%, Cabernet Franc 15%, Malbec 8%, Petit Verdot 8%. Alcohol 14.1%. Aged 11 months in French and American oak (35% new). Production 106 cases.

WINERY TASTING NOTES "Intense notes of blackberry, black cherry, plum, and vanilla on the nose and palate. Full-bodied and complex with a long finish." Drink by 2018.

Nichol Vineyard

SYRAH

Ross Hackworth, the owner of Naramata's Nichol Vineyard since 2004, is torn between his flagship red wines. "Syrah is what we are known for," he says, "but if I had my druthers, I'd make four different kinds of Cabernet Franc." It is a recipe for the production of more than one collectible wine.

Some collect Nichol Syrah because this was the first Okanagan winery to plant Syrah. The founders of the winery, which opened in 1993, were Alex and Kathleen Nichol. In his previous career, winemaker Alex had played double bass with the Vancouver Symphony Orchestra. His taste for a big instrument extended to wines as well. That was why he imported enough Syrah vines in 1991 from a certified French nursery, Morisson-Couderc, to plant about half a hectare (1.25 acres), a quarter of the entire vineyard. "I wanted it to produce a big monster," Alex admitted. The Canadian government had not yet approved Syrah for general planting, so Alex was required to quarantine the vines for three years and not allow any plant material to leave the vineyard.

The Syrah block is located against a cliff that absorbs the heat of the sun and reflects it across the vines. The cool 1996 vintage was the only one in which Alex did not release Syrah on its own (the wine was too tannic) but blended it with Cabernet Franc. In exceptionally warm vintages like 1994, Alex produced the Syrahs big in flavour and robust in alcohol that built the winery's reputation. Other Okanagan wineries followed with additional Syrah plantings, occasionally marketed as Shiraz, the varietal name used in Australia.

"I wouldn't want to call it Shiraz because everybody expects a big, huge Australian wine and this is not Australia," Kathleen said. They developed a style more comparable to one used in the south of France, which was more appropriate to the Naramata terroir. "What it does give me," Alex explained, "is a wine that has got crisp acidity and lots of aromatics along with raw power." The tasting notes on the 2001 Syrah gave a clue to his stylistic model: "Nichol Vineyard's Syrahs are similar to those of Hermitage, where five years from the vintage date is just when the wine begins to think about going out in the world."

Ready to retire in 2004, the Nichols sold the winery to Ross Hackworth. A pulp-and-paper sales executive, Ross had grown up on a Naramata orchard. He wanted to return to his agricultural roots and pursue a lifestyle that included time for a family and for sailing on Okanagan Lake.

The wines Alex made in 2004 included a muscular Syrah. "Alex had a bruiser of a vintage in 2004," Ross remembers. "It came in at just under 16 percent. It was well balanced and well done—a delicious wine. But it absolutely is not my style." Since taking over Nichol Vineyard, Ross has made changes in viticulture and winemaking to moderate the alcohol and produce Syrahs that have become consistent, even when wild yeast is used during fermentation. "If I have a 12.5 percent to 13 percent Syrah or Cabernet Franc, I am thrilled," Ross says.

The barrels in which the wine is aged for 10 to 14 months are two to five years old, to preserve the fruit flavours and ripe tannins. "We have been known for consistently approachable wine on release with the ability to hold its own for years down the road," Ross says. Despite having a fondness for Cabernet Franc, he has more than doubled the Syrah planting since acquiring the winery. Beginning with the 2013 vintage, Syrah made from vines planted in 1990 and 1991 is designated Old Vines. The Syrah from younger plantings, called Nate's Vineyard, is made in an early-drinking style.

Old Vines Syrah 2014 ($40)

Alcohol 13.2%. Aged 16 months in French oak (mostly neutral).

AUTHOR'S TASTING NOTES "Dark in colour, the wine begins with earthy plum and fig aromas accented with black pepper. On the palate, there are flavours of plum, black cherry, black pepper, and charcouterie herbs and spices. The tannins are ripe but firm, supporting the wine's concentrated texture and long finish." Drink by 2026.

Old Vines Syrah 2013

Alcohol 12.6%.

WINERY TASTING NOTES "The 2013 vintage is a return to the classically styled, perfumed, and feminine Nichol Syrah. Nothing changed in the winery but the vintage gave us very pretty, aromatic, substantial but detailed fruit. Medium ruby, vibrant lilac in colour. Aromas of sweet red/black fruits, black pepper, and roasted herbs. On the palate, this is very youthful but accessible with red fruit, moderate tannins, and fresh acidity." Drink by 2025.

Syrah 2012

WINERY TASTING NOTES "The 2012 vintage is one of the most open and accessible in years. Nothing changed in the winery, but the vintage gave us very open-knit fruit. Dark, vibrant purple/lilac in colour. Aromas of sweet red/black fruits, black pepper, and roasted herbs. On the palate, this is very youthful but accessible with dark red fruit, moderate tannins and fresh acidity." Drink by 2022.

Syrah 2011

WINERY TASTING NOTES "Dark ruby core with a vibrant ruby rim. Aromatics of lilac, sweet game meats, pepper, and sage. Full-bodied with red to dark berry fruit, damson plum, and sage." Drink by 2021.

Syrah 2009

Production 400 cases.

Tasting notes unavailable. Drink by 2020.

Syrah 2008

Alcohol 13%. Production 470 cases.

WINERY TASTING NOTES "Colour: dark bing cherry, opaque. Nose: dark cherry, plum, blackberry. Palate: dark cherry, plum, roasted meats. Full-bodied. Finish: smooth, hint of black pepper, black cherry, roasted meat." Drink by 2018.

Syrah 2006

TASTING NOTES courtesy of Gismondionwine.com: "Coffee, leather, meaty, peppery, tobacco, spicy, floral nose. Dry, slightly lean entry with light tannins. Earthy, black cherry, savoury, coffee, tobacco, dried herb flavours. Finish is quite tart and somewhat tannic." Drink now.

Syrah 2005

Alcohol 13.3%. Production 451 cases.

WINERY TASTING NOTES "The 2005 Syrah is dark Bing cherry in colour [with] aromas of cherry and hints of roasted meat. Flavours [of] bright cherry and black raspberries [with] ripe plum and bitter chocolate on the finish." Drink now.

Syrah Reservare 2003

Alcohol 14.5%. Production 335 cases.

WINERY TASTING NOTES "Opaque dark Bing cherry in colour [with] aromas of brandied cherries, pepper, and roasted meat. Flavours follow with those of cherries and Saskatoon berries [with] bitter chocolate and liquorice on the finish." Drink now.

Syrah 2001

WINERY TASTING NOTES "Great colour! Almost like the velvety red of a brocade tapestry, Syrah 2001 is dark plum in colour. Look for a hint of roast meat. Flavours include cherries, roast meat, and liquorice." Drink now.

Syrah 2000

Production 375 cases.

WINERY TASTING NOTES "Dark Bing cherry in colour [with] an earthy nose that is a panoply of aromas—brandied cherries, smoky salmon, roast beef, and a hint of sourdough. The flavours follow with hints of Saskatoon berries [with] a finish where bitter chocolate and a note of black liquorice linger." Drink now.

Syrah 1999

WINERY TASTING NOTES "A truly meaty wine, it has a plum colour with a pink rim. A wild bouquet of blackberries with hints of roasted meat is complemented by a mouthful of ripe cherries and raspberries." Drink now.

Syrah 1998

Production 660 cases.

WINERY TASTING NOTES "Deep plum in colour. But now [summer 2000], and for some time, it has a very closed nose. What sneaks through is tarry and smoky. A long finish wraps itself around the mouth." Drink now.

Syrah 1997

Production 115 cases.

WINERY TASTING NOTES "Fermented totally from [wild] yeasts, Syrah 1997 is the colour of brilliant rubies [with aromas of] cherries, black pepper, and roast beef. Round in the mouth, more intense than the 1995. Cellaring potential of 10 years." Past its prime.

Syrah Barrel Reserve 1995

WINERY TASTING NOTES "The 1995 Syrah has hints of pepper on the nose; with smoke, pepper, blackberries, and a touch of vanilla on the palate; silky and smooth in the mouth." Past its prime.

Syrah 1994

Production 300 cases.

WINERY TASTING NOTES "Fruity, jammy nose with a touch of tar, this wine is robust, with hints of smoke and wood." Past its prime.

Nk'Mip Cellars

MER'R'IYM

The precursor to Mer'r'iym, Nk'Mip Cellars' icon Bordeaux red, was the winery's 2002 Meritage. Equal parts Merlot and Cabernet Sauvignon, it won several major awards and drew attention to the winery. Nk'Mip was North America's first Aboriginal-owned winery, having been launched as a joint venture between the vineyard-owning Osoyoos Indian Band and Vincor (subsequently Constellation Brands).

A few years after opening in 2002, Nk'Mip developed an 8.5-hectare (21-acre) estate vineyard around its Osoyoos winery, planted largely with the Bordeaux varieties that enabled it to make Mer'r'iym. The winery's first vintages, in 2000 and 2001, were made off-site, and the wines were competent but not memorable. Then the winery recruited Randy Picton, who had been the assistant winemaker at CedarCreek Estate Winery. With a dedicated winemaker and new equipment in its modern winery, Nk'Mip was able to establish itself as a producer of quality wines. It soon added a premium tier designated Qwam Qwmt, which means "achieving excellence" in the language of the Osoyoos Indian Band.

The icon wine was added to the portfolio after the estate vineyard had come into production. "Two thousand and eight was the first year that we had a chance to work with all five of the classic red Bordeaux varietals," Randy says. "Other wineries had their iconic red blends. We thought this was our opportunity." Malbec and Petit Verdot, always a small part of the blend, are from a Constellation vineyard near Oliver. The three varieties that make up the major part of Mer'r'iym are all from the estate.

Because of the terrain, the vineyard is planted primarily with rows running east-west, meaning that the south side of each row gets more sun exposure. "We'll pick the south side [of each row] first and we will pick the north side later," Randy says. He prefers the riper flavours of Merlot from the south side and the brighter fruit of Cabernet Sauvignon from the north side of the vines.

The estate vineyard yields about 350 barrels of Bordeaux reds. From that, the winemaker cherry-picks 20 barrels of the best wine for Mer'r'iym, producing about 450 cases each vintage. None was made in 2011, an exceptionally cool year. The wine, aged in French and American oak for 18 months, invariably displays an accessible texture, savoury berry flavours, and a long-lasting finish.

The name of the wine, also from the Osoyoos band's language, is pronounced *mur-eem* and means marriage—"the perfect union of varietals." It also sets up Randy's standard quip about the wine's age-ability. "I tell them that Mer'r'iym means marriage, and like any good marriage, it should probably last seven to 10 years," he says. He and his wife, Lynele, have been married since 1981.

2014 ($50)

Cabernet Sauvignon 55%, Merlot 30%, Cabernet Franc 10%, Malbec 5%. Alcohol 14.75%. Aged 18 months in French oak. Production 431 cases.

WINERY TASTING NOTES "Aromas of blackberry, tobacco, juniper, and mint lead to flavours of berry fruits and chocolate. This is a full-bodied wine with a soft entry that gives way to a fully structured palate with balanced acidity and great length." Drink by 2024.

2013 ($50)

Merlot 76%, Cabernet Sauvignon 12%, Malbec 7%, Cabernet Franc 5%. Alcohol 14.7%. Aged 18 months in French oak. Production 900 cases.

WINERY TASTING NOTES "Aromas of blackberry, cassis, and tobacco with flavours of black cherry and chocolate. The palate is full-bodied with great length." Drink by 2021.

2012

Merlot 59%, Cabernet Sauvignon 22.7%, Malbec 12.3%, Cabernet Franc 6%. Alcohol 15.09%. Aged in predominantly French oak barrels for 18 months.

WINERY TASTING NOTES "Merlot, Cabernet Sauvignon, Cabernet Franc, Petit Verdot, and Malbec all come together to create an elegant wine that is all about balance, texture, and length. Aromas are of blueberries, blackcurrant, smoke, and tobacco with flavours of dark fruit and cherry leading into a lengthy, structured finish." Drink by 2020.

2010

Cabernet Sauvignon 58%, Merlot 28%, Cabernet Franc 6%, Malbec 6%, Petit Verdot 2%. Alcohol 14.5%.

WINERY TASTING NOTES "The wines were fermented in separate lots and pressed into a combination of French and American oak barrels. We began with 28 potential lots from various vineyard blocks within the three vineyards and a total of 350 barrels—all to make a 20-barrel blend. In the end, we hope we got it right. It is a wine that is not necessarily about power but more of balance and harmony—about elegance and length—important qualities in any marriage." Drink by 2019.

2009

Merlot 46%, Cabernet Sauvignon 42%, Cabernet Franc 5%, Malbec 5%, Petit Verdot 2%. Alcohol 14.5%.

AUTHOR'S TASTING NOTES "This is a wine that is texturally ripe and rich, with mouth-filling flavours of blackcurrant, blackberry, and chocolate. Five years after the vintage, the wine was closing in on a satisfying peak of aroma and flavour. It is a level of quality that should not fade for at least five more years." Drink by 2019.

2008

Cabernet Sauvignon 54%, Merlot 35%, Malbec 7%, Cabernet Franc 2%, Petit Verdot 2%. Alcohol 14.3%.

AUTHOR'S TASTING NOTES "This savoury wine has spice, blackcurrant, chocolate, and tobacco in the aroma and on the palate. The longer but slightly cooler 2008 vintage yielded slightly firmer and longer-lived wines than 2009." Drink by 2020.

Noble Ridge Vineyards

KING'S RANSOM

The 2006 vintage created King's Ransom. Philip Soo had joined Noble Ridge in August as consulting winemaker. "He came in and said that there is something going on in the vineyard that is spectacular," recalls Jim D'Andrea, one of the winery's owners. "He recommended that we do something special with the block of grapes. He was extremely excited about it." The winery bought new French oak barrels and set out to make a Bordeaux blend of international quality.

That first King's Ransom defined the Noble Ridge icon wine strategy. So far, three of the King's Ransom wines have been Meritage blends, two have been Pinot Noir, and one is a Chardonnay. Each wine is simply the best of the vintage. And no King's Ransom is made in vintages when nothing vaults the rigorously high bar set by the winery owners.

"As long as we do our work in the vineyard, these premium wines are going to come out," Jim believes. "And we will get better and better. It is the passion. We can make a great wine, and a wine that can compete with other wines of the world."

Jim, a retired lawyer, and his wife, Leslie, have had a long and serious interest in wine. They even considered investing in a French vineyard before recognizing the potential of the Okanagan. In 2001, they bought an Okanagan Falls vineyard with 18-year-old Merlot and Cabernet Sauvignon vines and raw land for additional vines. Because they love Champagne, they planted Pinot Noir, Chardonnay, and Pinot Meunier with sparkling wine in mind. And they bought a neighbouring vineyard with more Bordeaux varietals.

The unique terroir of Okanagan Falls allows Noble Ridge to make more styles of wine from one vineyard than the D'Andreas could ever have made in France. The cooler slopes—those with northern or eastern exposure—suit Pinot Noir and Chardonnay. The sunbathed slopes with southern and western exposures suit the Bordeaux varieties. The ripest Cabernet Sauvignon grows on sandy soil in a block so hot that, in summer, the vineyard crew tries to do its work between 6:00 AM and 9:00 AM.

That vineyard configuration explains why the King's Ransom mantle is not used for the same blend each time but rests on whatever wine is judged best in a given vintage. In 2012, a Pinot Noir emerged as the winery's very best wine. A Meritage blend was in the running until the winery's tasting panel decided it was merely an exceptional Meritage Reserve, not an icon wine.

The Meritage comes from select vineyard blocks that are fermented and aged separately in premium oak barrels reserved for the King's Ransom program. When it comes time to make the blend, the best barrels are selected, with the remaining wine directed to the winery's reserve tier.

The D'Andreas challenge themselves and their staff to raise the bar each year. "The goal I have set is that we want to make the best," Jim says. "There is no compromise on quality. Canadian wine is going to be top-quality wine, and I am convinced we can do it."

King's Ransom Chardonnay 2013 ($45)

Alcohol 13.8%. Production 60 cases.

AUTHOR'S TASTING NOTES "This elegant wine has citrus aromas mingled with lightly toasted oak. On the palate, there are flavours of marmalade, butter, and toasted almonds, with a persistent finish." Drink by 2020.

King's Ransom Pinot Noir 2013 ($55)

Alcohol 14%. Production 93 cases.

AUTHOR'S TASTING NOTES "This wine begins with aromas of cherries and raspberries. The palate is intense, with flavours of spicy cherries mingled with toasted oak. The texture is full, leading to a velvet polish on the finish." Drink by 2023.

King's Ransom Pinot Noir 2012

Pinot Noir (five clones). Alcohol 14.2%. Aged in French oak (50% new). Production 95 cases.

WINERY TASTING NOTES "Dark and richly concentrated, this wine has aromas of spice and cherry leading to voluptuous flavours of earthy black cherries. The structure and power of this wine indicates ability to cellar up to 10 years." Drink by 2022.

King's Ransom Meritage 2013 ($65)

Cabernet Sauvignon 60%, Merlot 40%. Alcohol 13.7%. Aged 16 months in French and American oak barrels (80% new). Production 120 cases.

WINERY TASTING NOTES "The blend boasts rich, complex aromas of ripe cherry, cassis, and cocoa. Flavours of plum and spice are balanced with hints of fresh cedar and vanilla. Smooth, velvety tannins linger on the finish." Drink by 2027.

King's Ransom 2009

Cabernet Sauvignon 50%, Merlot 50%. Alcohol 14.6%. Aged 18 to 24 months in barrels, 75% French, 25% American (60% new). Production 148 cases.

WINERY TASTING NOTES "The higher percentage of specially selected Cabernet Sauvignon in combination with our Merlot brings characteristic dark cherry, raspberry, tobacco, leather, and dark chocolate flavours. The aromas of cherries and liquorice are rich and complex. Round, full-bodied mouth feel is complemented by soft yet firm tannins." Drink by 2021.

King's Ransom 2006

Merlot 65%, Cabernet Sauvignon 35%. Alcohol 14.5%. Production 100 cases.

AUTHOR'S TASTING NOTES "The wine still had grip at eight years, suggesting it would peak in 2016 and retain that plateau for several more years. The wine has aromas of cassis and plum. On the palate, the blackcurrant flavours are intertwined with notes of leather, coffee, and cedar. The texture and finish are reminiscent of fine Bordeaux-classified growth." Drink by 2020.

Okanagan Crush Pad Winery
HAYWIRE PINOT NOIR

In 2005, Christine Coletta and her husband, Steve Lornie, impulsively bought an orchard near Summerland. Their subsequent money-losing experience with apricots triggered the conversion of the 4 hectares (10 acres) to Pinot Gris in what is called Switchback Vineyard. And the winery they opened in 2010 has become one of the Okanagan's most innovative.

The most dramatic example is the winery's daring decision on cooperage. Alberto Antonini, a consulting winemaker from Tuscany who has worked with Crush Pad since 2011, advised the winery to use concrete eggs and casks for the fermentation and aging of wines. "Concrete is a nice environment," Alberto said at the time. "When you smell an empty concrete tank, you smell life. You smell something which is important for making a premium wine. If you do the same with a stainless steel tank, you smell nothing. You smell death. To me, the making of premium wine is about life; it is not about death." By 2015, the winery had replaced all of its barrels with 59,000 litres of concrete vessels (stainless steel is used for storage and blending needs). He also influenced the winery's decision to convert to organic viticulture and to rely on indigenous yeasts.

Wines fermented and aged in concrete exhibit more generous textures than wines fermented in steel. This is apparent in the winery's Pinot Gris and surprisingly with Pinot Noir. "We are getting more complexity from the concrete, more richness, more depth of flavour, longer flavours, and more femininity, which is where we are trying to go," says Matt Dumayne, Crush Pad's veteran New Zealand–born winemaker. "Concrete has proved itself, that it can be just as texturally generous, if not more so [than barrels], and more expressive of the site and the grape."

Since 2010, which was the winery's second vintage, it has purchased Pinot Noir to develop into its flagship wine. One critical source has been the 3-hectare (7.5-acre) Canyonview Vineyard near Summerland. The vineyard is owned by an Algerian-born winemaker, Krimo Souilah, who made wine for many years in Napa before representing a French barrel maker. In 2003, on a sales trip to the Okanagan, he acquired this property. He planted Pinot Noir and a little Chardonnay and sells the grapes every year. Crush Pad took them from 2011 through 2014. Subsequently, Crush Pad switched to vineyards that are organic.

Much of Crush Pad's future growth depends on the success of its new organic vineyard in the nearby Garnet Valley. Six hectares (15 acres) of Pinot Noir have been planted since 2012, with the potential to quadruple the plantings on virgin soil at one of the highest elevations in the Okanagan. The pace at which the Garnet Valley vineyards will be completed depends on how good the wines are. Christine, Steve, and their colleagues intend to be on the industry's leading edge without being foolhardy about the risks they take on.

Haywire 2014 ($39.90)

Pinot Noir clones 115, 667. Alcohol 13%. Canyonview Vineyard. Fermented with wild yeast and aged 11 months in concrete. Production 530 cases.

WINERY TASTING NOTES "Classic aromas of wild berries, barnyard, and herbs dominate, while concrete aging adds a lush texture of sweet red fruits and juicy, mouth-watering acidity." Drink by 2021.

Haywire 2013

Pinot Noir clones 115, 667. Alcohol 13.5%. Canyonview Vineyard. Aged 14 months in concrete. Production 500 cases.

AUTHOR'S TASTING NOTES "The wine begins with bright aromas of cherry and raspberry that are echoed in the flavours, along with hints of herbs and spice. It is a lively wine with a silken texture." Drink by 2020.

Haywire 2012

Pinot Noir. Alcohol 13.2%. Canyonview Vineyard. Aged 2 months in used French oak and 18 months in concrete eggs. Production 515 cases.

AUTHOR'S TASTING NOTES "Dark in colour, the wine has aromas of toast and cherries, with deep cherry flavours. The texture is silken." Drink by 2018.

Haywire 2012

Pinot Noir. Alcohol 12.4%. Secrest Mountain Vineyard. Aged in old French oak. Production 750 cases.

WINERY TASTING NOTES "Loaded with bright cherry aromas and flavours, with soft texture and light tannins." Drink now.

Haywire 2011

Pinot Noir. Alcohol 13.4%. Canyonview Vineyard. Aged in old French oak and concrete eggs. Production 413 cases.

WINERY TASTING NOTES "This wine started with low crop levels, extreme patience during harvest, and slave-like manual punch-downs in the tanks. It was aged in old French oak barrels then moved into egg-shaped concrete tanks for further rest time. The wine has the hallmark cherry fruit intensity of the previous vintage, with soft, lush tannins, and will continue to improve and evolve with bottle aging." Drink now.

Haywire 2010

Pinot Noir. Alcohol 13%. Secrest Mountain Vineyard.

WINERY TASTING NOTES "The late ripening and warm fall of 2010 provided excellent flavour development that produced pure strawberry and cherry characters." Drink now.

Orofino Winery

BELEZA

Several years ago, a collector of Orofino wines (a Vancouver doctor) bought a double magnum of one of the reds. In his hurry to drive home from the winery's Similkameen tasting room, he left it behind. I am familiar with the incident because I visited Orofino shortly after he did and agreed to bring the wine to Vancouver for him.

I do not think the doctor was absent-minded. He had purchased other wines and had been so engaged in conversation with John and Virginia Weber, the captivating owners, that the large-format bottle just remained on the floor of the tasting room. John and Virginia, who are natives of Saskatchewan, purchased the 2-hectare (5-acre) vineyard in 2001. "We spent the first year on a huge learning curve," remembers John, a former teacher. Virginia is a nurse. They opened Orofino Winery in 2005, and it has become one of the most highly regarded wineries in the Similkameen Valley.

Almost every wine in the portfolio is collectible. The flagship is a Bordeaux blend called Beleza. "It means 'beauty' in Portuguese," Virginia says. "John spent some time in Brazil. When we were thinking of a proprietary name for our Merlot/Cabernet blend, that came to mind. It describes a perfect moment, not just beauty. Someone asks, 'How are you?' and the reply will be 'Beleza.'"

All but one wine from Orofino is made with Similkameen grapes. (The exception is Red Bridge, a Merlot formerly made with fruit from a Kaleden

vineyard). The winery vineyard includes blocks of five varietals planted in 1989, augmented by various plantings since 1999. The most recent addition, in 2010, was 0.2 hectares (0.6 acres) of Petit Verdot. The nearby Passion Pit Vineyard grows Cabernet Sauvignon. Hendsbee Vineyard, with 3.3 hectares (8.2 acres) of vines next door to Orofino, grows several varieties including a notable Riesling. At Scout Vineyard, a 1.7-hectare (4.2-acre) property beside the Similkameen River, owners Murray and Maggie Fonteyne grow Syrah, Pinot Gris, and more Riesling for Orofino. Also nearby is Celentano Vineyard, owned by Carmela and Antonio Celentano, which has a half-acre block of mature Gamay that Orofino has been buying since 2007. The 28-hectare (70-acre) Blind Creek Vineyard south of Cawston provides Sauvignon Blanc and Chardonnay to Orofino.

"Minimal intervention is the key to the development of this wine," the winery says of its approach to making Beleza. "The grapes were hand harvested and then gently destemmed and lightly crushed into half-ton open-top fermenters, where they were hand-punched three times per day until completion of fermentation. The wine was then pressed straight to new, one- and two-year-old French barrels. Each varietal lot was kept separate and aged carefully for 20 months before blending, racking, and bottling (unfiltered). Only the best barrels were included in the final blend."

Beleza 2013 ($34)

Cabernet Sauvignon 35%, Merlot 35%, Petit Verdot 20%, Cabernet Franc 10%. Alcohol 14.2%. Aged separately in French oak for 20 months before blending. Production 600 cases.

WINERY'S TASTING NOTES "A seductive wine full of complex notes of violets, exotic spice, and chocolate-dipped black cherries. The finish is full of satisfying tannins with hints of sweet vanilla and coffee." Drink by 2023.

Beleza 2012

Cabernet Sauvignon 40%, Merlot 40%, Cabernet Franc 10%, Petit Verdot 10%. Alcohol 14.8%. Aged separately for 20 months in French oak before blending.

AUTHOR'S TASTING NOTES "The wine is a powerhouse of almost port-like fruit that creates a rich, intense mid-palate. It begins with aromas of dark fruits and chocolate, leading to flavours of plum, black cherry, and chocolate, with a touch of sage on the finish." Drink by 2022.

Beleza 2011

Merlot 50%, Cabernet Sauvignon 30%, Cabernet Franc 10%, Petit Verdot 10%. Alcohol 14.3%. Aged in barrels (30% new). Production 490 cases.

AUTHOR'S TASTING NOTES "The wine begins with aromas of red fruit and violets, leading to flavours of blackcurrant. Typical of the vintage, the fruit flavours are bright and the texture is lean." Drink by 2020.

Beleza 2010

Cabernet Sauvignon, Merlot, Cabernet Franc, and Petit Verdot. Alcohol 14.1%. Aged separately for 20 months in barrel before blending. Production 285 cases.

WINERY TASTING NOTES "The wine begins with aromas of red fruits, vanilla, and dust. Earthy yet bright. On the palate, there are flavours of red and black fruits with dried herbs and wet rocks. Bright with elevated acidity. Juicy. Good length and promises to be a very good wine to cellar. The wine is from a cool vintage. Not a big bruiser like we can make in hotter years, it is slightly leaner but ripe and juicy." Drink by 2020.

Beleza 2009

Merlot 50%, Cabernet Sauvignon 30%, Petit Verdot 15%, Cabernet Franc 5%. Alcohol 14.8%. Aged 16 months in French (30% new) and American oak. Production 364 cases.

AUTHOR'S TASTING NOTES "This is a bold wine: dark and broody, dense and chewy. There are aromas and flavours of black cherry, vanilla, and graphite." Drink by 2020.

Beleza 2008

Merlot 60%, Cabernet Sauvignon 20%, Cabernet Franc 10%, Petit Verdot 10%. Alcohol 14.7%. Aged 16 months in a combination of French and American oak. Production 498 cases.

AUTHOR'S TASTING NOTES "It begins with aromas of currants and chocolate, continuing to flavours of plum, black cherry, vanilla, and spice. It has substantial weight on the palate and ripe tannins that will allow it to age well." Drink by 2018.

Beleza 2007

Merlot 68%, Cabernet Sauvignon 15%, Cabernet Franc 13%, Petit Verdot 4%. Alcohol 14.3%. Production 352 cases.

AUTHOR'S TASTING NOTES "The Petit Verdot, which was added to the blend starting in 2007, brings lovely floral notes to the aromas of red fruit. The concentrated palate has flavours of blackcurrant and blackberry." Drink now.

Merlot Cabernet 2006

Merlot 76%, Cabernet Franc 12%, Cabernet Sauvignon 12%. Aged in French and American oak (45% new). Production 375 cases.

AUTHOR'S TASTING NOTES "Tasted in 2014, the wine still has a firm structure, with developed fruit aromas and flavours of blackcurrant and plum." Drink now.

Osoyoos Larose Winery

LE GRAND VIN

Osoyoos Larose turned the Bordeaux formula on its head with Le Grand Vin, launching it in the 2001 vintage as the premier wine from the estate, not as the second label. It was a surprise because one of the two partners behind Osoyoos Larose (and now the sole owner) was Groupe Taillan of Bordeaux.

Taillan operates several chateaux in Bordeaux, including Château Gruaud-Larose, a distinguished second-growth winery in Saint-Julien. In Bordeaux, grapes from young vines—vines less than 15 years old—are almost never blended into an estate's top wine. They are usually reserved for an estate's second label.

At Osoyoos Larose, Le Grand Vin 2001 was made with fruit from three-year-old vines. The second label, Pétales d'Osoyoos, was not even launched until the 2005 vintage. Even then, it was not created as a home for fruit from young vines but rather for the barrels of quality wine left over after the blend for Le Grand Vin had been decided.

"At the beginning, we intended to have two labels, and the first release in 2001 would be the second label," says Pascal Madevon, the French-born winemaker who managed Osoyoos Larose for 10 years. Referring to Le Grand Vin, he says: "The first label was to be for the later years because the 2001 is from young vines. That was not the case. The wine is so good, we decided to put Osoyoos Larose on the 2001 label, and we decided to put 95 percent of the 2001 vintage into the blend—except six or seven barrels of hard-press wine. Incredible!"

Groupe Taillan had been asked to partner in an Okanagan vineyard and winery by Vincor International (now Constellation Brands). The strategy was to bring the experience of a seasoned Bordeaux producer to the Okanagan. Taillan's consultants chose the vineyard site and the varietals. The vineyard was as densely planted as a Bordeaux vineyard. The French company recruited Pascal, who already had almost two decades of experience in Bordeaux. He arrived in the Okanagan a month or so before the first grapes were picked at Osoyoos Larose.

"I was surprised after I arrived here," Pascal remembers. "It was a big gap from France. The first surprise was the quality of the grapes." Alain Sutre, Taillan's consultant, asked what Pascal thought of the grape quality. "I think it is close to a classified growth," he said. From that insight flowed the ultimate decision that Osoyoos Larose would produce an icon wine from the very first vintage.

In the manner of the great Bordeaux châteaux, Osoyoos Larose achieves a consistent style with Le Grand Vin that appeals to collectors. The wine is released three to four years after the vintage. While it can be enjoyed on release, it rewards those prepared to wait five to 10 years before opening it. This is entirely reminiscent of reds from top Bordeaux châteaux and is one of the reasons that Le Grand Vin stands out among Okanagan wines.

NOTE: The majority of the author's tasting notes were written in 2014.

2013 ($45.99)

Merlot 57%, Cabernet Franc 17%, Cabernet Sauvignon 16%, Petit Verdot 6%, Malbec 4%. Alcohol 14%. Aged 18 to 20 months in French oak (60% new).

AUTHOR'S TASTING NOTES "The wine is structured with a Bordeaux-inspired firmness that portends aging potential. It begins with aromas of mint, blackcurrant, and cedar. On the palate, there are flavours of blackcurrant, espresso, dark chocolate, and graphite-like minerality." Drink by 2025.

2012 ($45)

Merlot 50%, Cabernet Sauvignon 24%, Petit Verdot 13%, Cabernet Franc 9%, Malbec 4%. Alcohol 13.8%. Aged 18 to 20 months in French oak (60% new). Production 6,500 cases.

AUTHOR'S TASTING NOTES "The wine begins with aromas of vanilla and cassis and continues with flavours of black cherry and blackcurrants, along with hints of espresso and dark chocolate on the finish. The wine has great elegance and polish." Drink by 2024.

2011

Merlot 48%, Cabernet Sauvignon 33%, Petit Verdot 10%, Cabernet Franc 6%, Malbec 3%. Alcohol 13.8%. Aged 18 to 20 months in French oak (60% new). Production 3,000 cases.

WINERY TASTING NOTES "The 2011 vintage features a very deep, intense colour. The nose is rich and complex with toasty caramel and espresso aromas, opulent blackcurrant notes, spices, and eucalyptus. Ripe, velvety tannins enrobe a silky texture." Drink by 2023.

2010

Merlot 67%, Cabernet Sauvignon 20%, Petit Verdot 6%, Cabernet Franc 4%, Malbec 3%. Alcohol 13.8%. Aged 18 to 20 months in French oak (60% new). Production 3,000 cases.

WINERY TASTING NOTES "Exhibiting all the hallmarks of a classic Bordeaux, the 2010 vintage reveals a deep ruby colour, complex aromas of rich vanilla, currant, and coffee bean that are all wrapped around a core of luscious red berry fruits. Perfectly balanced, the powerful, velvet tannins seamlessly integrate with the concentrated flavours, creating a finish that is long and lingering." Drink by 2022.

2009

Merlot 58%, Cabernet Sauvignon 26%, Cabernet Franc 7%, Petit Verdot 7%, Malbec 2%. Alcohol 13.87%. Aged 20 months in French oak (60% new). Production 8,000 cases.

AUTHOR'S TASTING NOTES "Dark in colour and concentrated in texture, this wine still shows its youthful tannins. Decanting helps reveal aromas of sage, blueberry, and cedar with lush layers of plum and blackcurrant." Drink by 2021.

2008

Merlot 60%, Cabernet Sauvignon 25%, Cabernet Franc 7%, Malbec 5%, Petit Verdot 3%. Alcohol 13.9%. Aged 20 months in French oak (60% new). Production 9,000 cases.

WINERY TASTING NOTES "This rich, full-bodied wine features a deep, intense ruby colour and deliciously persistent aromas of ripe red raspberry, dark chocolate with toasty caramel and vanilla notes. Opulent notes of blackberry fruit, spice, and pepper grace the palate with a well-rounded tannin structure and fruit-driven, lingering finish." Drink by 2020.

2007

Merlot 70%, Cabernet Sauvignon 21%, Cabernet Franc 4%, Petit Verdot 3%, Malbec 2%. Alcohol 13.9%. Aged 20 months in French oak (60% new). Production 7,500 cases.

AUTHOR'S TASTING NOTES "The tannins are silky and the texture is juicy. There are notes of cassis and mocha in the aroma and on the palate. The balance is elegant." Drink by 2018.

2006

Merlot 69%, Cabernet Sauvignon 20%, Cabernet Franc 4%, Petit Verdot 4%, Malbec 3%. Alcohol 13.8%. Aged 16 months in French oak (60% new). Production 10,125 cases.

AUTHOR'S TASTING NOTES "This wine has a dense, chewy texture with ripe tannins supporting earthy notes of blackcurrant and coffee." Drink now.

2005

Merlot 67%, Cabernet Sauvignon 23%, Cabernet Franc 4%, Petit Verdot 4%, Malbec 2%. Alcohol 13.8%. Aged 16 months in French oak (60% new). Production 10,475 cases.

AUTHOR'S TASTING NOTES "This is an elegant wine with silky tannins. It seems to have less power than either the preceding or succeeding vintages, but the wine is more polished and rather pretty." Drink now.

2004

Merlot 68%, Cabernet Sauvignon 21%, Petit Verdot 5%, Cabernet Franc 4%, Malbec 2%. Alcohol 13.5%. Aged 18 months in French oak (60% new). Production 9,250 cases.

AUTHOR'S TASTING NOTES "Bottle age has given this wine an alluring cassis perfume. There is concentrated fruit on the palate—blackberries and black-currant—with a touch of chocolate and espresso on the finish." Drink now.

2003

Merlot 75%, Cabernet Sauvignon 11%, Malbec 6%, Petit Verdot 5%, Cabernet Franc 3%. Alcohol 13.4%. Aged 16 months in French oak (60% new). Production 9,850 cases.

AUTHOR'S TASTING NOTES "This wine begins with glorious aromas of cassis and red fruit and delivers rich flavours and a full weight to the palate." Drink now.

2002

Merlot 57%, Cabernet Sauvignon 19%, Malbec 12%, Cabernet Franc 7%, Petit Verdot 5%. Alcohol 13.6%. Aged 16 months in French oak (60% new). Production 3,387.5 cases.

AUTHOR'S TASTING NOTES "The colour is browning. The cassis aromas and flavours mingle with hints of cigar box." Fully mature.

2001

Merlot 66%, Cabernet Sauvignon 25%, Cabernet Franc 9%. Alcohol 13.9%. Aged 16 months in French oak (60% new). Production 2,200 cases.

AUTHOR'S TASTING NOTES "The flavours are drying out and the tannins, while not hard, seem somewhat dusty." Fully mature.

Painted Rock Estate Winery
RED ICON

Few Okanagan wineries are as greatly influenced by Bordeaux consultant Alain Sutre as John and Trish Skinner's Painted Rock Estate Winery. Alain's advice to them covers the full scope of winemaking, from viticulture and barrel selection to blending the winery's flagship Red Icon.

"I will tell you how Alain found me," says John. "Alain heard about me from the nursery in Bordeaux. I had contacted the nursery directly because I wanted to get very specific clones. A year later, Alain showed up at the vineyard one day when we had just planted. He introduced himself and said, 'I love what you have planted here, but no one in the Okanagan knows how to blend these clones.' That was the beginning of the journey."

John needed such expertise to fully realize his wine-growing ambitions. Born in 1958, he had been a successful Vancouver investment adviser. His growing passion for wine triggered a decision to retire from the investment business at 50 and take up wine-growing. In 2004, after a careful study of potential vineyard sites, he bought a 24-hectare (60-acre) former apricot orchard near the Skaha climbing bluffs. The site was shaped to produce an ideal southwestern vineyard exposure that he began planting in 2005.

He had a clear vision for his wines. "This journey is not about making a Bordeaux blend," he told Alain. "This is about making an Okanagan wine with clones I sourced from Bordeaux." Alain, he discovered, was on the same page. The consultant has had a hand in making Okanagan wines at other distinguished producers including Osoyoos Larose and, latterly, Culmina Family Estate Winery.

To date, Alain has blended every vintage of Red Icon. The blending decisions reflect the strengths of the Painted Rock vineyard in any given vintage. "Our 2012 Red Icon is kind of an inverted Bordeaux blend because it leads with 31% Malbec," John says. "It's Okanagan."

The blends vary from year to year and are somewhat unorthodox, with higher percentages of both Malbec and Petit Verdot. In most Okanagan red Meritages, Petit Verdot is a minor portion of the blend, bringing a touch of spice. Not so at Painted Rock. "I have never tasted a Petit Verdot like this," Alain once said, advocating that the variety play a significant role in the blend.

The varietals all have roles to play. The Cabernets provide structure; Merlot fleshes out the mid-palate; Malbec brings bright flavour notes. "Petit Verdot," John says, "is the attack and the finish." While the components move around from vintage to vintage, Red Icon is united in style year after year by its harmony, as John discovered when tasting a vertical of the first five vintages. "Those five wines, all different blends, were all quite similar because they were complete wines," he explains.

2014 ($55)

Merlot 33%, Cabernet Franc 21%, Malbec 19%, Petit Verdot 16%, Cabernet Sauvignon 11%. Alcohol 14.3%. Aged 18 months in French oak (30% new). Production 1,153 cases.

WINERY TASTING NOTES "This wine invites you in with rich aromas of blackberry, dark plums, cassis, and sweet spices. The palate, with its velvety tannins and high acid, offers bold and juicy black fruit layered with pepper, baking spices, vanilla, and chocolate." Drink by 2029.

2013

Merlot 33%, Cabernet Franc 29%, Petit Verdot 21%, Malbec 12%, Cabernet Sauvignon 5%. Alcohol 14.9%. Aged 18 months in French oak (30% new). Production 985 cases.

WINERY TASTING NOTES "Dark and rich, cassis, blackberry, vanilla, and spice on the nose. On the palate, more ripe black fruit, dark chocolate, vanilla, and baking spice with mouth filling ripe tannins and high acidity. Give this wine maximum cellar time for the ultimate reward." Drink by 2028.

2012

Malbec 31%, Merlot 28%, Cabernet Franc 26%, Petit Verdot 15%. Alcohol 14.9%. Aged 18 months in French oak (50% new). Production 1,156 cases.

WINERY TASTING NOTES "This wine is rich and seductive with dark chocolate, coffee, and black cherry combining with vanilla, showcasing the predominant varieties in the blend. More mocha and rich tones of black cherry, tobacco, and cassis." Drink by 2027.

2011

Malbec 30%, Cabernet Franc 27%, Merlot 20%, Petit Verdot 20%, Cabernet Sauvignon 3%. Alcohol 14.5%. Aged 18 months in French oak (50% new). Production 717 cases.

AUTHOR'S TASTING NOTES "In the glass, this wine announces itself dramatically with perfumed aromas that include cherry, plum, and vanilla. The wine is ripe and rich on the palate, with flavours of black cherry, cassis, and mocha. The balance is exquisite, with a suave and polished texture and a very long finish." Drink by 2026.

2010

Cabernet Franc 39%, Merlot 21%, Petit Verdot 18%, Malbec 11%, Cabernet Sauvignon 11%. Alcohol 14.5%. Aged 18 months in French oak (80% new). Production 656 cases.

WINERY TASTING NOTES "The blend is well balanced and complex. The nose reveals notes of leather, berries, smoke, ink, and a touch of dusty earth. The palate is well structured, striking the perfect balance between acidity and bold tannin. The long finish unfolds with berries, smoke, and savoury tones." Drink by 2025.

2009

Merlot 30%, Cabernet Franc 29%, Cabernet Sauvignon 25%, Petit Verdot 15%, Syrah 1%. Alcohol 14.3%. Aged 18 months in French oak (95% new). Production 1,309 cases.

WINERY TASTING NOTES "Dark, dusty cocoa and espresso flavours contribute to a good earthy backbone, while blackberries, black Kalamata olives, prunes, and currants provide healthy fruit character. An Okanagan dusty sage element . . . becomes a slightly minty element on the long, beautiful, chocolaty finish." Drink by 2024.

2008

Merlot 30%, Cabernet Franc 25%, Malbec 25%, Petit Verdot 20%. Alcohol 13.9%. Aged 18 months in new French oak. Production 464 cases.

AUTHOR'S TASTING NOTES "The 2008 begins with inviting areas of cassis and spice cake, leading to sweet berry flavours . . . a touch of cherry, a touch of blackberry and currant, and a hint of vanilla and chocolate. The tannins are ripe and silky. The wine is very elegant with a long, long finish." Drink by 2023.

2007

Cabernet Franc 33%, Petit Verdot 20%, Cabernet Sauvignon 16%, Merlot 16%, Malbec 15%. Alcohol 14.5%. Aged 18 months in new French oak. Production 735 cases.

AUTHOR'S TASTING NOTES "This is a radical blend among Okanagan Meritage wines, most of which are built on Merlot or Cabernet Sauvignon. However, thinking outside the box has produced a delicious wine. It begins with spectacularly lifted aromas of blackcurrants, plums, blackberry, vanilla, and mocha. All of these elements follow through to the taste. The long, ripe tannins contribute to the wine's elegance and power and ageability." Drink by 2022.

Pentâge Winery

PENTÂGE BLEND

Pentâge Winery only opened its tasting room in 2011, eight years after opening the winery. The reason: it took Paul Gardner 11 years to plan and dig the massive 500-square-metre (5,400-square-foot) cave from the crown of hard rock dominating this vineyard's million-dollar view of Skaha Lake. Cool and spacious, the cave accommodates barrels and square stainless-steel tanks custom-made by a Croatian firm called Letina. "I didn't want to waste floor space," he explains. The ambience can be grasped without a tour simply by peering through the gigantic glass doors at the mouth of the cave.

This was a derelict orchard in 1996 when Paul and his wife, Julie Rennie, were so enchanted with the property that they decided to change careers. Subsequently, they have planted two vineyards near to each other with 19 grape varieties on 6 hectares (15 acres). Paul, born in Singapore in 1961, spent 20 years as a marine engineer before tiring of going to sea. "I got caught up in winemaking in the early '90s," he recalls.

The winery now produces about 5,000 cases a year, divided into a remarkable kaleidoscope of 26 wines from entry level (called Hiatus) to premium.

The Croatian tanks—whose gleaming workmanship is remarkable—are sized to facilitate Paul's penchant for making small-lot wines. "I would still rather make small lots of interesting wine than big tanks full of wine," he says. An example of an eccentric but delicious wine is the 2011 Cabernet Franc Appassimento Style, where he mimicked Amarone by drying the grapes for 58 days before crushing them.

The winery name, a play on the Greek word for five, was chosen after Paul planted five red varieties for the flagship red, also called Pentâge. The wine is built primarily with Merlot and Cabernet Sauvignon; small amounts of Cabernet Franc, Syrah, and Gamay add complexity and personality. Each variety is hand-picked, hand-sorted, and barrel-aged separately. During fermentation of each wine, the bins are punched down three times a day for maximum extraction of colour and tannins. When fermented dry, the wines are racked to French and American barrels ranging from new to two years old. After an average of 15 months in oak, the blending trials begin. This wine is unfined and unfiltered.

2012 ($30)

Cabernet Sauvignon 43.5%, Cabernet Franc 32%, Merlot 18%, Petit Verdot 5%, Syrah 1.5%. Production 440 cases.

WINERY TASTING NOTES "This current release of our flagship wine offers aromas of dark plum and blueberry mixed with toasted oak and dried mint. Flavours of ripe plum and cherry mingle on the palate and are supported by balanced acidity and youthful, leathery tannins. Well structured with a long, supple finish." Drink by 2020.

2011

Cabernet Franc 50%, Cabernet Sauvignon 30%, Merlot 11%, Petit Verdot 6%, Syrah 2%, Gamay 1%. Alcohol 13.5%. Production 200 cases.

WINERY TASTING NOTES "Aromas of black cherry, red berries, and dried plum are combined with notes of vanilla, cedar, and spice. Flavours of red berry, dried cherry, toasted oak, and spice mingle on the palate. The youthful and bright balanced acidity makes this an ideal wine for drinking now." Drink by 2018.

2010

Cabernet Sauvignon 39%, Cabernet Franc 27%, Merlot 17%, Petit Verdot 13%, Syrah 3%, Gamay 1%. Production 200 cases.

WINERY TASTING NOTES "This wine is deep garnet red in colour, with aromas of blackcurrant, red berries, chocolate with a hint of leather and spice. Flavours of blackberries, ripe cherries, toasted oak all blend harmoniously. Rich and smooth, this elegant wine offers a soft, smooth finish."

2007

Cabernet Sauvignon 42%, Merlot 38%, Cabernet Franc 16%, Gamay 2%, Syrah 2%. Production 400 cases.

WINERY TASTING NOTES "This wine is deep garnet red in colour, with aromas of blackcurrant, chocolate, leather, and a hint of spice. Flavours of blackberries, ripe cherries, toasted oak all blend harmoniously. Rich and smooth, this wine offers fine tannins with an elegant finish." Drink by 2019.

2006

Merlot 46%, Cabernet Sauvignon 35%, Cabernet Franc 15%, Syrah 2.5%, Gamay 1.5%. Production 360 cases.

Tasting notes unavailable.

2005

Merlot 46%, Cabernet Sauvignon 35%, Cabernet Franc 15%, Syrah 2.5%, Gamay 1.5%. Production 180 cases.

WINERY TASTING NOTES "The wine is a dark purple colour with a vivid ruby red brim. Aromas of caramel and chocolate-covered cherries, while the palate is rich and smooth with layers of cherries, blackberries, anise, and rich mocha coffee flavors. These flavours, along with the fine-grained tannins, will linger on your palate. With decanting or by leaving the bottle open for an hour before drinking, the wine comes to life." Drink by 2018.

2004

Merlot 41%, Cabernet Sauvignon 40%, Cabernet Franc 17%, Syrah 1.5%, Gamay 0.5%. Production 200 cases.

Tasting notes unavailable.

2003

Merlot 62%, Cabernet Sauvignon 20%, Cabernet Franc 15%, Syrah 2%, Gamay 1%. Production 160 cases.

Tasting notes unavailable.

Perseus Winery

INVICTUS

Perseus is an urban winery located in a 60-year-old house within walking distance of downtown Penticton. The house does not look its age, after a $500,000 update several years ago added an elegant and spacious tasting room overlooking the city. There is a glimpse of the country, however: Perseus's Lower Bench Vineyard, a 2-hectare (5-acre) Pinot Gris planting, is just beyond the parking lot at the rear of the winery.

The winery released its first wine in 2009 under the Synergy name. It was then renamed the less corporate-sounding Perseus, the constellation in the Okanagan night sky during harvest. "We feel the symbolism of this constellation overlooking the entire valley to be quite fitting, much in the way we cover the Okanagan looking for the finest grapes," the winery says.

Perseus is owned by Terrabella Wineries Ltd., a winery holding company headed by Summerland chartered accountant Rob Ingram. In 2015, it also opened the Hatch Winery in West Kelowna. The Hatch's wine shop is an artfully renovated barn. In keeping with the Terrabella strategy of having highly visible wineries in high-traffic locations, the Hatch is just up the road from popular Quails' Gate Winery.

Over the years, ownership, management, and winemaking duties have been in flux at Perseus. One constant, however, is the winery's production of small-lot wines, with Invictus as the flagship.

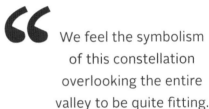

We feel the symbolism of this constellation overlooking the entire valley to be quite fitting.

2013 ($44.99)

Cabernet Franc 42%, Merlot 38%, Cabernet Sauvignon 13%, Malbec 7%. Alcohol 14.5%. Production 700 cases.

WINERY TASTING NOTES "Our 2013 Invictus showcases the true potential that Bordeaux-style wines can achieve here in the South Okanagan. This wine bursts out of the bottle with concentrated aromas of black cherry, ripe plum, and dark chocolate. The bouquet is echoed on the palate with additional hints of clove, eucalyptus, and smoked meats. This well-structured, balanced wine has a velvety mouth-feel with long, lingering tannins." Drink by 2024.

2012

Cabernet Franc 58%, Merlot 21%, Cabernet Sauvignon 19%, Malbec 2%. Alcohol 14.5%. Production 400 cases.

WINERY TASTING NOTES "This wine bursts out of the bottle with concentrated aromas of black cherry, truffle, and shades of pencil lead that lead into an opulent yet well-structured wine of impressive complexity. Flavours here straddle both Old World and New, with boysenberry, anise, and dark chocolate hints. The mouth-feel is all velvet with long, lingering tannins." Drink by 2020.

2011

Merlot 40%, Malbec 21%, Petit Verdot 18%, Cabernet Sauvignon 11%, Cabernet Franc 10%. Alcohol 14.5%. Production 300 cases.

WINERY TASTING NOTES "French oak–warmed tannins on an outpouring of fresh, bright, black fruit elegance. Suggestion of violet blossoms. A bold and age-worthy blend." Drink by 2022.

2010

Merlot 56%, Cabernet Sauvignon 29%, Petit Verdot 9%, Cabernet Franc 4%, Malbec 2%. Alcohol 14%. Production 200 cases.

WINERY TASTING NOTES "A commanding wine of structure and balance that displays an outpouring of elegant black fruit, leather, rich earthy tones, and a trace of cigar box: bold, intriguing, and age-worthy." Drink by 2018.

2009

Cabernet Sauvignon 44%, Merlot 34%, Petit Verdot 10%, Cabernet Franc 9%, Malbec 3%. Alcohol 14%. Production 200 cases.

WINERY TASTING NOTES "Plum, cacao, dark cherry, and aged leather aromas dominate the nose. The mouth feel is silky with dark fruit flavours and hints of dark chocolate." Drink now.

2008

Cabernet Sauvignon 50%, Cabernet Franc 21%, Merlot 19%, Malbec 8%, Petit Verdot 2%. Alcohol 13.7%. Production 200 cases.

AUTHOR'S TASTING NOTES "Elegant and full-bodied with lovely ripe fruit, the wine tastes of currants, blueberries, and blackberries with an appealing spicy finish." Drink now.

Poplar Grove Winery

THE LEGACY

Since launching in the 2004 vintage, the Legacy has been positioned as the best wine in the Poplar Grove portfolio. Winemaker Stefan Arnason, with his endless pursuit of what he calls marginal improvement, promises there is even better to come. "You can always make it better," he believes. "Perfection is by definition unattainable. Excellence is what you are after. Don't let perfection get in the way of excellence."

The bar was always set high. Ian Sutherland, the self-taught founding winemaker, had trained his palate by collecting and drinking fine Bordeaux reds. The winery's initial vintage, in 1995, was made in a garage with minimal tools. Yet on release two years later, his Merlot and Cabernet Franc won gold and silver medals in their first competition. In the 1998 vintage, Ian began blending the forerunner of the Legacy, a reserve that was 80 percent Merlot and 20 percent Cabernet Franc. He added Cabernet Sauvignon to the blend in 2002, establishing the template for the Legacy. Remarkably, he made great wines in small volumes despite the rustic production facilities.

In 2008, Tony Holler, a Naramata Bench neighbour, acquired control of Poplar Grove. The son of Austrian immigrants, Tony, who was born in 1951 and grew up on his family's Summerland orchard, went to medical school, and succeeded in the pharmaceutical industry. He also liked Poplar Grove wines and believed in the Okanagan's potential to produce wines that rank among the best in the world. "I wasn't that interested in having a tiny boutique winery," Tony said in 2012. So after acquiring a controlling interest in the winery, he invested in vineyards so the business could become largely self-sufficient with grapes; he built a well-equipped, modern winery.

"Ian and his winemaking team were working from a 4,000- to 5,000-square-foot building, producing this wine with very little technology," Tony notes. "The question in my mind was what if we had the proper infrastructure—a winery with the right cooling systems, with the right tanks and the right barrels—what can this winery really become?"

Stefan Arnason, who joined the winery in 2008 and became winemaker two years later, says that older Poplar Grove reds sometimes reminded him of Rioja reds that had spent a little too much time evaporating in older barrels. The humidity controls in the new Poplar Grove winery curb the evaporation during the 18 to 21 months the Legacy ages in barrel. And now, 30 percent of the barrels are new French oak, resulting in the wines remaining fresh longer.

The 2010 vintage, one of the Okanagan's coolest, demonstrated the importance of the winery controlling its own vineyards. To ensure that the red varieties ripened adequately, Poplar Grove reduced its crop so aggressively that more than half the grapes were dropped on the ground.

Production of the 2010 Legacy, at 350 cases, was the lowest ever, but the quality of the wine was not compromised. The potential, in a great vintage like 2012, is 2,000 cases. The actual production was about half that, allowing the winery to satisfy the rising demand for its other Bordeaux reds, which also appeal to collectors.

2012 ($49.90)

Cabernet Franc 35%, Malbec 23%, Merlot 22%, Cabernet Sauvignon 20%. Alcohol 13.9%. Production 900 cases.

AUTHOR'S TASTING NOTES "This wine begins with aromas of blackcurrants and spice. The wine is rich on the palate with flavours of black cherry, blackberry, espresso, and mocha. The ripe tannins give it a polished texture." Drink by 2023.

2011

Merlot 43%, Cabernet Franc 41%, Malbec 13%, Cabernet Sauvignon 3%. Alcohol 14.5%. Production 550 cases.

AUTHOR'S TASTING NOTES "This firmly textured wine begins with aromas of blackcurrant and black cherry, which are echoed on the palate, along with flavours of coffee and dark chocolate. There are spicy fruit flavours on the lingering finish." Drink by 2022.

2010

Merlot 33%, Malbec 24%, Cabernet Sauvignon 23%, Cabernet Franc 20%. Alcohol 13.3%. Production 350 cases.

WINERY TASTING NOTES "Rich ruby red in colour. The Legacy bouquet delivers enticing aromas of fresh tobacco, plum, and blackcurrant. Fresh vanilla and espresso greet the palate, while lush tannins of blackberry and dark cherry linger in between. A soft yet structured mouth feel is complemented by notes of plum and sagebrush on the finish. This age-worthy red blend will only become more expressive with time." Drink by 2020.

2009

Merlot 56%, Cabernet Sauvignon 21%, Cabernet Franc 20%, Malbec 3%. Alcohol 15.3%. Production 500 cases.

WINERY TASTING NOTES "Deep crimson red in colour. Distinct aromas of plum, leather, and cedar mingle in the glass. The first sip delivers cassis, plum, and vanilla flavours infused with orange zest on the palate. Mature integration of fine tannins and balanced acidity create depth of flavour in the mid palate with a long exploratory finish. A glorious expression of the 2009 vintage that will age gracefully for over a decade." Drink by 2020.

2008

Cabernet Franc 55%, Merlot 26%, Cabernet Sauvignon 19%. Alcohol 14.5%.

WINERY TASTING NOTES "Deep garnet red in colour. Complex aromas of tobacco, tea leaf, and cassis mingle in the glass. The first sip delivers blackberry, cherry, and plum flavours infused with anise and subtle notes of sage. Balanced acidity and fine tannins create a long, intense finish. Cabernet Franc, Cabernet Sauvignon, and Merlot are seamlessly blended together to offer a big, brooding wine that will continue to impress as it ages." Drink by 2021.

2007

Merlot 71%, Cabernet Franc 17%, Cabernet Sauvignon 12%. Aged 2 years in French oak.

WINERY TASTING NOTES "The Legacy 2007 offers deeply concentrated and mature colour. The nose gathers aromas of currant, coffee, and cedar. Initial flavours of blackberry, briar, and ripe plums are followed by hints of leather, spice, and vanilla. Silky tannins and elegant fruit meet a balanced backbone of acidity creating depth and complexity. A sweet ripeness makes this wine dangerously delicious. The finish is heartbreakingly long, like a French kiss goodbye at the train station." Drink by 2020.

2006

Merlot 70%, Cabernet Franc 24%, Cabernet Sauvignon 6%. Alcohol 14.8%.

WINERY TASTING NOTES "Dark cherry, floral notes of iris and Callebaut chocolate arrive on the nose. The first sip of this signature blend delivers dark berry fruit infused with more cocoa flavours. Subtle notes of briar and vanilla are wrapped in generous ripe tannins that build length on the finish." Drink by 2019.

2005

Merlot 65%, Cabernet Franc 20%, Cabernet Sauvignon 10%, Malbec 5%. Alcohol 14.2%.

WINERY TASTING NOTES "The strength of the blend begins with the elegance of Merlot and the power of Cabernet Franc. Add the richness of Cab Sauvignon to bring out a medley of fruit components and let Malbec pick up the backbeat in mid-palate. Ripe tannins build length and breadth in the finish. As big and brooding as it is now, it will develop further in the years to come." Drink by 2018.

2004

Merlot 65%, Cabernet Franc 20%, Cabernet Sauvignon 10%, Malbec 5%. Alcohol 14.8%. Production 760 cases.

WINERY TASTING NOTES "This is our interpretation of the Bordeaux Right Bank Blend from around Pomerol and St. Emilion, where Merlot is queen of the vintage. Combined with Cabernet Franc, Cabernet Sauvignon, and Malbec, it produces a classic wine demonstrating wonderful integration and finesse, with blackberry, leather, and currants in a big chewy matrix." Those notes no longer apply a decade later—unfortunately, Poplar Grove used synthetic closures in the 2004 vintage, which led to the wines aging prematurely. The Legacy 2004 is now hard and dried out.

Privato Vineyard and Winery
PINOT NOIR

By launching their Privato winery in Kamloops, where they lived, John and Debbie Woodward gave themselves some daunting challenges. The first was planting Pinot Noir and Chardonnay. Their vineyard on the bank of the North Thompson River, a 30-minute drive north of downtown Kamloops, is one of the most northerly vineyards in British Columbia.

"Debbie has always wanted a vineyard," says John, who was born in Kamloops in 1954. He is a professional forester, while Debbie is a certified general accountant. Since 1987, they have grown trees for Christmas and for landscaping on their 32-hectare (80-acre) farm. Several years ago, they took time off from this bucolic life to tour in Italy during harvest. Seeing tiny wineries harvesting and processing grapes inspired them. "It was just the fuel we needed to get going," Debbie says. There was nothing holding them back: they had land and their elegant farm buildings were easily turned into a winery and tasting room. In 2010, they planted 1.2 hectares (3 acres) of vines—Pinot Noir, Chardonnay, and one row of Maréchal Foch.

Since John had limited winemaking experience, he retained a consultant, Gustav Allander of Foxtrot Vineyards. Gustav coached him in making a trial lot of Pinot Noir in 2010 and enough in 2011 for commercial release. In 2013, when Gustav stopped consulting, the Woodwards turned to New Zealand-trained Jacqueline Kemp for guidance on sourcing Okanagan grapes and making wine. She is the consulting winemaker at several Okanagan wineries, including One Faith Vineyards.

The challenge for collectors of Privato's Pinot Noirs is the winery's penchant for identifying small-lot wines with different labels. Tesoro and Fedele are Pinot Noirs from different vineyards. From 2013 forward, these wines succeed the Woodward Collection Pinot Noir. The Grande Réserve Pinot Noir will be released only in exceptional vintages. None was made in 2013, but a 2014 is likely to be released. Pinot Noirs released under the Privato Collection label might be considered the "regular" Pinot Noirs.

 Debbie has always wanted a vineyard.

Woodward Family Collection Pinot Noir Fedele 2013 ($38)

Dijon clone 115. Alcohol 12.5%. Aged 18 months in François Frères barrels (25% new, 40% second fill, 35% third fill), followed by one full year lying down before release in fall 2016. Production 119 cases.

WINERY TASTING NOTES "Fedele (Italian for Faithful—and named after our beloved Labrador Retriever Maddy) Pinot Noir is a deep ruby red colour. Raspberry, cherry, blackcurrant, and orange blossoms intermingle with toasty oak. The palate finishes long and its juicy acidity lends it to aging for a good 10 years." Drink by 2025.

Woodward Family Collection Pinot Noir Tesoro 2013 ($38)

Dijon clones 115, 777. Alcohol 13.5%. Aged 18 months in François Frères barrels (35% new, 40% second fill, 25% third), followed by one full year lying down before release in fall 2016. Production 95 cases.

WINERY TASTING NOTES "Garnet red in colour, our Tesoro Pinot Noir (Tesoro is Italian for treasure, for we treasure this wine and all that life brings us) captures the essence of this warm growing season. Black liquorice, tobacco, pomegranate, wild mushrooms, and a hint of thyme set the tone for this wine, whilst supple tannins and juicy acidity leave you wanting more." Drink by 2025.

Woodward Family Collection Pinot Noir Grande Reserve 2012 ($49)

Dijon clones 115, 777. Alcohol 13.6%. Aged 18 months in François Frères barrels (30% new, 35% second fill, 35% third fill), followed by 1.5 years lying down before release, following the European Reserve rules. Production 200 cases.

WINERY TASTING NOTES "Choosing the top 8 barrels from this already exceptional vintage, this reserve is absolutely tantalizing! This vintage just gets better and better with age and in fact will have taken 3 full years to bring this wine to aficionados and collectors alike. Also ruby-red in colour the berry notes fill the nose, bursting out of the glass with black pepper, spice, and ripe blackberry coulis to a satisfyingly long finish." Drink by 2025.

Woodward Family Collection Pinot Noir 2012 ($38)

Dijon clones 115, 777. Alcohol 13.7%. Aged 18 months in François Frères barrels (30% new, 35% second fill, 35% third fill), followed by one full year lying down before release. Production 337 cases.

WINEMAKER'S TASTING NOTES "Receiving top honour of Double Gold in the 2015 All Canadian Wine Championship, this Pinot Noir is well, just simply yummy! Ruby-red in colour it has haunting aromas of wild raspberries, ripe strawberries, leather, violets, and smoky oak. It exhibits soft, approachable tannins and juicy acidity. It will benefit from decanting in its youth and will age for a good 10 years." Drink by 2025.

Pinot Noir 2011 ($35)

Dijon clones 115, 777. Alcohol 14.3%. Aged 18 months in François Frères barrels (40% new, 60% second fill), followed by one full year lying down before release. Production 360 cases.

WINEMAKER'S TASTING NOTES "Privato's Pinot Noir has quite a developed style with long aging and significant amounts of red fruit, spice, and vegetal notes. The structure leaves a great mouth feel with juicy acidity and silky tannins filling the palate. Flavours of ripe cherries round out the experience, maintaining a mouth-filling balance. The presence on the palate lingers, creating a long, enjoyable finish." Drink by 2024.

Quails' Gate Winery

STEWART FAMILY RESERVE PINOT NOIR

The Okanagan's first successful block of Pinot Noir was planted on the slopes of Mount Boucherie in 1975. It was another 14 years before a winery opened there: Quails' Gate Winery, which has become one of Canada's leading Pinot Noir producers.

The Stewart family, owners of Quails' Gate, have been pioneers in Okanagan agriculture since their forebears emigrated from Ireland in 1908. Viticulture began with Richard Stewart, who planted grapes in what was then called Mount Boucherie Vineyards in 1961. The winery was founded by his two sons. Ben was president initially; when he went into politics, his younger brother, Tony, succeeded him. They hired a succession of winemakers trained in Australia and New Zealand, who unlocked the potential of Pinot Noir, starting with Jeff Martin, who had 20 years of experience making wines in Australia when he arrived in 1994. The next year, he began the practice of bottling the best Pinot Noir in the cellar under the Family Reserve tier.

The 1975 planting was a modest self-rooted block of the so-called UC Davis Clone 1, said to have been developed at the University of California at Davis. Richard Stewart decided to grow Pinot Noir after researching the variety in France. That block, even though it was subsequently replaced by better Dijon clones, encouraged the Stewart family to plant additional clones over two decades, beginning in 1987. Currently, there are eight or nine clones here, each of which brings flavour and aroma profiles crucial to building great wines. The Pinot Noir flourishes on the complex soils. "Above the Mt. Boucherie Road," a winery document says, "the soils are heavily influenced by feldspar, the deposits of the youngest volcanic flow in the Kelowna area."

Canadian-born winemaker Grant Stanley, who specialized in Pinot Noir in New Zealand, joined Quails' Gate in 2003. He refined the Pinot Noir program, significantly extending skin contact during fermentation to three or four weeks in a quest for more intense flavour. He adopted fermentation with native yeasts, introducing added complexity to the wines, and he refined the choices of French oak barrels.

Grant left in 2013 to become a partner in another winery. His successor, Nikki Callaway, a French-trained Canadian winemaker, shares his affinity for Pinot Noir. She previously made the Martin's Lane Pinot Noir at Mission Hill Family Estate, which was judged best in the world in its price range at a Decanter competition in London.

2014 ($45)

Alcohol 13.5%. Fermented with indigenous yeast on the skins for nearly a month. Aged 10 months in French oak barrels (50% new). Production 974 cases.

WINERY TASTING NOTES "A New World–style Pinot Noir with aromas of rich, ripe red berries, cherry jam, and the sweet spices of clove and nutmeg. The palate is very seductive and complex, full of intense red-berried fruits with intriguing, exotic spices and a long, lingering finish." Drink by 2023.

2013

Alcohol 14%. Fermented with indigenous yeast on the skins for nearly a month. Aged 10 months in French oak barrels (50% new). Production 1,015 cases.

WINERY TASTING NOTES "A beautifully balanced wine that demonstrates a youthful nose with a mélange of ripe red berries, sweet tobacco, exotic spices, and subtle oak notes. The palate is very refined and complex with a silky and seductive mouthfeel and a long, lingering finish." Drink by 2022.

2012

Alcohol 14%. Fermented with indigenous yeast on the skins for nearly a month. Aged 10 months in French oak barrels. Production 887.5 cases.

WINERY TASTING NOTES "The nose is rich and complex with hints of dark cassis and aged oak mixed with chocolate, plum, and floral notes. This elegant wine is fruit-forward with notes of ripe cherry layered with roasted nut flavours." Drink by 2020.

2011

Alcohol 14%. Fermented with indigenous yeast on the skins for nearly a month. Aged 10 months in French oak barrels. Production 1,013.5 cases.

WINERY TASTING NOTES "With a bright luminescent garnet colour, the [wine] offers sweet red fruit fragrances mingled with delicate floral garden roses and perfume notes that leap out of the glass. The mouth feel is enticing, showing exceptional tension between the concentration of fruit weight and an almost airy lightness on the palate." Drink by 2019.

2009

Alcohol 14.5%. Grapes from four blocks and one clone were fermented individually with both indigenous and cultivated yeasts and aged 11 months in French oak (40% new, 60% 1-year-old) before blending and bottling. Production 1,031.5 cases.

WINERY TASTING NOTES "[The wine] is fragrant, with plum, dark chocolate, and cocoa notes. Hints of leather and sweet tobacco mingle with exotic spice. With long-term cellaring, this Pinot Noir will reveal earthy notes and gamy forest-floor complexities." Drink by 2018.

2008

Alcohol 14%. Best barrels of four clones were selected for this wine. Aged 11 months in French oak barrels (40% new, 60% 1-year-old). Production 1,556 cases.

WINERY TASTING NOTES "A fruit forward wine with light oak and vanilla, this wine is defined by firm, supple tannins with gamy complexity. This wine exhibits aromas of plum, cherry, and accents of exotic spice." Drink now.

2007

Alcohol 14%. Best barrels of four clones were selected for this wine. Aged 11 months in French oak barrels (40% new, 60% 1-year-old).

AUTHOR'S TASTING NOTES "It is a seductive wine, beginning with a rush of berry aromas in the glass. The velvet texture adds to the wine's seduction." Drink now.

2006

Alcohol 14%. Four clones were blended. Aged 11 months in French oak barrels.

WINERY TASTING NOTES "Ripe plum characters mingle with delicate spice and sweet vanilla oak. There are rich savoury notes and fine tannins that float evenly across the palate. The aromas are layered and complex, revealing vivid red fruits, fresh plum, and ripe black cherry notes with hints of spice, dark chocolate, and earth." Drink now.

Quinta Ferreira Estate Winery

OBRA-PRIMA

A few years after Quinta Ferreira opened its tasting room in 2007, two visitors—businesswomen from Vancouver—asked to taste wines that were still in barrel or tank.

"'I have the perfect tank,'" proprietor John Ferreira replied. "We are about to release a new wine, and it has no name. We went in the cellar and I poured a little for them. They could not believe how good it was. So I said, 'If you guys like it so much, name it.'" They came up with Obra-Prima, a Portuguese term that means masterpiece. The name was not even in the vocabulary of the modest Ferreira family, who immigrated to the Okanagan from Portugal in 1960, when John was 14.

After two decades as a farm labourer, John and his wife, Maria, bought a Black Sage Road orchard in 1979. After another two decades, with tree fruit prices in decline, John replaced their fruit trees with 6.3 hectares (15.5 acres) of grapes. The winery was housed in their former fruit-packing house, which was renovated in the style of a grand Portuguese bodega.

John and Maria's winemaker son, Michael, crafted the first Obra-Prima from the 2006 vintage in order to create the winery's first blend. "We had too much Merlot," he says candidly. The masterpiece, which is a regular award winner, has remained in the portfolio ever since. It has been complemented by Alagria (Portuguese for joy), a blend similar to Obra-Prima except that Zinfandel is added to make it fruitier and accessible at an earlier age.

The wine began as a three-variety blend. With the addition of Carmenère in 2013, it now includes six Bordeaux varieties, all estate-grown. Each individual component of Obra-Prima is aged about 28 months in barrel (90 percent French, 10 percent American oak) before Michael starts blending Obra-Prima from the best barrels. "It gets blended right at the end," he says. "That way, I can select my barrels at the end." The wine is then bottled and aged another 12 months before being released.

The 2008 vintage was so strong that the winery even released an Obra-Prima Reserve. "It was put together from the best of our best barrels," Michael says. "Only 60 cases were produced. We did not do that in 2009 or 2010. We might do it with our 2012."

On each bottle of Obra-Prima, the winery advises drinking the contents within three to five years. Quinta Ferreira is likely understating the wine's ageability. When Michael opened a 2007 Obra Prima in 2015, he thought the wine had at least three more years of life.

2010 ($34.90)

Cabernet Sauvignon 40%, Merlot 35%, with Cabernet Franc, Malbec, and Petit Verdot. Alcohol 14.1%.

AUTHOR'S TASTING NOTES "The wine begins with aromas of bell pepper, black-currant, vanilla, and cigar box. On the palate, there are flavours of blackcurrant, black cherry, chocolate, and leather, with a smoky note on the finish. The firm tannins signal an ability to age." Drink by 2023.

2009

Production 600 cases.

WINERY TASTING NOTES "Wonderful bell pepper and black cherry notes greet your first impression as the coffee, light cedar, and sweet vanilla flavours keep this wine very enjoyable to drink from start to finish. Take note of the beautiful hard-candy flavours on the long, spicy finish [and] the velvety tannins." Drink by 2020.

Reserve 2008

Alcohol 14.3%. Production 60 cases.

AUTHOR'S TASTING NOTES "The wine was tasted in late 2015. It begins with aromas of cassis, cherry, and vanilla, leading to flavours of cassis, cherry, lingonberry, and spice. Bottle age has accentuated the chocolate, tobacco, and exotic spice on the palate and the finish, a spice reminiscent of a fine slice of fruit-cake. The ripe but firm tannins give this wine good aging ability." Drink by 2020.

2008

Alcohol 13.4%. Production 820 cases.
Tasting notes unavailable. Drink by 2020.

2007

Alcohol 14.4%. Production 525 cases.

AUTHOR'S TASTING NOTES "The wine begins with aromas of vanilla, black cherry, and chocolate. These are echoed on the palate. The wine is concentrated in texture, with firm, ripe tannins. There are lingering notes of dark chocolate and black licorice on the finish." Drink by 2018.

2006

Cabernet Sauvignon 48%, Merlot 40%, Malbec 12%. Production 433 cases.
Tasting notes unavailable. Drink now.

Red Rooster Winery

GOLDEN EGG

Red Rooster Winery created Golden Egg in the 2001 vintage as a Meritage blended from third-leaf grapes. The winery was then owned by its founders, Beat and Prudence Maher. They had come to the Okanagan in 1990 from Switzerland, where they had operated fitness centres. In the Okanagan, they replaced fruit trees in a Naramata orchard with grapes and opened the winery in 1997.

Full of energy and ambition, the Mahers were some of the earliest producers to come to market with a prestige red wine. The debut 2001 Golden Egg, priced at $47.90 a bottle, was a blend of 65 percent Merlot, 25 percent Cabernet Sauvignon, and 10 percent Cabernet Franc. No Golden Egg was made in 2002 (the grapes were required in other wines), while the 2003 Golden Egg was the last under the Maher ownership. At that time, it was difficult to sell any Okanagan table wine at that price. Almost all the other wines in the Red Rooster portfolio were priced between $14 and $20. Secondly, personnel issues resulted in the winery having a succession of winemakers, which interrupted the production of icon wines (there were five winemakers during Red Rooster's first decade). Finally, the relocation of the winery in 2004 absorbed the energy of the owners. Their

production had quickly outgrown their first winery. They moved to a much larger winery on Naramata Road that included a grand château designed by architect Robert Mackenzie.

In 2005, Red Rooster was acquired by Andrew Peller Ltd., a well-financed national wine producer with several experienced winemakers. One was Karen Gillis, who took over the Red Rooster cellar in 2007. Born in Vancouver, she grew up in a family of chefs. She had that career in mind when she completed a diploma in food technology at the British Columbia Institute of Technology in 1996. But after three years of developing food products, she zeroed in on wine and joined Andrés (as Andrew Peller was then called) as an assistant winemaker.

Karen resurrected Golden Egg soon after joining Red Rooster. "After many years of fascination with 'Rhône-style' reds, I decided to work with a couple of our passionate growers, who are innovative, thirsty for knowledge, and enjoy a challenge," she has explained. "We decided in 2007 to plant some Mourvèdre, Syrah, and Grenache vines in the heart of the Okanagan Valley. In 2009 we harvested the grapes for the icon wine at Red Rooster called the 'Golden Egg.'"

2012 ($50)

Syrah 42%, Mourvèdre 30%, Grenache 28%. Alcohol 13%. Each varietal was aged separately for 12 months in French oak; after blending, the wine was aged another 6 months, half in barrel and half in a concrete egg. Production 196 cases.

WINERY TASTING NOTES "This iconic rooster really expresses its 'Rhône-style' image with flair and panache while strutting through the hen house. The clutch of hens immediately noticed that perfect shade of garnet and enticing bouquet of blue plum and black cherry, accented by notes of marzipan, almond, sweet spice, leather, oak, and forest floor. This dry, medium-bodied wine has soft, velvety tannins and food-friendly acidity. Flavours of blackberry, plum, and cherry provide that perfect, juicy fruit-forward excitement, while notes of baking spice add interest. Blueberry, blackberry, and cherry with a touch of black tea and spice provide that lasting memory." Drink through 2018.

2011

Mourvèdre 40%, Grenache 35%, Syrah 25%. Alcohol 12.2%. Each varietal was aged separately in French oak barrels. The wines were blended together after 12 months, and the final assemblage was aged a further 7 months before bottling. Production 193 cases.

WINERY TASTING NOTES "This iconic rooster really expresses its 'Rhône-style' image with flair and panache while strutting through the hen house. The clutch of hens immediately noticed that perfect shade of garnet and enticing bouquet of cherry, blueberry, and plum accented by notes of vanilla, sweet smoky oak, leather, and tobacco. This dry, medium-bodied wine has soft, delicate tannins and food-friendly acidity. Flavours of cherry, red berry, and blueberry provide that perfect tangy, juicy fruit-forward excitement, while notes of sweet vanilla extract and white pepper add interest. Cocoa, sweet spice, and red fruit notes provide that lasting memory." Drink through 2017.

2010

Grenache 33.33%, Mourvèdre 33.33%, Syrah 33.33%. Alcohol 12.5%. Aged 14 months in French oak and American oak. Production 75 cases.

WINERY TASTING NOTES "This iconic rooster really expresses his 'Rhône-style' image with flair and panache while strutting through the hen house. The clutch of hens immediately noticed that perfect shade of deep ruby red and enticing bouquet of raspberry and strawberry accented by notes of bay leaf and violet. This dry, medium-bodied wine has soft, delicate tannins and food-friendly acidity. Flavours of red berry, cherry, and plum provide that perfect tangy, juicy fruit-forward excitement, while notes of red licorice and delicate spice add interest. Red fruits, spice, mineral, and plum notes provide that lasting memory." Drink now.

2009

Mourvèdre 59%, Syrah 24%, Grenache 17%. Aged in French and American oak barrels. Production 186 cases.

WINERY TASTING NOTES "This wine has a complex, enticing bouquet. The body is rich and luxurious, with gentle tannins and juicy flavours of currants, cherry, strawberry, and raspberry all wrapped around notes of cedar, cigar box, toasty oak, and spice. Juicy black cherries, cocoa, white pepper spice, and black tea flavours provide that lasting memory." Drink now.

River Stone Estate Winery

CORNER STONE

Ted Kane had Corner Stone in mind back in 2003, when he began planting the River Stone vineyard on Tuc El Nuit Drive, just outside Oliver. In the French tradition, he planted Bordeaux varietals—Merlot, Cabernet Sauvignon, Cabernet Franc, and Malbec—in the proportions he believed he needed for his blend.

"I knew at the beginning it was going to be a Merlot-forward, Right Bank Bordeaux style because of our cool-climate growing conditions," Ted says. "Merlot is the most reliable ripener as opposed to Cabernet Sauvignon, which I knew would be the last to ripen." Consequently, Merlot was the biggest block on the well-drained south-facing slopes. Subsequent experience led him to increase the planting of Cabernet Franc, another reliable ripener. He also replaced five rows of Cabernet Sauvignon with Petit Verdot in order to grow the full suite needed for a Bordeaux-type blend.

Ted says some have drawn parallels between Corner Stone and Bordeaux's Château Cheval Blanc, although in the latter's vineyard, Cabernet Franc takes the lead, followed by Merlot. While he does not mind the compliment inherent in that comparison, Ted says that Corner Stone is made in the New World style, closer to reds from California or Chile. "I wanted to produce wines that had concentration and weight," he says. "I also found after a short time in France that what I didn't want was the astringency that was still there after year six on some of the wines."

Ted, who was born in Edmonton in 1962, began making wines from tree fruits when he was 19. Even as he began a career as a respiratory therapist, he was obsessed with wine-growing. "I built a small greenhouse by my house in Edmonton," he says. "I bought grapevines from Eastern Canada and propagated and grew them, just so I could learn pruning and trellising and irrigation techniques." By the late 1990s, while his wife, Lorraine, was completing a medical degree, Ted was anxious to find an Okanagan property before, in her words, "It was all gone." Good properties were still available in 2001, when they found 3.8 hectares (9.5 acres) of raw land near Oliver, on a hill beside the Okanagan River. They moved there in 2002, planting a 3-hectare (7.5-acre) vineyard while Lorraine began a family medicine practice.

After selling grapes for several years, Ted took advantage of the superb 2009 harvest to make River Stone's debut vintages. He was mentored in his first vintage by a consulting winemaker, New Zealand–trained Jacqueline Kemp. She remains on call when another palate is needed, but Ted is now comfortable in his ability to grow grapes and make wine.

The individual varietals are fermented in small lots that are aged separately in French oak barrels for 14 to 18 months. By blending time, Ted has identified the best barrels of each varietal. Wine not needed for Corner Stone is blended into Stones Throw, which, in the French tradition, is made for earlier consumption. He also bottles modest volumes of single varietals, offering them in the wine shop and to his wine club.

Perhaps the most notable of these single varietals is the Cabernet Franc, which grows very successfully in the River Stone vineyard. "If I knew back when I planted what I know now, I would have planted more Cabernet Franc," Ted admits. Much like Cheval Blanc.

2012 ($31.90)

Merlot 57%, Cabernet Sauvignon 21%, Cabernet Franc 14%, Malbec 8%. Alcohol 14.3%. Aged in French oak barrels (33% new) for approximately 14 months. Production 339 cases.

WINERY TASTING NOTES "This full-bodied Bordeaux-style blend is rich and concentrated with bold ripe fruit and concentrated textures from mature tannins representative of the great growing season. This wine is presently showing flavours reminiscent of blackberry, cherry, blueberry, and hints of sage and wild thyme. Loads of dark berry flavours, coffee, and chocolate, supported by French oak. It has balanced acidity and moderate tannins that will soften in time." Drink by 2022.

2011

Merlot 53%, Cabernet Franc 40%, Cabernet Sauvignon 16%, Malbec 11%. Alcohol 12.35%. Production 344 cases.

WINERY TASTING NOTES "This bold Bordeaux-style blend is presently showing ripe varietal fruit character with hints of blueberry, blackberry, cherry, sage, and wild thyme. Loads of berry flavours, coffee, and chocolate, supported by French oak. It has balanced acidity and moderate tannins that will soften in time." Drink by 2021.

2010

Merlot 59%, Cabernet Sauvignon 23%, Cabernet Franc 18%. Alcohol 14.4%. Production 415 cases.

WINERY TASTING NOTES "This bold Bordeaux-style blend is presently showing ripe varietal fruit character with hints of mocha, vanilla, liquorice, blackcurrant, wild thyme, and smoky oak. It has balanced acidity and moderate tannins that will soften in time." Drink by 2020.

2009

Merlot 49%, Cabernet Sauvignon 29%, Malbec 18%, Cabernet Franc 4%. Alcohol 14.6%. Production 349 cases.

WINERY TASTING NOTES "This bold Bordeaux-style blend is presently showing dark ruby red color and ripe varietal fruit character with hints of blackcurrant, blackberry, black cherry, and nuances of French oak. Layered and dense. The fruit is supported by fresh acidity and fine juicy tannins that linger and give it great length." Drink by 2019.

Road 13 Vineyards

5TH ELEMENT

In the 2005 vintage, Road 13's winemaker at the time, Michael Bartier, set out to create a premium Bordeaux-inspired blend. Michael liked to work with complex wine blends. In this vintage, he fermented 27 different lots of red wine. The wines were kept separate in barrel until the following August when, after two months of blending trials, the first 5th Element was assembled, to be aged further in barrel until the wine was bottled in June 2007. The name was inspired by the dash of Syrah, a non-Bordeaux varietal, in the final blend. "Of course, subsequent vintages weren't necessarily composed from five varietals, traditional or not, but the name stuck," says Michael, who left Road 13 after the 2010 vintage.

That first vintage was released under the name Golden Mile Cellars, the moniker of the winery for 10 years from its opening in 1998. A modest venture making just enough wine for the wine shop each summer, Golden Mile was notable chiefly because the founders, Peter and Helga Serwo, had built a replica castle as their winery. Pam and Mick Luckhurst, who bought the winery in 2003, soon outgrew the castle, with its drafty offices and cramped cellars. The strikingly modern extensions added in the subsequent decade now dwarf it.

In 2008, the name was changed to Road 13, the street that ends at the castle door. The change eliminated confusion with the surrounding wine-growing region. In 2015, the Golden Mile became the Okanagan's first sub-appellation, home to a dozen wineries.

The 5th Element blends are made with grapes from several appellations. J-M Bouchard, who took over as winemaker in 2011, also began getting grapes from the Blind Creek Vineyard in the Similkameen Valley as well as Road 13's own Castle Vineyard.

"In the past, 5th Element was made more by barrel selection than anything else. Road 13 never grew the Cabernet Sauvignon and the Cabernet Franc for it," J-M said in 2014. "Both varietals are needed for the 5th Element. In 2011 and 2012, I was not happy with the source of fruit for those varietals, so it would have to be a barrel selection to make the 5th Element. Now I am truly excited because they all come from the Blind Creek Vineyard (now 50% owned by Road 13). I control the yield there and the quality is unbelievable, just because of the site and how the vineyard is managed."

The quality of the fruit allowed J-M to increase the volume of 5th Element, with it moving toward the quantity made in 2007. The winery made none in 2008, thinking the quality was weak, and soon heard from customers who were unhappy that the vertical had been interrupted. Several subsequent releases of 5th Element were small as the winery rebuilt a following for the wine. J-M's vintages, however, have grown to around 800 to 1,100 cases. In 2016, J-M left Road 13, handing over the cellar to Jeff Del Nin, formerly the winemaker at Church & State, where he created Quintessential, that winery's icon.

2012 ($49)

Merlot 47%, Syrah 19%, Cabernet Sauvignon 16%, Cabernet Franc 9%, Malbec 5%, Petit Verdot 4%. Alcohol 14.9%.

WINERY TASTING NOTES "Ample notes of cigar box, leather, and blackcurrant dominate the nose on this wine. It has a rich mouthfeel with full flavours of blackberries and dark cherry, rounded off with baking spices and an extremely long finish." Drink by 2022.

2011

Merlot 57.47%, Cabernet Franc 21.2%, Syrah 10.88%, Cabernet Sauvignon 7.07%, Petit Verdot 1.87%, Malbec 1.51%. Alcohol 14.4%. Aged 16 months in French oak. Production 588.5 cases.

WINERY TASTING NOTES "[The wine] has an attractive dark ruby colour and a nose that is lifted, complex, and very 'Old World' with aromas of dark soya sauce, grilled almond, blackberry, blackcurrant, sage, and violet. All six varieties work together to deliver complex flavours of black cassis, blackberry, dark chocolate, and cedar. The rich and silky palate is structured by extremely fine tannins." Drink by 2021.

2010

Merlot 48.7%, Syrah 20.4%, Cabernet Franc 17.1%, Cabernet Sauvignon 8.1%, Petit Verdot 4%, Malbec 1.7%. Alcohol 14.2%. Production 248 cases.

WINERY TASTING NOTES "[The wine] has a beautiful and rich dark ruby colour. The nose is lifted, savoury, and very complex, showing aromas of black olive tapenade, blackberry, blueberry, violet, garrigue, and hazelnut. [There are] flavours of dark prune, black cassis, blackberries, and black sage brush [with] fine ripe tannins and fresh acidity." Drink by 2020.

2009

Merlot 68%, Syrah 22%, Cabernet Franc 10%. Alcohol 14.9%. Production 250 cases.

WINERY TASTING NOTES "Be prepared for an alluring medley of intense black fruits that are supported by an engaging, sultry, savoury characteristic that is notoriously Okanagan. The nose and palate project pure harmony and continue to amaze with integrated, complex layering of tobacco and black sage. The intensity of the Syrah gains momentum on the finish and has the classic notes of braised red and green peppercorns." Drink by 2018.

2007

Cabernet Sauvignon 38%, Cabernet Franc 33%, Merlot 29%. Alcohol 14.3%. Production 2,044 cases.

WINERY TASTING NOTES "A very complex mix of aromas and flavours including smoke, cherry, vanilla, and mocha. Especially mocha. The tannic and acid structure is quite fine, balanced with excellent fruit." Drink now.

2006

Merlot 38%, Cabernet Franc 28%, Cabernet Sauvignon 22%, Malbec 6%, Petit Verdot 6%. Alcohol 14.3%. Production 1,262 cases.

WINERY TASTING NOTES "There is a lot going on in the aroma and even more on the palate. The flavours run from tobacco through chocolate with much fruit between, while the texture is mouth filling . . . The tannins and acidity hold the wine together." Drink now.

Golden Mile Cellars 5th Element 2005

Merlot 65%, Cabernet Sauvignon 28%, Petit Verdot 4%, Syrah 2%, Cabernet Franc 1%. Alcohol 13.7%.

WINERY TASTING NOTES "The aromas are explosive and, like any wine that ages, the flavours in this wine are transient. The dark berry characters that exist on release will caramelize over the years, though themes of coffee and chocolate will persist. There are fine and edgy tannins in this wine that will help it to age well." Drink now.

Robin Ridge Winery

GAMAY

The second variety that Tim Cottrill planted was Gamay Noir. That was in 1999, three years after he and his wife, Caroline, had begun converting a hayfield near Keremeos to vineyard. The first variety he planted was Chardonnay; in subsequent plantings, he added Merlot, Pinot Noir, Cabernet Sauvignon, Cabernet Franc, and Petit Verdot. Yet in 2012, when the winery began a second vineyard nearby, more Gamay was planted. Robin Ridge has made such a name for itself with that variety that it charges more for the wine than for its Pinot Noir. If Gamay is generally regarded as the lesser of the two varieties, that is not the case at Robin Ridge.

The winery made that clear in a newsletter item recalling famous hostility toward the variety from two dukes of Burgundy, as recounted on Wikipedia: "The Gamay grape is thought to have appeared first in the village of the Gamay, south of Beaune, in the 1360s," the newsletter recounted. "The grape brought relief to the village growers following the decline of the Black Death. In contrast to the Pinot Noir variety, Gamay ripened two weeks earlier and was less difficult to cultivate. It also produced a strong, fruitier wine in a much larger abundance."

The newsletter continued: "In July 1395, the Duke of Burgundy Philippe the Bold outlawed the cultivation of the grape, referring to it as the 'disloyal Gaamez' that in spite of its ability to grow in abundance was full of 'very great and horrible harshness' due in part to the variety's occupation of land that could be used for the more 'elegant' Pinot Noir. Sixty years later [his grandson] Philippe the Good issued another edict against Gamay in which he stated the reasoning for the ban is that 'The Dukes of Burgundy are known as the lords of the best wines in Christendom. We will maintain our reputation.' Robin Ridge vigorously disagrees with the Dukes of Burgundy, indeed, our reputation is built on this formidable grape!"

Collectors might also consider Big Bird, the new Meritage blend added to the Robin Ridge portfolio in the 2011 vintage. The wine is a blend of Merlot, Cabernet Sauvignon, Cabernet Franc, and Petit Verdot. Only $6 more than the Gamay, it shows good length and refinement, especially in the 2012 vintage.

> The Gamay grape is thought to have appeared first in the village of the Gamay, south of Beaune, in the 1360s.

2013 ($24)

Alcohol 13%. Production 13 barrels (25 cases in each barrel).

WINERY TASTING NOTES "Intense aromas of purple flowers, raspberry, cinnamon, liquorice, red currant, and graphite. The palate is fresh and juicy with vibrant acidity and cherry and red berry fruit given complexity by dried wild thyme, clove, black pepper, and a long, mineral finish." Drink by 2020.

2012

Alcohol 14%. Aged 11 months in French oak (20% new) and Hungarian oak (10% new). Production 10 barrels.

WINERY TASTING NOTES "Brooding floral notes with raspberry and blueberry fruit and complex clove, cinnamon, and paprika spice. The palate is juicy and fresh with lively acidity and plum, dried strawberry, oak, and pepper with a long, meaty finish." Drink by 2019.

2011

Alcohol 13.9%. Production 8 barrels.

WINERY TASTING NOTES "Juicy and complex showing the cinnamon, mixed red berry, floral, and graphite notes of the fantastic Gamay variety. The palate is elegant, crisp and juicy, and full of raspberry, cherry, strawberry, mineral, and spice flavours that linger on the intense, long and silky finish." Drink by 2018.

2010

Alcohol 14.3%. Production 8 barrels.

WINERY TASTING NOTES "Intense and welcoming aromas of plum, cherry, ripe strawberry, and complex floral and meaty notes. The palate has a velvet texture and is elegant yet powerful with ripe red fruits, roasted herbs, and great length. The juicy acidity and complexity will leave the palate insisting on more." Drink now.

2009

Alcohol 14.8. Production 9 barrels.

WINERY TASTING NOTES by Rhys Pender, MW: "A lively medium-ruby colour with seductive aromas of ripe cherry, violets, strawberry, vanilla-spiked cream, and toasted almonds. The palate is lush and soft, silky textured with intense raspberry, cherry, floral, and graphite flavours, balanced acidity, and a long finish." Drink now.

2008

Alcohol 14.8%. Production 7 barrels.

WINERY TASTING NOTES "Dried tobacco and leather with some raspberry and cherry aromas on the nose. On the palate, more raspberry, cherry, and small berry flavours combined with the toast from the (heavy toast) oak barrels in the program that give that spicy finish." Drink now.

2006

AUTHOR'S TASTING NOTES "All [of Robin Ridge's debut wines] are solid but the star of the show, in my judgment, is the fat and full-bodied Gamay Noir, with a quality approaching that of a good Beaujolais Cru. This generous wine has aromas and flavours of plums and cherries, backed up with notes of mocha and a touch of oak." Fully mature.

Sage Hills Vineyard

PINOT NOIR

Rick Thrussell, the owner of Sage Hills, rejects the cliché that Pinot Noir is the "heartbreak" grape. "I don't believe that making a great Pinot is some black art," he says. "Any great grape can be a heartbreak grape if you are growing it in the wrong location. We planted Pinot Noir on the best site in our entire vineyard, where it would do the best."

The 4-hectare (10-acre) organic vineyard was planted in 2007. The French consultant retained by Rick advised planting just three varieties—Pinot Gris, Gewürztraminer, and Pinot Noir. The latter, at just over half a hectare, is the smallest block. But in just three vintages, starting with 2012, Pinot Noir has become the winery's *tête de cuvée*.

"I am following the grand cru model from France," Rick says. "I am growing my grapes organically; I am keeping my yields very low; I am using the finest barrels that are available to me. I am not over-oaking the wine because the quality of the fruit we are using is really high." It must be working. A French wine connoisseur dining in a Whistler restaurant thought he was drinking a fine Burgundy until the sommelier showed him the Sage Hills bottle.

Born in Vancouver in 1959, Rick pursued a series of careers from project management to home building after graduating in geography, political science, and communications from Simon Fraser University. An Okanagan weekend in the 1980s planted the desire to become a wine grower. The ambition was realized when Rick planted vines on this Summerland vineyard, dramatically situated on a plateau high above Okanagan Lake. The seductive panorama seen from his living room is exactly the view that draws so many to the wine-country lifestyle.

Tom Di Bello, the consultant who made the 2012 vintage for Sage Hills and returned to make the 2015, inculcated the discipline of keeping the Pinot Noir yield low. At Sage Hills, it is a mere 1.3 tons (or less) per acre, one of the lowest in the Okanagan for this variety. "The amount that Tom was dropping in our first vintage was painful," Rick recalls. "But he kept telling me that if you are going to make good Pinot Noir, this is what you have to do. We follow our procedure year after year." The result is Pinot Noir with vibrant flavours, depth of body, and the structure to age gracefully.

2015 ($45)

Alcohol 12.7%. Aged 3 months in new French oak, 6 months in older French oak. Production 158 cases.

WINERY TASTING NOTES This is a "beautifully expressive Pinot Noir embracing complex aromas of chocolate-covered cherries, dried cocoa, blackcurrant, blueberries, and savoury spices. The wine is wonderfully balanced and has a lively fruit structure wrapped in fine, smooth tannins." Drink by 2022.

2014

Alcohol 12.6%. Aged 9 months in new and used French oak. Production 120 cases.

WINERY TASTING NOTES "Our multi-layered Pinot Noir balances elegance and power. The finely nuanced nose offers plums, red currants, black cherries, chocolate, spice, and white pepper—we could go on. Whole berry fermentation at low temperatures preserved the delicacy of the fruit. The fine, ripe tannins are well integrated and this wine is drinking beautifully now." Drink by 2021.

2013

Alcohol 14%. Production 191 cases.

AUTHOR'S TASTING NOTES "This wine explodes with aromas and flavours of spicy cherry and raspberry with a backbone of minerality. The texture is silky." Drink by 2020.

Sandhill Wines

SANDHILL SMALL LOTS ONE

Sandhill One, a Bordeaux blend, was launched in the 2000 vintage with grapes from the Phantom Creek Vineyard on Black Sage Road. Just 3 hectares (7 acres) in size, the vineyard was planted in 1996 by Richard Cleave, one of the Okanagan's most highly regarded growers.

Sandhill One is an anchor in a portfolio composed exclusively of single-vineyard wines, both red and white. The first vintage of Sandhill was produced in 1997 by winemaker Howard Soon as a premium label distinguishing the wines from those of sister winery Calona Vineyards. Calona, founded in 1931, is the oldest winery in the Okanagan. It was burdened by a colourful history that placed a ceiling on what consumers expected to pay for the wines. The Sandhill strategy successfully broke away from that reputation.

The Sandhill approach celebrates terroir. Every bottle of Sandhill wine is made with grapes only from the specific vineyard named on the label. Currently, five vineyards in the Okanagan Valley and Vanessa Vineyard in the Similkameen Valley grow grapes for Sandhill. "The collaboration between the land, the grower and the winemaker allows the unique character of each vineyard to reveal itself in your glass," Howard has written.

Born in Vancouver in 1952, Howard studied biochemistry and business administration and worked in a brewery before joining Calona in 1980. His lengthy experience won him the winemaking assignment when Sandhill was launched.

Sandhill collectors have other choices besides Sandhill One. There is Sandhill Two, another Bordeaux blend, and Sandhill Three, a blend of Sangiovese with Bordeaux varietals. Both of these wines are made with grapes from the Sandhill Estate Vineyard. This vineyard is almost across the road from Phantom Creek. However, the soil is sandier. The wines from the estate vineyard are different in aroma and flavour, vividly showing the impact of terroir. "Terroir is the expression of the fruit quality," Howard says. "What the grape is giving you, that's what terroir is to me—a true expression of what is in the fruit. Our slogan is 'a true expression of the vineyard,' and that is what we are trying to do."

In 2016, the Phantom Creek Vineyard was sold to owners who are building a showcase winery called Phantom Creek Estates. Howard will source fruit for Sandhill One from the 30-hectare (75-acre) Vanessa Vineyard in the Similkameen Valley.

2013 ($37)

Cabernet Sauvignon 66%, Malbec 11%, Petit Verdot 9%, Syrah 9%, Cabernet Franc 3.5%, Merlot 1.5%. Alcohol 14.2%. Phantom Creek Vineyard. Production 20 barrels.

WINERY TASTING NOTES "Deep garnet colour with an intriguing bouquet of blackcurrant, violet, leather, vanilla, sweet oak, and black licorice. A full-bodied wine with soft, drying tannins, moderate acidity, and a terrific mouth-feel. Ripe fruit flavours of blackcurrant, blackberry, and blueberry are enhanced by notes of vanilla and sweet oak. Notes of tart black fruits and sweet spice linger on the finish." Drink by 2020.

2012 ($35)

Cabernet Sauvignon 66%, Malbec 11%, Petit Verdot 9%, Syrah 9%, Cabernet Franc 3.5%, Merlot 1.5%. Alcohol 13.5%. Phantom Creek Vineyard. Aged in new American oak for 14 months. Production 1,000 cases.

WINERY TASTING NOTES "Deep garnet colour with an intriguing bouquet of blackcurrant, violet, leather, vanilla, sweet oak, and black liquorice. A full-bodied wine with soft, drying tannins, moderate acidity, and a terrific mouth-feel. Ripe fruit flavours of blackcurrant, blackberry, and blueberry are enhanced by notes of vanilla and sweet oak. Notes of tart black fruits and sweet spice linger on the finish." Drink by 2018.

2011

Cabernet Sauvignon 75%, Malbec 13%, Petit Verdot 12%. Alcohol 13%. Phantom Creek Vineyard. Aged in new American oak for 20 months. Production 500 cases.

WINERY TASTING NOTES "Garnet colour with an intriguing bouquet of blackcurrant, smoky oak, sweet vanilla, molasses, violet, and leather. A full-bodied wine with velvety tannins, moderate acidity, and a terrific mouth-feel. Rich black fruit flavours are enhanced by notes of cedar, vanilla extract, roasted nuts, and charred oak barrel. Notes of spice, roasted nuts, coffee bean, white pepper, and currant linger on the long finish." Drink now.

2008

Cabernet Sauvignon 68%, Petit Verdot 17%, Malbec 9%, Cabernet Franc 3%, Merlot 3%. Alcohol 14.9%. Phantom Creek Vineyard. Aged 20 months in new American and French oak. Production 300 cases.

WINERY TASTING NOTES "A deep garnet colour with an intriguing bouquet of blackberry, blackcurrant, violet, sweet spice, espresso, and oak. Plenty of rich black fruits on the palate provide a more fruit-driven style. Black tea, cocoa powder, spice, and charred barrel notes on the finish." Drink now.

2007

Cabernet Sauvignon 67%, Petit Verdot 20%, Malbec 10%, Syrah 3%. Alcohol 14%. Phantom Creek Vineyard. Aged 20 months in new American and French oak. Production 498 cases.

WINERY TASTING NOTES "A deep black purple colour with a complex bouquet of sweet oak, rich vanilla, sweet Chai spice, blackcurrant, cocoa, plum, and black tea Plenty of rich black fruits, accented by cloves, allspice, vanilla, and a whiff of humidor evolve on the palate. The wine lingers on the finish with notes of black fruits, sweet spice, and smoke." Drink now.

2005

Cabernet Sauvignon 70%, Petit Verdot 17%, Malbec 9%, Merlot 4%. Alcohol 13%. Phantom Creek Vineyard. Aged 18 months in new French and American oak. Production 532 cases.

WINERY TASTING NOTES "Aromas of red and black berries, violets, and a hint of oak. Soft tannins and flavours of blackberry, a touch of spice, and sweet vanilla notes." Drink now.

2004

Cabernet Sauvignon 82%, Malbec 9%, Petit Verdot 9%. Alcohol 14%. Phantom Creek Vineyard. Aged 20 months in new American oak. Production 511 cases.

WINERY TASTING NOTES "Deep mulberry purple with rich plummy fruit on the nose. Complex, rich fruit with good acidity and soft, smooth tannins." Drink now.

2002

Cabernet Sauvignon 92%, Petit Verdot 5%, Malbec 3%. Alcohol 14.5%. Phantom Creek Vineyard. Aged 17 months in new American oak. Production 148 cases.

WINERY TASTING NOTES "Full of blackberry fruit, toast, and spice from being aged 17 months in new American oak barrels, the smooth, lengthy ripe roundness of the tannins shows the unique quality of Phantom Creek's terroir." Mature.

2001

Petit Verdot 55%, Cabernet Sauvignon 35%, Malbec 10%. Alcohol 12.5%. Phantom Creek Vineyard. Individual varietals aged 8 months in new American oak; blend aged a further 2 months in older French oak. Production 373 cases.

WINERY TASTING NOTES "This wine has lovely rich fruit and hints of chocolate and berry character. It is medium-bodied with solid, polished silky tannins and a bright fruity finish." Mature.

2000

Cabernet Sauvignon 33%, Malbec 33%, Petit Verdot 33%. Alcohol 13%. Phantom Creek Vineyard. Individual varietals aged 8 months in new American oak; blend aged a further 2 months in older French oak. Production 75 cases.

Tasting notes unavailable. Mature.

Seven Stones Winery

THE LEGEND

George Hanson, the owner of Seven Stones Winery, was invited to his first vertical wine tasting not long after coming to the Similkameen Valley from the Yukon in 1999. The tasting featured nine vintages of the premium red blend from Lebanon's Château Musar. This is a legendary winery owned by the Hochar family, whose ancestors were French crusaders who never returned to France. In 1930, the family planted French vines in a vineyard near the border of Lebanon and Syria. The winery has survived several regional wars to become one of the world's leading wine brands, with wines appealing to collectors like the Penticton psychiatrist who hosted George. "It was a life-changing event," George says of the tasting. It was one of the inspirations for the production of the Legend.

George was a Yukon telephone company manager who, in his spare time, had become the territory's best amateur winemaker. An early retirement package at age 42 freed him to plant an 8-hectare (20-acre) vineyard in the Similkameen. "I planted the vineyard with the intention of making a Bordeaux-style red and one white," he says. The white variety is Chardonnay. He also added Syrah and Pinot Noir and opened the winery in 2007.

At the time, several Okanagan wineries had begun to release icon reds. When George first decided that he would make an icon at Seven Stones, his wife, Vivianne, teased him that it was an ego wine that "didn't make marketing sense."

Undeterred, George made 50 cases in the 2008 vintage. When it sold well, Vivianne suggested doubling the production. The Legend was capped at 100 cases a year until the 2013 vintage, when production was doubled to satisfy demand from the Seven Stones wine club.

The wine, like a Left Bank Bordeaux blend, is built around Cabernet Sauvignon. "Cabernet Sauvignon is not an easy grape to get ripe," George acknowledges. "It can be a bit risky. But I am confident here because our Cabernets ripen really, really well."

Secure in the consistency of his vineyard, George blends the Legend from the best barrels aging in the underground cave at Seven Stones. "When the grapes first come in, we treat them all the same," he says. "I separate the wines by barrel in the cellar. I taste every barrel every month. I start developing my favourites. The next thing I know, it is blending time and I have picked out those that go into the Legend." The wine is always aged in new French oak for 18 months.

George likens blending to building a person. "You make the body, which is the Merlot and Cabernet Sauvignon together," he explains. "Then you put the personality in the final dress. That would be Petit Verdot and Cabernet Franc." Except for vintage variations, the Legends share a familial personality because, so far, George has hardly departed from his successful blending formula.

2013 ($50)

Cabernet Sauvignon 48%, Merlot 32%, Petit Verdot 12%, Cabernet Franc 8%. Alcohol 14.2%. Production 208 cases.

WINERY TASTING NOTES "Aromas of ripe dark fruit, spicy sage, coffee, green olives, and cedar leap out of the glass. The [wine has] astounding complexity of flavours, a satisfying mouth-feel, and an exquisite finish." Drink by 2025.

2012

Cabernet Sauvignon 52%, Merlot 28%, Petit Verdot 12%, Cabernet Franc 8%. Alcohol 14.1%. Production 100 cases.

WINERY TASTING NOTES "Aromas of ripe dark fruit, spicy sage, coffee, green olives, and cedar leap out of the glass. The [wine has] astounding complexity of flavours, a satisfying mouth-feel, and an exquisite finish." Drink by 2024.

2011

Cabernet Sauvignon 48%, Merlot 32%, Petit Verdot 12%, Cabernet Franc 8%. Alcohol 13.9%. Production 104 cases.

AUTHOR'S TASTING NOTES "The wine begins with aromas of bright berries and sage, leading to flavours of cassis and red currants, with Bordeaux-like cedar on the finish." Drink by 2023.

2010

Cabernet Sauvignon 50%, Merlot 30%, Petit Verdot 12%, Cabernet Franc 8%. Alcohol 13.6%. Production 100 cases.

AUTHOR'S TASTING NOTES "This is a bold and complex red, with floral, spicy, and berry aromas and with flavours of blackcurrant, raspberry, blackberry. On the finish, there are notes of dark chocolate." Drink by 2022.

2009

Cabernet Sauvignon 48%, Merlot 32%, Petit Verdot 12%, Cabernet Franc 8%. Alcohol 14.5%. Production 100 cases.

AUTHOR'S TASTING NOTES "The wine begins dramatically in the glass with aromas of red fruit, vanilla, and chocolate. On the palate, this is a muscular wine with long, ripe tannins and a very complex array of flavours: currants, plums, coffee, and cedar. The wine finishes with flavours reminiscent of spice cake." Drink by 2021.

2008

Cabernet Sauvignon 50%, Merlot 30%, Petit Verdot 12%, Cabernet Franc 8%. Alcohol 14.3%. Aged 17 months in new oak barrels. Production 50 cases.

WINERY TASTING NOTES "Aromas of ripe fruit, spicy sage, leather, green olives, and cedar leap out of the glass. Complex layers of chocolate, plum, blueberry, and coffee flavours are complemented by an exquisite mouth-feel and a satisfying, smooth, and long finish." Drink by 2020.

Silkscarf Winery

ENSEMBLE

When Roie Manoff and his family moved to the Okanagan from Israel in 2003, they were impressed with the region's white wines but less impressed with its reds. "My dream when I became a wine-maker was to make a good Cabernet Sauvignon," Roie says.

Roie, who was born in Argentina in 1951 but grew up in Israel, has loved wine for a long time. He began technical wine studies somewhere between his career as an Israeli jet pilot and his subsequent ownership of a Tel Aviv software firm. When the family decided to leave Israel, a study of wine-growing regions brought them to the Okanagan and the quiet beauty of a Summerland orchard, most of which they have converted to 3.4 hectares (8.5 acres) of vines.

The varieties planted include Pinot Gris and Gewürztraminer. Much of the vineyard has been planted to Merlot, Pinot Noir, and Cabernet Sauvignon. Roie did not plant Cabernet Franc because he did not care for the wine—until he began tasting the vibrant Okanagan Cabernet Francs. "It is just the perfect grape to grow here," he maintains. With purchased grapes and those from his vineyard, Roie began to produce award-winning red wines. His 2009 Cabernet Sauvignon was chosen the Best of Variety in a major Okanagan competition in 2014.

The flagship wine at Silkscarf is Ensemble, the winery's Bordeaux blend. "Behind a blend, there are two motivations," Roie says. "The most popular motivation, which is the driver behind blends, is this: when one of the attributes of a single variety is weak, you can balance it with the appropriate attribute from another variety. You make it far better. There is another motivation sometimes where you can exploit the synergies of three grapes which are so good—especially the Cabernet Franc of the Okanagan Valley. So you say one plus one plus one would be much more than three. That is what drives us with the Ensemble. Each variety is perfect as a single varietal. If we find the right proportion among the three, we come up with something that we are very proud of."

Unfortunately for collectors, the winery so far has released just three vintages of Ensemble, for various reasons. The production volume of recent vintages sustained sales over several years, including vintages like 2009, when the individual varieties were outstanding on their own. There were also several vintages when the retraining of Silkscarf's Merlot vines reduced their output. Ensemble is always anchored on Merlot and Cabernet Sauvignon, with just enough Cabernet Franc to brighten the aromas and flavours.

Ensemble is a long-lived wine. "One of the most exciting things about collecting wines is that you drink it while it progresses in the bottle," Roie says. "Every six months, we taste the wine to see how the profile changes. That is great fun to monitor how that wine makes such a big journey in the bottle."

2013 ($32.90)

Cabernet Sauvignon 52%, Merlot 40%, Cabernet Franc 8%. Alcohol 12.7%. Aged 18 months in French oak barrels. Production 482 cases.

WINERY TASTING NOTES "Full-body red wine with velvety texture and soft, round tannins. The Cabernet Sauvignon, with its blackberry and blackcurrant notes, provides the complexity and the mouth feel which nicely balance the Merlot's straightforward aromatic fruity flavour. The Cabernet Franc complements the blend with an elegant violet bouquet and a gentle tone of green bell pepper." Drink by 2023.

2008

Cabernet Sauvignon 46%, Merlot 46%, Cabernet Franc 8%. Alcohol 12.5%. Production 600 cases.

WINERY TASTING NOTES "The Ensemble complexity and caressing softness harmonically expresses the Merlot fruitiness, embraced by the deep full-bodied Cabernet Sauvignon and the gentle floral notes of the Cabernet Franc." Drink by 2019.

2006

Merlot 45%, Cabernet Sauvignon 42%, Cabernet Franc 13%. Alcohol 12.8%. Production 350 cases.

Tasting notes unavailable.

Sperling Vineyards

OLD VINES RIESLING

It's no coincidence that Sperling Vineyards and the nearby Tantalus Vineyards both produce an Old Vines Riesling. That variety was planted at both vineyards on the same day in 1978. These are among the oldest blocks of vinifera in the North Okanagan. The Riesling is Clone 21B, also called the Weis clone because it was developed by a Mosel viticulturist named Hermann Weis. It is widely planted around the world because it produces excellent wines.

Sperling Vineyards takes its name from Bert Sperling and his family. Bert farmed this East Kelowna property from 1960 until his death in 2012. The property, called Pioneer Ranch, was first planted with grapes, tree fruits, and vegetables in 1929 by Pete and Louis Casorso, the father and uncle of Velma Sperling, Bert's wife.

The winemaker at Sperling Vineyards is Bert and Velma's daughter, Ann Sperling, who has vivid memories of growing up on Pioneer Ranch. "All the grapes at that time were labrusca or labrusca hybrids," she says. "The exception was the Perle de Csaba. It is a vinifera and a Muscat type. It ripened early, in late August, and tasted wonderful. I certainly attribute my love of Muscat and Moscato d'Asti to having gorged myself as often as possible on those grapes."

Ann began making wine in 1984, armed with a food sciences degree from the University of British Columbia. She had had an illustrious career with major Canadian wineries by the time she and her siblings launched Sperling Vineyards in 2008. "It was always in the back of my mind that I wanted to make wine here, because I am so familiar with every foot and every slope and every grape on the property," she says.

Several of the Sperling wines appeal to collectors, including three sparkling wines (rosé, Brut, and Brut Reserve) and Pinot Noir. The Old Vines Riesling stands apart for its scarcity (the 1978 Riesling block is just two-thirds of a hectare in size), its Mosel-like style, and its longevity. The 15-year bottle lifespan noted here is just an educated guess. This mineral-laden wine with racy acidity and residual sugar might well live longer than that.

I certainly attribute my love of Muscat and Moscato d'Asti to having gorged myself as often as possible on [labrusca] grapes.

2014 ($32)

Alcohol 11.5%. Acidity 9.10 grams per litre. Residual sugar 12.29 grams per litre. Production 210 cases.

WINERY TASTING NOTES "Colour: pale straw. Medium-intensity nose with green apple, lime juice, and citrusy aromas. Still very youthful and tight. Off-dry, medium body, with nervy acidity. Apple and hints of white flowers and stone fruits, finishing with bright acidity. Mineral-driven." Drink by 2029.

2013

Alcohol 12.4%. Acidity 10.3 grams per litre. Residual sugar 17 grams per litre. Production 210 cases.

WINERY TASTING NOTES "Colour: bright straw. Ripe apples, white peach with subtle hints of flowers. Slight petrol and sweet fruit impressions. Round and fuller mouth feel with medium sweetness followed by balancing acidity." Drink by 2028.

2012

Alcohol 11.5%. Acidity 8.10 grams per litre. Residual sugar 18 grams per litre. Production 200 cases.

AUTHOR'S TASTING NOTES "The wine begins with aromas of lime with an appealing hint of botrytis, which contributes honey to the marmalade flavours. The wine has good weight and good minerality on the palate. The finish is crisp and tangy." Drink by 2027.

2011

Alcohol 10.2%. Acidity 10.5 grams per litre. Residual sugar 17 grams per litre. Production 197 cases.

WINERY TASTING NOTES "Aromas of apricot and citrus. On the palate there is an initial attack of bright citrus flavours, settling into the minerality, and finishing with apricot again." Drink by 2026.

2010

Alcohol 12.4%. Acidity 8.9 grams per litre. Residual sugar 12 grams per litre. Production 115 cases.

WINERY TASTING NOTES "Notes of key-lime pie and hints of quince open to a broad entry on the palate. Flavours of citrus and pom-fruits [apples, pears, and quince] narrow and tighten to a refined, tart and mineral finish, with just enough residual sugar to balance." Drink by 2025.

2009

Alcohol 10.4%. Acidity 8.75 grams per litre. Residual sugar 18 grams per litre. Production 208 cases.

TASTING NOTES by Rick Van Sickle on the Wines in Niagara website, June 27, 2011: "The nose is replete in lime, peach, flinty minerality, and a hint of petrol. It's made with 10.5% alcohol and explodes with flavour on the palate. Mineral, tart citrus, quince, grapefruit, and bracing acidity that suggests a youthful wine that will evolve for years to come." Drink by 2024.

2008

Alcohol 12%. Acidity 9 grams per litre. Residual sugar 18 grams per litre. Production 95 cases.

AUTHOR'S TASTING NOTES "This is a wine with a pristine, laser-like clarity of fruit and acidity. It begins with aromas of herbs and citrus, shows abundant flavours of lime, and has a refreshingly tangy finish." Drink by 2023.

SpierHead Winery

PINOT NOIR CUVÉE

The Gentleman Farmer Vineyard, as SpierHead Winery calls its estate vineyard in East Kelowna, was planted beginning in 2008. Because young vines need two or three years to produce a significant grape crop, the winery struck a contract with the Sundial Vineyard on Black Sage Road for Bordeaux varietals. Soon after SpierHead opened in 2010, the winery released red blends called Pursuit and Vanguard from the 2009 vintage. These would have been eminently collectible but for one thing: the final vintage for these was 2013.

"At SpierHead, we have decided to go all in with the heartbreak grape," says Bill Knutson, one of the proprietors, referring to Pinot Noir. "Our goal is to be one of the wineries mentioned in any conversation concerning the top Pinot Noir producers in BC."

The 8-hectare (20-acre) estate vineyard, a former apple orchard, was given its name because the winery's founders were all new to farming. Bill is a Vancouver lawyer, while partner Bruce Hirtle is a Vancouver investment dealer. A third partner, who has since sold his interest, was Brian Sprout, a leading photographer in Kelowna. Consultants advised SpierHead to plant Pinot Noir, Chardonnay, and Riesling. Those choices were affirmed when SpierHead's first Pinot Noir from young vines in 2010 received a gold medal in the 2012 Canadian Wine Awards.

Since then, SpierHead has committed itself almost entirely to Pinot Noir. Three-quarters of the 5 hectares (12 acres) under vine in 2014 was Pinot Noir, with additional plantings of that variety made over the following two years. "My plan is to establish a vineyard with a broad diversity of clones to enable some experimentation with combinations and possibly single-clone wines," Bill says. SpierHead initially planted three Dijon clones—the ubiquitous Clone 115, along with clones 777 and 828. The latter clone was particularly successful at this site, and a further 4,000 vines were planted in 2014. Clone 828 is well known as the one grown by Domaine de la Romanée-Conti, the most famous estate in Burgundy.

As well, SpierHead planted 3,000 vines of Dijon clone 667, following that in 2016 with a few thousand vines each of the Pommard clone and Dijon clone 943. The Pommard clone is widely planted in Oregon and is believed to add spicy notes to wines. Clone 943 is a relatively new clone that is highly praised by New Zealand vintners. Finally, SpierHead in 2015 planted a small block of a California heritage clone, Mt. Eden. When all clones are in full production, SpierHead will have an enviable number of winemaking options—more than most small producers. The winery's total annual production is 3,000 cases, and this will rise only to 5,000 cases.

All SpierHead Pinot Noirs are collectible. The Pinot Noir Cuvée, first produced in the 2013 vintage, is the flagship wine, selected each vintage from the best barrels (French oak, of course).

2015 ($35)

Pommard 30%, Dijon 667 21%, Dijon 777 21%, Dijon 115 14%, Dijon 828 14%. Aged in 100% French oak.

WINERY TASTING NOTES "This wine is made in limited quantity and is blended from a very few barrels which stood out to our winemaker." Drink by 2026.

2014

Dijon 115 46%, Dijon 777 21%, Dijon 828 17%, Dijon 667 8%, Pommard 8%. Alcohol 13.3%. Aged 10 months in French oak. Production 274 cases, 48 magnums, 12 double magnums.

AUTHOR'S TASTING NOTES "The wine's rich colour is immediately inviting, as are the complex aromas of cherry, strawberry, and raspberry that are echoed in the flavours. The wine is concentrated and the texture is seductive, as it should be in a fine Pinot Noir. There is a lingering finish with notes of spice, red fruit, and mocha." Drink by 2021; drink large-format bottles by 2025.

2013

Pommard 44%, Dijon 667 33%, Dijon 115 23%. Alcohol 13.5%. Aged 10 months in French oak. Production 100 cases, 24 magnums, 6 double magnums.

AUTHOR'S TASTING NOTES "This seductive wine is a hedonistic beauty. It begins with alluring aromas of raspberry jam with notes of cherry. The wine has just enough oak to support a rich bouquet of cherry, strawberry, and raspberry flavours. The texture is silky, with just enough tannin to take this wine to a peak at four or five years." Drink by 2020; drink large-format bottles by 2024.

Stag's Hollow Winery
RENAISSANCE MERLOT

In 1992, when Larry Gerelus and Linda Pruegger bought this 2.8-hectare (7-acre) Okanagan Falls vineyard, the four-year-old vines included Chasselas, a white variety from Switzerland. The vineyard was then supplying grapes to Mission Hill, whose winemaker at the time, Swiss-born Daniel Lagnaz, had suggested Chasselas. "The problem is that it would ripen in August, and I wasn't ready to pick in August," Larry says. In 1995, after his contract with Mission Hill ended, Larry promptly grafted Merlot onto the Chasselas roots. Stag's Hollow Winery opened the following year and, by the 1999 vintage, the best barrels of Merlot were bottled under the winery's reserve label, Renaissance.

"Renaissance is the name we have given to our premium wines," the winery explains. "The decision for what wines can be assigned to the Renaissance program is made in the cellar, based on the quality of wines in the best barrels from a vintage. Not necessarily made every vintage, our Renaissance wines are made in small lots only, and are meant to be tucked away in your cellar for two to five years."

The Renaissance Merlot is the most commonly collected Stag's Hollow wine because it can be aged for at least 10 years. But long before the wine had established a track record of longevity, its appeal to collectors grew through the winery's futures program. The wine is offered at a discount of 15 percent to those who commit to buying it (by the case) at least six months before its general release to the public. Bordeaux wineries have long had futures programs. Stag's Hollow was among the earliest Okanagan wineries to offer futures, and it has been rewarded by with a loyal following for its Renaissance Merlot.

Those who have collected verticals have tasted a significant evolution in the style of this wine. Larry, working with a succession of consultants and winemakers, initially made Merlots that were boldly ripe and occasionally over-extracted. About a third of the 2000 Renaissance Merlot was macerated on the skins for an astonishing 73 days and then barrel-aged for 22 months.

"Most of my wines pre-2004, although the label said under 15 percent alcohol, they were usually over—in the 15.2 percent range," Larry told me in a 2008 interview. "They were nice, extracted, and rich when you released them, but how much longevity was there?" With the 2005 vintage, Stag's Hollow began picking its Merlot a little earlier, paying more attention to the flavour of the grapes and not the Brix reading. In a vertical tasting at the winery a decade later, the best and most elegant wine was the 2005 Renaissance Merlot. Earlier vintages were mature and, in the case of the 2000, past their prime.

The wine has become even more refined since winemaker Dwight Sick joined Stag's Hollow in 2008. "I really want to take the level of this wine to the next notch," he says. He is doing this not just by finding the best barrels in each vintage. He and Larry have also identified the best block—the first four rows—in the 1.6-hectare (4-acre) Merlot vineyard. A serendipitous nursery error resulted in Cabernet

Sauvignon representing 12 percent to 15 percent of this block. "It has always played a significant role in the Renaissance Merlot," Dwight says, "but as we have a greater appreciation of the vineyard, it is the most important portion of this wine."

2013 ($40)

Merlot 91%, Cabernet Sauvignon 9%. Alcohol 14.5%. Stag's Hollow Vineyard. 87.5% aged in French oak (75% new, 25% second-fill), 12.5% in American oak (100% new). Production 100 cases.

WINERY TASTING NOTES "Darkest purple core with a brighter ruby brim colour. The nose is expressive showing dark berry, cocoa nibs, and smoky French oak. The wine shows bright aromas and flavours with a little time in the glass or decanting, of ripe plums, Bing cherries, mocha coffee, leather, and oak spice. This youthful wine shows a long finish with ripe, lingering tannins and natural acidity, which should ensure a long life ahead." Drink 2020 to 2025.

2012

Merlot 92%, Cabernet Sauvignon 8%. Alcohol 14.5%. Stag's Hollow Vineyard. Aged 15 months in new American oak (70%) and second-fill French oak (30%). Production 143 cases.

WINERY TASTING NOTES "Dark purple core with a brighter ruby brim colour. The nose is quite expressive showing dark berry, cocoa nibs, and earth. Tight palate at release but now much more integrated, the wine shows bright aromas of and flavours of ripe plums, Bing cherries, mocha coffee, leather, and spice." Drink by 2020.

2011

Merlot 97%, Cabernet Sauvignon 3%. Alcohol 14%. Stag's Hollow Vineyard. Aged 15 months in new American oak.

WINERY TASTING NOTES "A wine with an amazing bouquet, you will just want to leave your nose in the glass and breathe! The palate does not disappoint either with dark plums, blackberries, cedar, coffee, and spice." Drink by 2020.

2010

Merlot 95%, Cabernet Sauvignon 5%. Alcohol 14.2%. Stag's Hollow Vineyard. Aged 15 months in barrel (80% new American oak, 20% second-fill French oak). Production 200 cases.

WINERY TASTING NOTES "Concentrated and elegant, our Merlot shows dark purple in the core with a nice bright brim. Tight when first uncorked, with a little time it opens up with bright aromas and flavours of ripe plums, Bing cherries, mocha coffee, leather, and spice. The finish is long with lingering ripe tannins." Drink by 2020.

2009

Merlot 95%, Cabernet Sauvignon 5%. Alcohol 14.2%. Stag's Hollow Vineyard. Aged 15 months in new American oak (80%) and second-fill French oak (20%). Production 125 cases.

WINERY TASTING NOTES "Concentrated and elegant showing dark purple in the core with a brighter rim. Tight, but with a little time, showing bright aromas and flavours of ripe plums, Bing cherries, mocha coffee, leather, and spice." Drink by 2018.

2008

Merlot 95%, Cabernet Sauvignon 5%. Alcohol 14.5%. Stag's Hollow Vineyard. Aged 15 months in new American oak (20%) and second-fill French oak (80%). Production 115 cases.

WINERY TASTING NOTES "The darkest possible purple in colour without being black. Big, bright aromas and flavours of ripe plums, Bing cherries, mocha coffee, and spice. A long and lingering finish." Drink by 2019.

AUTHOR'S TASTING NOTES in 2014: "Rich aroma and palate of plums, cherries, and cassis, Stag's Hollow Winery's signature sage herbaceousness, very fine tannins, and elegant balance." Drink 2017 to 2020.

2007

Merlot 95%, Cabernet Sauvignon 5%. Alcohol 14.5%. Stag's Hollow Vineyard. Aged 50% in French, 50% in American oak. Production 125 cases.

WINERY TASTING NOTES "Dark ruby red/purple in colour with aromas of ripe Bing cherries, spicy Italian plums, and notes of coffee oak. Great structure and balance with flavours of dark cherries, blackberries, and a touch of sweet red liquorice candy that lead to fine grainy tannins and finish with a lingering dark chocolate note."

AUTHOR'S TASTING NOTES in 2011: "Colour—brilliant red ruby; nose—smoky notes over sweet cherry; palate—tight pencil lead tannins, tart pie cherries, bright acidity, finishing in notes of red licorice and an elegant finish of French oak tannins." Drink now.

2006

Merlot 95%, Cabernet Sauvignon 5%. Alcohol 14.8%. Stag's Hollow Vineyard. Aged 20 months in barrel, 60% French, 40% American. Production 225 cases.

WINERY TASTING NOTES "A rich and concentrated wine with lots of blueberry, blackberry and its signature chocolate finish." Drink now.

2005

Alcohol 14.2%. Stag's Hollow Vineyard. Aged in French oak (40% new). Extended maceration (20%).

AUTHOR'S TASTING NOTES "The wine begins with the perfume of cherries and plums, leading to flavours of plum and loganberry. The silky tannins give the wine a polished elegance and a lingering finish." Drink now.

2004

Stag's Hollow Vineyard.

AUTHOR'S TASTING NOTES "Dark in colour, the wine has black cherry and vanilla aromas. Generous in texture, it has flavours of plum, black cherry, and cassis." Drink now.

2003

Stag's Hollow and Harmony vineyards.

WINERY TASTING NOTES "This wine [shows] blueberry, blackberry, and cherry on the palate. Subtle hints of chocolate, vanilla and mint add to the palate." Fully mature.

2002

Alcohol 14.8%. Noble Ridge Vineyard. Aged 18 months in new American barrels (15%), new French barrels (15%), and older French oak (70%).

AUTHOR'S TASTING NOTES "Dark in colour, the wine has a brooding earthy aroma, a chewy texture, and flavours of plum and espresso." Fully mature.

2001

Alcohol 14%. Stag's Hollow Vineyard. Aged 20 months 67% in French oak (33% new), 33% in American oak.

WINERY TASTING NOTES "Unusually small berries in our 2001 vintage meant a high ratio of skins to juice, resulting in tremendous extraction and concentration. With a deep plum colour and rich layers of fruit, this wine shows remarkable complexity."

AUTHOR'S TASTING NOTES from a winery tasting in 2005: "This wine is developing some unique and attractive character. The nose is characterized by pepper and meat drippings that one taster noted as 'dry salami.' Flavours of dark cherry dominate the palate and harmonize well with the tannins." Drink now through 2018.

2000

Alcohol 14.5%. Stag's Hollow, Remuda, and Hest vineyards. Aged 22 months in a combination of new and used French, Slavonian, and American barrels.

WINERY TASTING NOTES "A big wine [with] beautiful flavours of dark cherry, plum, cigar box, cassis, blackberry with a warm mouth feel, soft tannins, and a long smoky finish." Fully mature.

1999

WINERY TASTING NOTES "1999 was an interesting growing year in the Okanagan. Those that carried light crops and were able to avoid early frosts were rewarded with rich, intense fruit. The wines are rich, soft, and incredibly flavourful." Fully mature.

Steller's Jay

STELLER'S JAY BRUT

Steller's Jay Brut, a Champagne-method sparkling wine, emerged from sparkling-wine trials begun in 1985 by Sumac Ridge Estate Winery founder Harry McWatters and his winemaking team. That vintage was not released; it is said that Harry drank it all. He is a great lover of sparkling wine, often saying that it is what he drinks while deciding what wine to have for dinner.

The first commercially available Steller's Jay Brut was a blend of 1987 (85 percent) and 1985 (15 percent) wines. The cuvée was 70 percent Pinot Blanc, 15 percent Chardonnay, and 15 percent Pinot Noir. The wine, which was named in honour of BC's official bird, was released in July 1989 after just two years on the lees. Most subsequent vintages have benefited from three years *en tirage*.

The cuvée has always included Pinot Blanc, Chardonnay, and Pinot Noir. Pinot Blanc, while not a traditional sparkling wine varietal, contributes subtle fruitiness to the wine. The proportion was reduced to about 40 percent of the cuvée as more Chardonnay and Pinot Noir became available. The wine is balanced to finish crisp and dry. A typical blend has 10 to 12 grams of residual sugar and 7 to 9 grams of acidity per litre. The wine is made in the traditional style of Champagne. The wines for the cuvée are fermented to dryness. They are blended, then bottled with a dosage of sugar and yeast, undergoing a second fermentation in heavy bottles capable of containing six or so atmospheres of pressure. The time spent aging in bottle and on the yeast lees creates the fine bubbles and toasty aromas typical of fine sparkling wine.

Over the wine's first two decades, Steller's Jay Brut grew in volume to about 7,000 cases a year, with a quality that has made it among the most awarded Canadian sparkling wines. As a result of its success, this former flagship of Sumac Ridge was promoted to become a stand-alone brand (even if the wine is still made and sold at the Sumac Ridge winery). Over the years, Sumac Ridge produced other bottle-fermented sparkling wines. Limited volumes of Blanc de Blanc (Chardonnay) and Blanc de Noir (Pinot Noir) sparkling wines were made in 1988. While Blanc de Blanc was discontinued, Blanc de Noir was renamed Pinnacle. From the 2000 vintage, the winery produced Prestige Cuvée Brut, a dry sparkling wine with a blend of grapes similar to that of Steller's Jay. On other occasions, the winery also released a sparkling Shiraz, a style that was developed in Australia, as well as Sparkling Gewürztraminer.

Steller's Jay Brut 2009

($25)

Cuvée of Pinot Noir, Chardonnay, and Pinot Blanc. Alcohol 12.5%. Three years *en tirage*. Residual sugar 10.5 grams per litre. Acidity 7.3 grams per litre.

WINERY TASTING NOTES "White peach and golden hues flatter the ripe orchard fruit and citrus blossom aromas in this crisp and complex sparkling wine. Rich flavours of toasted nut and red berries layer the palate, resolving to a soft and creamy floral mousse finish." Drink now.

Sumac Ridge Steller's Jay Brut 2008

Cuvée of Pinot Noir, Chardonnay, and Pinot Blanc. Alcohol 12%. Three years *en tirage*.

AUTHOR'S TASTING NOTES "In the glass, the wine puts on a wonderful display of fine and long-lasting bubbles. The aroma is slightly bready from its time on the lees. The wine has citrus and apple flavours, and an attractive nutty undertone. The finish is crisp and bright." Drink now.

Sumac Ridge Steller's Jay Brut 2007

Cuvée of Pinot Noir, Chardonnay, and Pinot Blanc. Three years *en tirage*.

AUTHOR'S TASTING NOTES "This is as fine a vintage as the winery has yet released, with notes of toast and yeast on the nose (classic Champagne!), with delicious fruity flavours and a creamy texture. The bubbles create an active and long-lasting display. The finish is clean and dry." Drink now.

Sumac Ridge Steller's Jay Brut 2006

Cuvée of Pinot Noir, Chardonnay, and Pinot Blanc. Three years *en tirage*.

TASTING NOTES by Beppi Crosariol: "There's an intriguing coppery-pink tinge to this 'white' sparkling wine due to some bleeding from the Pinot Noir skins (which are normally removed quickly before sparkling wine fermentation). It's bone-dry, with a pear and bitter lemon essence, rich texture, and crusty, well-baked-bread finish." Drink now.

Sumac Ridge Steller's Jay Brut 2001

Cuvée of Pinot Blanc, Chardonnay, and Pinot Noir. Alcohol 12.1%. Three years *en tirage*. Residual sugar 12.1 grams per litre. Acidity 9.3 grams. Production 2,500 cases.

WINERY TASTING NOTES "The wine leads off with toast and citrus aromas, followed by a smooth, creamy palate and a crisp, mineral finish."

Stoneboat Vineyards
ROCK OPERA PINOTAGE RESERVE
SOLO PINOTAGE RESERVE
PINOTAGE

The Pinotage grape was developed in South Africa in 1925 when a professor of viticulture at Stellenbosch University, Abraham Perold, pollinated Pinot Noir with a Rhône variety, Cinsault. After the first commercial planting in 1943, it was planted modestly and now comprises just six percent of South Africa's vineyards. However, the variety has an international following. Peter F. May, a British wine writer and an honorary member of the producers' Pinotage Association, has run a web-based fan club, The Pinotage Club, for more than a decade.

The vine was brought to the Okanagan in 1995 by a South African immigrant, Paul Moser, who established Lake Breeze Vineyards. He bought a limited number of Pinotage vines from the University of California (South African vines were not allowed into Canada because of virus concerns). Paul asked Lanny Martiniuk, an Oliver vine propagator, to multiply them. Lanny was impressed with the vines and propagated some that he planted, beginning in 1998, in one of his own vineyards. Five years later, he expanded the planting to another of the Martiniuk family vineyards. Today, the Stoneboat Pinotage blocks total 3.23 hectares (8 acres) and are the largest planting in the South Okanagan.

"Though it originated in South Africa," the winery commented when releasing the 2012 vintage, "we have found over the past 15 years that Pinotage on the Black Sage Gravelbar expresses itself differently from its counterpart abroad. Usually last to be harvested, in late October, Pinotage never fails to deliver intense, exotically flavoured wines."

"Pinotage is great to work with in the cellar," said Alison Moyes, Stoneboat's winemaker until 2015. "It is the complete opposite of Pinot Noir in how we treat it. With Pinot, everything is gentle, with lower temperature fermentation. Pinotage is a bigger animal. I am trying to get more extraction so it ferments with more heat. I don't extract a lot of unpleasant characters in doing that. Pinotage is not overly prone to bitterness and astringency."

The winemaking is straightforward. The grapes, after a five-day cold soak, are fermented in small stainless-steel tanks, followed by a short maceration. Then the wine is transferred to oak. The first vintage, in 2005, had just 10 months in barrel. Subsequently, the winery has concluded that the variety needs at least 13 months in barrel "to restrain the variety's flamboyant wild berry characters and bring forth its rich, plummy undertones."

The winery also produces Solo, a reserve Pinotage, when vintages are exceptional or when several barrels stand out as being "the best of the best." Solo gets 22 months' aging in the barrel. Beginning with the 2013 vintage, the wine was renamed Rock Opera Pinotage Reserve—a reference to stones in the field, not to music.

Pinotage wines are juicy and drinkable on release but are capable of aging at least seven to 10 years.

Rock Opera Pinotage Reserve 2013 ($34.90)

Alcohol 14%.

WINERY TASTING NOTES "This limited production reserve is crafted using our finest Pinotage lots, showcasing the best of the vintage. Bold, dark sweet fruits, baking spice, and chocolate flavours framed by lush, sturdy tannins lead to a lengthy, smooth finish." Drink by 2023.

Solo Pinotage Reserve 2012

Alcohol 14%. Aged 15 months in oak barrels. Production 95 cases.

WINERY TASTING NOTES "Bold layers of dark cherry fruit, baking spice, and chocolate are integrated beautifully, with luscious tannins leading to a warm finish." Drink by 2022.

Solo Pinotage Reserve 2010

Alcohol 13.6%.

Tasting notes unavailable.

Solo Pinotage Reserve 2007

Alcohol 14.1%.

TASTING NOTES by Peter F. May, founder of the Pinotage Club: "It is a bright red-black colour with a ripe fruit richness and cedar-wood flavours and is absolutely beautiful." Drink now.

Pinotage 2012 ($24.90)

Alcohol 13.9%. Aged 15 months in French (90%) and American (10%) oak barrels. Production 1,092 cases.

WINERY TASTING NOTES "The 2012 vintage delivers intense, exotic fruit flavours with notes of mocha, black cherry, and vanilla on a bold, rounded palate." Drink by 2020.

Pinotage 2010

Alcohol 13.5%.

AUTHOR'S TASTING NOTES "This is bigger in texture and flavour than one usually sees in Pinotage, with tastes of black cherry, spice, and chocolate." Drink by 2019.

Pinotage 2009

Alcohol 13.5%. Production 1,013 cases.

AUTHOR'S TASTING NOTES "This wine is dark in colour and begins with aromas of vanilla and mocha. On the palate, there are flavours of plum, blueberry, lingonberry, and mocha, with a lingering spicy finish." Drink by 2019.

Pinotage 2008

Alcohol 14.1%.

TASTING NOTES by Peter F. May, founder of the Pinotage Club: "Dense and complex with black fruits, damsons, cherries, and a spiciness that makes it so drinkable." Drink now.

Pinotage 2007

Production 715 cases.

TASTING NOTES by Peter F. May, founder of the Pinotage Club: "Pinotage 2007 had a leathery nose and was lively in the mouth. It is an exciting wine with cedar wood and spices in abundance. This wine won the Lieutenant Governor's Award for Excellence in British Columbia Wines." Mature.

Pinotage 2005

Alcohol 14%. Aged 10 months in French and American oak. Production 416 cases.

WINERY TASTING NOTES "Our 2005 Pinotage presents cedar box and cassis on the nose, complemented by soft strawberry basket notes. Intense flavours of ripe plum, Bing cherry, and raspberry jam are wrapped in bold tannins, finishing with rich boysenberry and subtle black pepper." Mature.

Summerhill Pyramid Winery
CIPES SPARKLING WINES

If the word *Champagne* were not an exclusively French appellation, Summerhill founder Stephen Cipes would have called the winery Champagne House when it opened in 1992. "I hate the term 'sparkling wine,'" he said at the time. "People misunderstand it and confuse it with the cheap junk they do not like." He was referring to carbonated sparkling wines best suited to launching boats.

Summerhill, which markets its sparkling wines under the Cipes label, was an early producer in the Okanagan of sparkling wines fermented in bottle, just like Champagne. Stephen participated in a 1990 winemaking trial in the Okanagan led by California's Schramsberg Champagne Cellars. (Some American producers have ignored the French Champagne trademark.) When Schramsberg decided against producing wine in Canada, Stephen recruited a Canadian-born but German-trained winemaker, Eric von Krosigk, to launch his so-called Champagne House.

The most enduring and best-selling sparkling wine in the portfolio is Cipes Brut, a crisply dry wine originally made just with Riesling grapes, perhaps because Eric had learned to make that type of wine when he was studying at Geisenheim University. More recent releases have included Chardonnay and Pinot Blanc in the cuvée.

A former New York real-estate developer, Stephen had the flair to get a high profile early for Cipes (rhymes with "stripes") Brut. In 1993, US president Bill Clinton and Russian president Boris Yeltsin met on a yacht in Vancouver harbour. Stephen managed to get some Cipes Brut onto the yacht for any toasts that were required. Subsequently, Stephen, who is inclined to mysticism, built a pyramid at the winery, contending that aging wines were improved by the spiritual energy generated inside the pyramid.

Summerhill's founder also set an early example of responsible viticulture. The East Kelowna vineyard he bought when he moved to the Okanagan in 1986 was soon converted to organic production. His sons Ezra and Gabe, who now run the winery, have gone further. They require Summerhill's growers to be organic and have adopted organic and biodynamic practices in both the estate vineyard and the winery.

The winery has been noted for its highly unusual packaging. Cipes Ariel 1998, its prestige sparkling wine, is in a conical bottle. The subsequent vintages of Ariel, however, will be in conventional sparkling wine bottles. Currently, Ariel 2000 and Ariel 2004 are resting on the lees.

Cipes Ariel Cuvée 1998 ($88)

Pinot Noir 59%, Chardonnay 40%, Pinot Meunier 1%. Alcohol 12.5%. Summerhill Vineyard. 100% organic grapes. Residual sugar 7.8 grams per litre. Acid 7.5 grams per litre. Sixteen years *en tirage*. Production 500 cases.

WINERY TASTING NOTES "Very rich and complex with notes of custard, vegemite, brioche, orange and lemon zest, ripe apple, dried apricot, nut, and ginger."

Cipes Blanc de Blanc 2010 ($44.85)

Chardonnay. 100% organic.

AUTHOR'S TASTING NOTES "The wine has bready aromas and flavours of yeast lees, leading to flavours of fresh apple and citrus, with a hint of anise on the finish. The mid-palate is creamy, but the finish is crisp."

Cipes Blanc de Noirs 2008 ($34.90)

Pinot Noir. Alcohol 12.9%. 100% organic. Residual sugar 12.6 grams per litre. Acidity 8.6 grams per litre. The wine rests on the lees, with tranches disgorged as sales require.

WINERY TASTING NOTES "Extended *sur lie* bottle aging results in deep, complex flavours and a fine mousse. Notes of marmalade, raspberry, brioche, white almond, ginger, and lime."

Cipes Brut NV ($26.95)

Riesling, Chardonnay, Pinot Blanc. Alcohol 12.5%. *En tirage* for 12 months.

WINERY TASTING NOTES "Cipes Brut is a beautiful Riesling-and-Chardonnay-based traditional method sparkling wine with aromas of apple, lime, pear, almonds, and grapefruit. On the palate, Cipes Brut exhibits crisp acidity, a soft, creamy mousse, and a long finish."

Cipes Rosé NV ($26.95)

Pinot Noir; 75% of the juice spent 48 hours on the skins to extract colour and flavour. Alcohol 12.5%. Residual sugar 9.3 grams per litre. Acidity 7.9 grams per litre.

WINERY TASTING NOTES "Pinot Noir cuvée grown at multiple vineyard locations around the Okanagan Valley that were planted and are maintained specifically for sparkling wine production to express a crisp, bright style. Notes of raspberry, strawberry, kiwi, blood orange, vanilla, almond, and white toast."

Cipes Traditional Cuvée 1996 ($101.20)

Pinot Noir, Chardonnay, Pinot Meunier. Residual sugar 14.5 grams per litre.

This wine was disgorged and released in 2015. The winery judged it to need 19 years aging on the lees to tame the bracing acidity of the 1996 vintage.

AUTHOR'S TASTING NOTES "The acidity has preserved almost youthful brightness in the wine. It has complex aromas and flavours of marmalade, ginger, and oyster shells. The bubbles are extremely fine."

Synchromesh Wines

STORM HAVEN VINEYARD RIESLING

Long before opening this Okanagan Falls winery, Alan Dickinson was collecting Rieslings, especially ones from Germany. "I really like old Rieslings," he says. "To me, the German Riesling vintage that tastes the best now is 1983." He has a ways to go at Synchromesh, where the first Storm Haven Vineyard Riesling was made in 2010. In recent vintages, however, Alan has begun bottling the wines under cork. "When you start laying Riesling down past 15 years, there is magic that happens under cork."

Alan began his personal cellar when he was a partner in a Vancouver business that helped collectors source and store fine wines. When they decided to participate in the wine industry directly, Alan and his wife, Amy, searched the Okanagan for good Riesling sites for 18 months. In early 2010, they bought a 2-hectare (5-acre) piece of land that included a four-year-old block of Clone 21B Riesling. They have since replaced all the other varieties on the property with Riesling and Pinot Noir.

Alan and Amy christened the vineyard Storm Haven after observing weather patterns in the area. The most prominent geological feature of Okanagan Falls is 600-metre-high Peach Cliff,

north of the vineyard. The updrafts around it after Peach Cliff absorbs the summer heat deflect rain and hail from the vineyard. The wide diurnal temperature swing—as much as 20°C between night and day—make this "perfect Riesling country," Alan believes.

In his first vintage here, Alan took the vineyard "off the cheeseburger diet" by replacing synthetic fertilizers with natural nutrient additions. The lean, complex, mineral-laden soils limit the vines to producing a spare 1.5 kilograms of intensely flavoured grapes per vine. "The greatest German Rieslings are basically grown in slate, with no soil whatsoever and very little nutrient," Alan says.

The style of Storm Haven and the four other Rieslings produced by Synchromesh is influenced by German Rieslings. The 2010 vintage of Storm Haven Riesling was even labelled *halbtrocken*, or off-dry. Alan has not used German on the labels since, but what's inside remains true to the style: significant residual sugar balanced with bracing acidity. While the wine is released when young, Alan recommends cellaring it until it is at least five years old. It will certainly age comfortably beyond that, perhaps even as long as some of the great German Rieslings in his own collection.

2015 ($34.90)

Alcohol 8.2%. Acidity 12.2 grams per litre. Residual sugar 35 grams per litre. Production 120 cases, 300 magnums.

WINERY TASTING NOTES "Mineral-driven apricot, mango meat, citrus, and Asian pear aromatics lead to a complex and concentrated mouth with delicate tension and pure Storm Haven expression. Tremendously long finish with creamy balance of acid and a kiss of honeyed lemon sweetness." Drink after 2020.

2014

Alcohol 9.4%. Acidity 12.6 grams per litre. Residual sugar 35 grams per litre.

WINERY TASTING NOTES "The 2014 vintage was very hot and dry but this special site showed its unique ability to retain excellent range of acid and delicacy even in these conditions. Hand-picked and gently processed, the 2014 shows the vineyard's characteristic minerality, mango meat, ripe pie apple, and honeysuckle aromatics. A viscous mouthfeel with broad acid leaves an endless lemon-kissed, mango, and applesauce finish." Drink after 2019.

2013

Alcohol 8.2%. Acidity 12.2 grams per litre. Residual sugar 35 grams per litre.

WINERY TASTING NOTES "Mineral-driven apricot, mango meat, citrus, Asian pear aromatics lead to a complex and concentrated mouth with delicate tension and pure Storm Haven expression. Tremendously long finish with creamy balance of acid and a kiss of honeyed lemon sweetness." Drink after 2018.

2012

Alcohol 10%. Acidity 12.4 grams per litre. Residual sugar 29 grams per litre. Production 54 cases.

WINERY TASTING NOTES "With a straw tint to the colour, this wine is incredibly complex on the nose. Ripe crab apple, pineapple, mango meat, coconut, banana, lemon, and applesauce are all prevalent. In the mouth the wine shows the same, adding Asian and Anjou pear, honey, sweet apple blossom, lime, rose petal, lemon curd, and banana. The finish is an enduring, fragrant honeyed sweetness balanced beautifully against a broad range of acids and stony minerality." Drink after 2017.

2011

Alcohol 9.3%. Acidity 12.3 grams per litre. Residual sugar 55 grams per litre. Production 41 cases.

AUTHOR'S TASTING NOTES "This wine presents a rich, generous texture with a backbone of minerals. The aromas include notes of petrol and lemon. On the palate, there are flavours of lemon and lime. The wine shows exquisite balance of acidity and sugar." Drink now through 2021.

2010

Alcohol 11.4%. Acidity 12.7 grams per litre. Residual sugar 25 grams per litre. Production 74 cases.

WINERY TASTING NOTES "The wine displays an explosive nose of Granny Smith and McIntosh apples, green pear, honey, apricot and undertones of petrol and wet stone. On the palate, fresh fruit flavours continue with mouth-watering acidity that is in perfect balance with residual sugar. Apricot, honey, and minerality take over the finish that lasts nearly a minute." Drink now through 2020.

Tantalus Vineyards

OLD VINES RIESLING

This winery's storied Old Vines Riesling was born in 1978 with the planting of Clone 21B Riesling in its vineyard, one of the oldest in the Okanagan. The foundation of the vineyard, with southwestern exposure overlooking Kelowna, was laid in 1927 when J.W. Hughes, a horticulturist from Iowa, planted both table and wine grapes here and on nearby properties. By 1944, he had about 121 hectares (300 acres) of vines, mostly labrusca hybrids. Hughes then sold the vineyards to his three foremen, one of whom was Czech-born Martin Dulik.

At the urging of Jordan & Ste-Michelle, the winery buying the grapes, Martin and his son, Daniel, gradually replanted the entire vineyard with better varieties, including Clone 21B. This was the renowned clone that was developed in the Mosel by Hermann Weis. To secure Canadian sales for his vines, he had it planted both in Ontario and in the Okanagan. "I recall planting the first vine of Riesling at Dulik's," recounts Lloyd Schmidt, a consulting viticulturist whose father was also a Hughes foreman. The vine was planted "with much ceremony," Lloyd says. "I recall toasting the vine with German Riesling, then pouring the wine onto that first vine, wishing it and the planting a good future."

In 1997, Susan Dulik, Martin's granddaughter, opened a winery called Pinot Reach Cellars. She planned to specialize in Pinot varieties, but the vineyard had another destiny. Helped by winemaking consultant Eric von Krosigk, she produced four vintages of Old Vines Riesling, beginning with the 1999. One of those vintages was the first Canadian wine to be praised by Jancis Robinson, the influential British wine writer.

No wine was made from the vineyard in 2003 because smoke from massive forest fires nearby saturated the fruit. The following year, the Dulik family sold the property to Vancouver investment dealer Eric Savics, who relaunched the winery in 2005 as Tantalus Vineyards. He arranged a further upgrading of the plantings while retaining the 1.2 hectares (3 acres) of old vines Riesling. Production of that wine resumed, and Jancis Robinson again singled it out for praise.

"It has to do with everything that encompasses terroir and very little to do with winemaking," suggests David Patterson, the Tantalus winemaker since 2008. "It is the age of the vines, the aspect, the elevation, the soils. The root system has gone down a long, long way and draws up a lot of minerality. The root system is so well established that it buffers the season. These vines buffer themselves against hot and cold vintages, and we get a very consistent product." Certainly, there is vintage variation. "But I think there is more of a commonality within the wines than there is a difference," he says. "There is that piercing mineral acidity in all the wines."

With its acidity and mineral content, the Old Vines Riesling can be aged for at least a decade and perhaps double that. As is the case with most fine Rieslings, this wine develops complex aromas and flavours that some describe as marmalade and others as petrol. "Occasionally, some clientele don't understand aged Riesling," David says. He refers them to Wikipedia's concise explanation of what happens when Riesling ages: the distinct taste is caused by a naturally developing compound and, far from being a defect, is a mark of quality.

Because of its crisp acidity when young, Old Vines Riesling is not released until it has two or three years of bottle age. The quantity is always small because a portion of Old Vines juice is blended with that from younger vines for the estate Riesling. As well, Tantalus produces a modest volume of Old Vines Riesling Natural Brut sparkling wine.

2013 ($30.35)

Alcohol 13.1%. Residual sweetness 9.2 grams per litre. Total acidity 10.7 grams per litre. Production 367 cases.

WINERY TASTING NOTES "Sun gold in colour, aromas of warm beeswax, granny smith apple, and citrus peel leap from the glass. The palate is focused and intense with concentrated notes of preserved lemon, pithy marmalade, and sour candies. Hints of minerality and a creamy meyer lemon curd character are beginning to emerge as a result of the wine's two-year cellaring time before release. The finish is long and dry with a bright, textured acidity." Drink now through 2026.

2012

Alcohol 12%. Residual sweetness 6.3 grams per litre. Total acidity 10.8 grams per litre. Production 260 cases.

WINERY TASTING NOTES "Morning sunshine in a glass—this wine is all about purity and balance. The nose invites with lime curd and mandarin marmalade lifted by hints of white flowers and wet stones. The palate is focused and textural. Ripe fresh-squeezed lemon, juicy pink grapefruit pith complemented by incredible minerality. This wine has great length and complexity and although delicious now, its long cellaring capability will richly reward those who wait." Drink now through 2025.

2011

Alcohol 12.7%. Residual sweetness 11.2 grams per litre. Total acidity 10.8 grams per litre. Production 150 cases.

WINERY TASTING NOTES "In the glass this wine shows a pure, star bright yellow. Fragrances of lemon oil, grapefruit pith, and Jasmine flowers define the bouquet. A captivating fresh rain on chalk aromatic also shines through. On the palate, the classic mineral intensity of our Block 5 old vines fruit is abundant, with flavours of granny smith apple, lemon zest, and key lime pie. Brilliant acidity and a hint of grapefruit pithiness stretches the wine out to a long and elegant finish." Drink now through 2024.

2010

Alcohol 12.6%. Residual sweetness 13.5 grams per litre. Total acidity 12 grams per litre. Production 150 cases.

WINERY TASTING NOTES "This is a wonderfully intense wine. The nose is brimming with fresh lemon and melon, coupled with wisps of wet stone and mineral. The palate's racy, citrus and granny smith apple flavours display a certain level of concentration that can only come from old vines planted on an exceptional site. Its unusually long finish is supported by an alluring minerality coupled with crisp acidity that hints at what is yet to come from this long cellaring wine." Drink now through 2023.

2009

Alcohol 13.4%. Residual sweetness 6.6 grams per litre. Total acidity 10.6 grams per litre. Production 100 cases.

WINERY TASTING NOTES "Intense aromas of lime and lemon with a hint of tropical fruit leap from the glass. On the palate, pineapple, melon, and citrus flavours envelope the tongue. It sings with balance and focus while displaying a depth of character only mature vines can create." Drink now through 2022.

2008

Alcohol 12.1%. Residual sweetness 14 grams per litre. Total acidity 13 grams per litre. Production 550 cases.

WINERY TASTING NOTES "Orange blossom, peach, and floral aromas leading into cooler-vintage flavour characteristics of grapefruit and lemon zest are offset by a subtle mineral core. Expect a sustained and intense finish." Drink now through 2021.

2007

Alcohol 13%. Residual sweetness 8 grams per litre. Total acidity 10.8 grams per litre. Production 268 cases.

AUTHOR'S TASTING NOTES "Dry on the finish, this is a restrained wine with flavours of lime and lemon. The old vines bring finely concentrated minerals as well as fruit to the taste and texture. This is a connoisseur's Riesling." Drink now through 2020.

2006

Alcohol 13%. Residual sweetness 9.3 grams per litre. Total acidity 10.8 grams per litre. Production 400 cases.

WINERY TASTING NOTES "[This wine] exhibits intense flavours of grapefruit, melon, passion fruit, and gooseberry. Bright acidity and a silky emollient mouth feel also contribute to the appeal of this exceptional vintage." Drink now through 2019.

2005

Alcohol 13%. Residual sweetness 6.9 grams per litre. Total acidity 11 grams per litre. Production 370 cases.

WINERY TASTING NOTES "[This wine] bursts with flavours of vibrant lime zest, refreshing grapefruit, and ripe apricot characters. Subtle notes of mineral and slate show in the wine's long finish." Drink now.

Tightrope Winery

PINOT NOIR

Graham O'Rourke characterizes this winery's Pinot Noir block, just over 0.75 hectare (2 acres) in size, as "a real stew of clones and rootstocks . . . and that is kind of my idea." This explains the complexity and depth of Tightrope's Pinot Noir.

He began planting the vineyard in 2007 when he and Lyndsay, his winemaker wife, started developing Tightrope. Before he installed a wind machine three years later, frost killed some of his vines. He replaced them by interplanting additional vines until he had six clones. It was an idea he took from New Zealand when he and Lyndsay studied winemaking and viticulture at Lincoln University.

"We are not harvesting all of the clones and rootstocks separately and then trying to blend them back together," Graham says. "That is the strategy of a lot of places—make the wines separately and rely on your palate to put it all together. Our vineyard puts it together just fine. There is no need to mess with it."

Both born in 1971, the pair found a shared interest in good wine while working in Whistler ski resort restaurants. "The thing about Whistler," Lyndsay says, "is that you get a lot of chances to try nice wines with good food." They moved to the Okanagan in 2003, studying viticulture at Okanagan College. That led them to enrol at Lincoln for honours degrees. On their return to the Okanagan, Graham managed vineyards for Mission Hill for six years before setting up his own consulting firm.

Lyndsay honed her winemaking skills at Ruby Blues Winery.

Lyndsay gained some experience working with Pinot Noir at a New Zealand winery. She refined her approach in the Okanagan, notably trading ideas with J-M Bouchard, then the winemaker at Road 13 Vineyards. In 2011, he bought grapes from Tightrope and a neighbouring vineyard to produce a stellar Pinot Noir that showed the O'Rourkes the potential of their terroir.

For the first Tightrope Pinot Noir in 2012, Lyndsay had just enough grapes to fill three small fermenters. She inoculated two with cultured yeast but, inspired by J-M, she relied on indigenous yeast for the third. "It was a little fruitier, more complex and interesting," she says. "So the following year, we did 100 percent wild ferment."

The winery is next to the Pinot Noir block so that the grapes are processed immediately after picking. Bunches are destemmed, with just whole berries going into the fermenters. After a five-day cold soak, the bins are warmed so that the yeast can get to work. After the ferment is complete in two to three weeks, the wine, after a day of settling, is aged in French oak for about 10 months. "We use 30 percent new French oak," Lyndsay says. "The rest is neutral. I like some oak to be present, but I don't want it to be overbearing."

"Pinot Noir is not meant to be overpowered by wood," Graham asserts. "We are trying to show off the brighter fruit characters."

2014 ($35)

Alcohol 12.8%. Fermented with indigenous yeast. Aged 10 months in French oak (30% new). Production 400 cases.

WINERY TASTING NOTES "This is a New World–style Pinot Noir that is fruit forward on the nose with aromas of black cherries, plum, and blackcurrants. On the palate, the fruit continues with hints of coffee, chocolate, vanilla, and spice. This Pinot Noir is rich and elegant with a lingering finish." Drink by 2021.

2013

Alcohol 13.3%. Production 180 cases.

WINERY TASTING NOTES "This is New World–style Pinot Noir that is fruit forward on the nose with aromas of black cherries, plum, and blackcurrants. On the palate, the fruit continues with hints of coffee, chocolate, and spice. This Pinot Noir is rich and full-bodied with a lingering finish." Drink by 2020.

2012

Alcohol 13.6%. Production 150 cases.

WINERY TASTING NOTES "Estate-grown and hand-picked, then fermented in small lots, this is indeed a nuanced production you'll want to reminisce about when you're old. Detect the balance of elegant black cherries, plums, and blackcurrants up front with hints of coffee, chocolate, and spice along for the ride." Drink by 2019.

Time Estate Winery
MCWATTERS COLLECTION MERITAGE

There's a reason why two red Meritage wines (and one white Meritage) are produced at Time Estate Winery. Harry McWatters, the winery's owner, in 1993 was the first person in Canada to be granted use of the term by California's Meritage Association. *Meritage* replaced the French appellations (like Bordeaux or Medoc) no longer appropriate to use on bottles of New World wine.

Sumac Ridge, the winery that Harry founded (with partners) in 1980, was the first Canadian winery to release Meritage wines. Numerous other Canadian wineries also adopted the term, including Time, the winery that Harry founded (again with partners) in 2012. Both the Time Meritage Red and the McWatters Collection Meritage are collectible, but the latter, according to Harry, has the structure for longer-term cellaring.

The launch of McWatters flows from Harry's insatiable fervour for wine and his determination to create a legacy for his family. He was passionate about wine before he was old enough to drink it, having started to make it at home when he was 16. (Harry was born in 1945.) In 1968, he quit his job as a United Van Lines manager in Vancouver to work in sales for Casabello Wines in Penticton. He was so enamoured with wine that, as Harry has often repeated, he only discovered he was earning less at the new job when he got his first paycheque.

But he stayed to provide critical leadership in the development of the Okanagan's wine industry.

The debut McWatters Collection Meritage was made in the 2007 vintage. Harry was just ending his association with Sumac Ridge, now corporately owned. The McWatters label was crafted to become a legacy for the McWatters family, based on superbly grown grapes in a mature 46-hectare (115-acre) vineyard on Black Sage Road. Planted in 1993, the vineyard was the largest block of Bordeaux varietals in Canada at the time.

The vineyard was owned almost equally by Sumac Ridge and Harry. When he retired from Sumac Ridge in 2008, his 24 hectares (60 acres) were renamed Sundial Vineyard. Its frontage on Black Sage Road proved an ideal location for the Time winery, which was under construction in 2015. In 2016, however, a buyer acquired both the vineyard and the incomplete winery to develop a new premium winery.

Meanwhile, Harry purchased a large, recently closed movie theatre in downtown Penticton. This is the new home for both Time and the McWatters Collection wines made, in future, from grapes purchased elsewhere in the South Okanagan. Both of these labels now operate under the umbrella company Encore Vineyards.

2013 ($24.99)

Cabernet Sauvignon 57%, Merlot 30%, Cabernet Franc 13%. Alcohol 14.1%. Sundial Vineyard. Matured in French oak for 15 months. Production 550 cases.

WINERY TASTING NOTES "Our 2013 vintage is big and elegant, with velvety tannins, well-balanced fruit, and oak characteristics with blackberry and cassis overtones. Our Meritage is comprised of several different clones to lend it depth and complexity including three Cabernet Sauvignon clones which give it structure and richness; two Merlot clones which impart a velvety texture, soft tannins, and blackberry and black cherry flavours; and one Cabernet Franc clone, which provides spiciness and black pepper." Drink by 2023.

2012

Cabernet Sauvignon 68%, Merlot 20%, Cabernet Franc 12%. Alcohol 13.7%. Sundial Vineyard. Aged 15 months in French oak. Production 650 cases.

WINERY TASTING NOTES "Our 2012 vintage is big and elegant with velvety tannins, well-balanced fruit, and oak characteristics with blackberry and cassis overtones." Drink by 2020 to 2022.

2011

Cabernet Sauvignon 40%, Merlot 31%, Cabernet Franc 29%. Alcohol 13.8%. Sundial Vineyard. Aged 15 months in French oak. Production 450 cases.

WINERY TASTING NOTES "Three Cabernet Sauvignon clones . . . give it structure and richness; two Merlot clones . . . impart a velvety texture, soft tannins, and blackberry and cherry flavours; Cabernet Franc provides spiciness and black pepper." Drink by 2019.

2009

Cabernet Sauvignon 44%, Merlot 32%, Cabernet Franc 24%. Alcohol 13.9%. Sundial Vineyard. Aged 15 months in French oak. Production 700 cases.

WINERY TASTING NOTES "Our 2009 vintage is big and elegant, with velvety tannins, well-balanced fruit, and oak characteristics with blackberry and cassis overtones." Drink by 2019.

2007

Merlot 60%, Cabernet Sauvignon 35%, Cabernet Franc 5%. Alcohol 13.8%. Sundial Vineyard. Aged 15 months in French oak. Production 500 cases.

WINERY TASTING NOTES "Big, elegant, with soft tannins, well-balanced with fruit and oak characteristics with blackberry and cassis overtones." Drink now.

Tinhorn Creek Vineyards

OLDFIELD SERIES 2BENCH RED

Tinhorn Creek, which made its first vintage in 1994, began producing reserve wines under the Oldfield label in 2004. A single variety Merlot was the first reserve; consequently, it remains one of the most-collected of Tinhorn Creek's wines. However, Sandra Oldfield, the former winemaker and now the winery's president, nudges collectors toward 2Bench Red. "It cellars better," she believes.

Historically, Tinhorn Creek has mainly produced single variety wines. The red blend called 2Bench was launched under that name because the winery has vineyards on both the Black Sage Bench and the Golden Mile Bench. Black Sage is on the east side of the Okanagan Valley; there, the vines grow in deep, sandy soil and get intense sunlight from morning until late evening. Golden Mile is on the west side of the valley. Its vines grow in gravel, clay, and volcanic soils, getting gentler sunlight from early morning until late afternoon. Only a few kilometres apart, the benches produce significantly different fruit flavours that complement each other in blends. The Golden Mile fruit has brighter acidity, while Black Sage fruit has riper flavours.

"The majority of the components [of 2Bench Red] come from the Black Sage Bench," Sandra says. "Only upwards of 10 percent of that wine will come from the Golden Mile Bench. But those components, the Malbec and the Petit Verdot, are unique on this side."

In 2007, the winery was ready to produce a Bordeaux blend that made a statement because its vineyards, planted mostly in 1993, were mature and premium blocks had been identified.

Initially, 2Bench Red was anchored with Cabernet Sauvignon. "But as the years went on, it is definitely dominated now by the Merlot," Sandra says. "That is a testament to how good Merlot is in this valley, and also how difficult it is sometimes to grow Cabernet Sauvignon in this valley. Even in cooler years, or years where we don't get Indian summers, the Merlot is going to add the power to that wine. It just does. In those years, the Cabernet Sauvignon adds a fruit component but not a tannin structure. Of course, the Cabernet Franc portion is always pretty strong with that wine."

Trained at the University of California at Davis, Sandra has always used American oak barrels as well as French oak. However, 2Bench Red has always been aged in French oak, if only to underline the intention that the wine be a premium Bordeaux blend. Only in recent vintages has Cabernet Franc aged in American oak been included in the blend because of the affinity of the spicy variety's flavours for the spicy oak.

The volume of 2Bench Red was modest during the early vintages. Now, the winery strives to make about 1,500 cases a year and to make it widely available so the wine can be collected. Those who are not interested in laying this wine down will find it immediately approachable because it will have had three years of barrel and bottle age before release.

2013 ($35)

Alcohol 14.7%. Aged 18 months in French oak. Production 1,684 cases.

AUTHOR'S TASTING NOTES "It begins with aromas of blackcurrants, mint, herbs, and cigar box. With breathing, the wine shows blueberry aromas as well. This is all echoed on the palate, along with notes of dark chocolate and black olive." Drink by 2025.

2012

Cabernet Sauvignon 41%, Cabernet Franc 28%, Merlot 28%, Petit Verdot 3%. Alcohol 14.7%. Aged 18 months in French oak (new and used). Production 1,683 cases.

WINERY TASTING NOTES "Lovely blueberry- and cassis-driven nose typical of Black Sage Bench Cabernet Sauvignon. Follows up with black cherries and subtle dried herb to finish out a powerful and expressive aroma. The palate carries through again with blueberries, cherries, and herbs . . . laced with a beautiful chocolate frame." Drink by 2024.

2011

Cabernet Franc 39%, Merlot 35%, Cabernet Sauvignon 24%, Petit Verdot 2%. Alcohol 13.4%. Aged 18 months in French oak (new and used). Production 1,446 cases.

AUTHOR'S TASTING NOTES "The wine begins with aromas of cherry, cassis, and plum. There is an elegant core of sweet fruit on the palate, including cassis, raspberry, and plum, with a touch of tobacco and cola on the finish. The texture evolved from lean to medium-bodied with decanting." Drink by 2020.

2010

Merlot 41%, Cabernet Franc 31%, Cabernet Sauvignon 24%, Petit Verdot 4%. Alcohol 14.3%. Aged 18 months in French oak (new and used). Production 1,172 cases.

AUTHOR'S TASTING NOTES "Dark in hue, the wine begins with seductively sweet aromas of cassis and blackberry. On the palate, it has flavours of plum, cassis, and vanilla. There is a hint of coffee and tobacco on the finish, as well as a touch of mint. The bright flavours and moderately angular texture reflect the cool vintage." Drink by 2020.

2009

Merlot 45%, Cabernet Sauvignon 30%, Cabernet Franc 22%, Petit Verdot 3%. Alcohol 14.8%. Aged 19 to 20 months in French oak barrels (both new and used).

AUTHOR'S TASTING NOTES "This is another big ripe red, beginning with aromas of spice, tobacco, and blackcurrant jam. On the palate, there are flavours of blackcurrants, plums, and figs, with an earthy note and a firm texture that becomes fleshy with breathing." Drink by 2019.

2008

Cabernet Sauvignon 40%, Merlot 40%, Cabernet Franc 20%. Alcohol 15%. Aged 18 months in new French oak barrels. Production 751 cases.

WINERY TASTING NOTES "The 2008 Oldfield Series 2Bench Red is densely extracted and ruby in colour. It is powerfully concentrated, with black cherries, blackberries and blackcurrant, notes of leafy tobacco, and menthol aromas. The wine has flavours of racy black fruit and delicate herbs. Fine tannins and refreshing acidity ensure that this wine will stand the test of time." Drink by 2018.

2007

Cabernet Sauvignon 42%, Cabernet Franc 29%, Merlot 29%. Alcohol 15%. Aged 18 months in new and used French oak. Production 355 cases.

WINERY TASTING NOTES "Both complex and subtle, this wine has aromas of blackberry, cassis, and herbs with notes of oak and cedar. On the palate the aromas carry through and are joined by dark chocolate and plum flavours." Drink now.

Township 7 Vineyards
RESERVE 7

Shortly after buying Township 7 Vineyards in 2006 from founders Corey and Gwen Coleman, Mike Raffan decided to add a flagship reserve red to the winery's portfolio. A former restaurateur (as were his partners), Mike understood the value of a prestige wine. He had inherited a capable winemaker, Brad Cooper, and grape contracts with good growers. He challenged the winemaker: "How do we go about making a high-performance red, the best of what we can do?"

The 2006 Okanagan vintage was one of the decade's best. When the wines had aged in barrel, Brad began the arduous task of identifying the best barrels in the cellar. The blend for the first Reserve 7 was selected from those barrels, a technique still employed by Township 7 (and by most producers of iconic reds).

That first vintage was released in 2008 with a label by Robb Dunfield, a quadriplegic Vancouver painter who became prominent in the early 1990s when Calona Vineyards began using his art on its labels. Township 7 contributed part of the proceeds from its first Reserve 7 to the Rick Hansen Foundation.

Fruit from the 6-hectare (15-acre) Blue Terrace Vineyard gives Reserve 7 its backbone and its consistency. Located on Tuc El Nuit Drive northeast of Oliver, it was planted in 1998 with Merlot, Cabernet Sauvignon, and Sauvignon Blanc. Township 7 began buying Blue Terrace grapes in 2000. Andy Marsel, the owner, subsequently planted and then sold a similar-sized vineyard nearby in a former gravel pit.

Now called Rock Pocket, it also supplies fruit for Township 7.

"It is at the north end of Black Sage Road," Mike says. "We are starting to identify that as a unique micro area. The biggest reason is that it is gravel, as opposed to the south end of Black Sage Road, which is all sand." Township 7 also buys Merlot from the Remuda Vineyard near Okanagan Falls and Cabernet Sauvignon (among other varieties) from Vanessa Vineyard in the Similkameen Valley. The winery's estate vineyard in Penticton provides a little Merlot as well as Malbec and Petit Verdot. The wine from the latter block of interplanted vines seldom exceeds a barrel in volume but is important in the spice jar of flavours for the Reserve 7 blend. Depending on the vintage, Reserve 7 has been anchored around Merlot or Cabernet Sauvignon. Merlot will likely play the leading role in the future because it ripens more reliably. In terms of volume, Reserve 7 will probably be limited to 500 or 600 cases a year.

Ontario-born Mary McDermott succeeded Brad in 2014 as Township 7's winemaker, bringing experience that should raise the bar further with Reserve 7 and its companions in the portfolio. A graduate of Brock University's winemaking program, Mary has worked at three top Ontario wineries: Stratus Vineyards, Cave Spring Cellars, and, from 2010 to 2014, Trius Winery. She brings techniques learned in producing the iconic Trius Grand Red, which currently sells for double the price of Reserve 7.

2013 ($37.99)

Merlot 60%, Cabernet Sauvignon 35%, Cabernet Franc 3%, Malbec 1%, Petit Verdot 1%. Alcohol 13%. Aged 24 months in French and American oak barrels. Production 468 cases.

WINERY TASTING NOTES "This blend is bursting with black cherry, eucalyptus, and lavender aromas. A robust wine, this vintage shows lingonberries, cherries, cedar box, and cocoa on the palate." Drink by 2025.

2012

Merlot 70%, Cabernet Sauvignon 11%, Malbec 11%, Cabernet Franc 5.5%, Petit Verdot 2.5%. Alcohol 13.5%. Aged 22 months in French and American oak barrels. Production 488 cases.

WINERY TASTING NOTES "This vintage has black cherry, sage, and fresh ground pepper in the nose. The palate shows cherry, boysenberry, hoisin, and cedar box. The texture displays great balance between the acidity and the tannins." Drink by 2024.

2011

Merlot 42%, Cabernet Sauvignon 38%, Cabernet Franc 12%, Malbec and Petit Verdot a combined 8%. Alcohol 13.8%. Unfiltered. Aged 24 months in French oak barrels. Production 328 cases.

WINERY TASTING NOTES "This vintage . . . shows great red berry presence and aromatics of cherry, vanilla, fall leaves and warm savoury spice." AUTHOR'S TASTING NOTES "It begins dramatically with aromas of spicy red fruit and chocolate. Firm but rich in texture, it has flavours of black cherry, blackberry, and licorice. As it breathes, the wine opens to offer a pleasing spoonful of sweet fruit to the palate." Drink by 2020.

2010

Cabernet Sauvignon 70%, Merlot 15%, Malbec and Petit Verdot a combined 15%. Alcohol 14.2%. Aged close to 30 months in French and American oak. Production 118 cases.

WINERY TASTING NOTES "The rich black cherry, chocolate and leather showcased in the Cabernet Sauvignon is made more interesting and complex in the true Bordeaux-style blend form, with cherry pie and sweet spice provided by the other varietals." Drink by 2021.

2009

Cabernet Sauvignon 55%, Merlot 43%, Malbec 2%. Alcohol 14.2%. Aged 22 months in French oak barrels. Production 118 cases.

WINERY TASTING NOTES "Bold bouquet of caramel, cherry, and Christmas spice. Flavours of cassis, cherry, cocoa, and cedar [with] hints of vanilla and toffee." Drink by 2019.

2008

Merlot 75%, Cabernet Sauvignon 17%, Cabernet Franc 8%. Alcohol 14.2%. Aged 25 months in French and American oak barrels. Production 217 cases.

WINERY TASTING NOTES "A rich and intense nose of red currant, toffee, and tea spices. This traditional Bordeaux-style blend opens with dark cherry and pomegranate flavours with undertones of cassis, cocoa, and cedar." Drink by 2018.

2007

Cabernet Sauvignon 55%, Merlot 40%, Cabernet Franc 5%. Alcohol 13.7%. Production 122 cases.

WINERY TASTING NOTES "Aromas of berry, vanilla, and spice . . . The palate is rich, with dark cherry, cassis, liquorice, and chocolate notes." Drink now.

2006

Cabernet Sauvignon 54%, Merlot 45%, Cabernet Franc 1%. Alcohol 13.9%. Aged in 60% American oak, 40% French oak. Production 200 cases.

WINERY TASTING NOTES "On the palate there are bold flavours of blackcurrant and cherry with subtle cedar and tobacco leaf on the finish. The nose has hints of liquorice, bell pepper and baked plums." Drink now.

Unsworth Vineyards

SYMPHONY

Unsworth Vineyards, in the south Cowichan Valley, opened in 2011 with just two wines: a Pinot Gris and Symphony, which is now emerging as the winery's flagship red. The initial vintages of Symphony were blends of equal parts Merlot from the Okanagan and Cabernet Libre from the Cowichan.

Those wines were well received. However, winemaker Daniel Cosman's enthusiasm for them was muted because they did not fully reflect the Cowichan terroir. It was only in the 2012 vintage that the maturing Unsworth vineyard provided enough fruit for a red made of grapes just from that vineyard. With the 2013 and 2014 blends aging in barrel, Symphony has become a collectible big red made entirely with hybrid Cabernet Libre grapes created by Swiss plant breeder Valentin Blattner.

The quality of Symphony will help validate the Blattner hybrids now being planted in numerous coastal vineyards. This began following a 2000 meeting between Paul Troop, a Salt Spring Island winemaker and viticulturist, and Valentin Blattner. The Swiss breeder had released 2,800 of his disease-resistant varieties for trials in 1998 at an Ontario nursery. Paul believed the vines might succeed in coastal British Columbia. He secured about 500 varieties to assess at his Salt Spring nursery. Subsequently, Daniel partnered with Paul and arranged for the planting of commercial quantities of promising Blattner varieties at several winery vineyards.

One of those was Unsworth, where he persuaded the owners, Tim and Colleen Turyk, to plant 2 hectares (5 acres) of Blattners after the Turyks bought this 13-hectare (32-acre) farm near Shawnigan Lake in 2010. They hedged their bets by also planting Pinot Gris and Pinot Noir.

The initial vintages of Symphony were blended primarily so that the winery could offer a red wine in the tasting room. That also gave Daniel time to refine viticultural and winemaking techniques for the Blattners until he hit upon an effective blend in 2012.

"It does not stand alone," he says of Cabernet Libre, a cross with Cabernet Sauvignon in its parentage. "I never expected it to. It has been a game of trying to subdue the negative flavours and encouraging the positive flavours. I am working with blending components to make it as close to a Chinon as I could possibly make it." Petit Milo, a white variety, provided crucial fruitiness and higher alcohol in the blend.

Daniel describes the characteristics of Cabernet Libre that are the foundation of the blend. "It has this floral component of violets, which I find compelling," he says. "And it smells like cherry, it tastes like cherry. That kind of fruit backbone is hard to get, no matter where you grow the fruit." Development was turned over in 2015 to Brock University–trained winemaker Dan Wright when Daniel, now the consulting winemaker, returned to maple-syrup farming in his native Quebec.

2014 ($25)

Cabernet Libre 85%, Petit Milo 15%. Alcohol 13.1%. Aged 23 months in French oak. Production 190 cases.

WINERY TASTING NOTES "Full-bodied, mahogany in colour. On the nose, aromas of cooked cherries, caramel, and vanilla give way to deep earthy flavours of dried fig, cedar, and subtle spice on the palate." Drink by 2024.

2012

Cabernet Libre 85%, Petit Milo 15%. Alcohol 13.7%. Aged 24 months in French oak. Production 160 cases.

TASTING NOTES by Daniel Cosman: "Full-bodied, mahogany in colour. On the nose, aromas of cooked cherries, caramel, and vanilla give way to deep earthy flavours of dried fig, cedar, and subtle spice on the palate." Drink by 2020.

2011

Cabernet Libre 50%, Merlot 50%.

TASTING NOTES from the dining room at Butchart Gardens' wine list: "This medium-bodied blend is great with food or on its own. Aromas of cooked red fruit give way to flavours of plum, cherry, and spice." Drink now.

2010

Cabernet Libre 50%, Merlot 50%.

WINERY TASTING NOTES "Mid-weight ruby red. [The wine] offers aromas of cooked red fruit and hints of resonant herbs that give way to deep, rich flavours of plum, ripe cherries, and subtle spice." Drink now.

2009

Cabernet Libre 50%, Merlot 50%.

AUTHOR'S TASTING NOTES "Deep in colour, the wine begins with the dusty, smoky aroma typical of Cabernet Libre. On the palate, the rich, sweet berry flavours of Merlot take over." Drink now.

Upper Bench Winery & Creamery

ESTATE MERLOT

The dilemma Upper Bench Winery presents for collectors is this: Should they choose the Estate Merlot or the Estate Cabernet Sauvignon?

This author believes that Merlot will ripen more consistently in this Penticton vineyard than Cabernet Sauvignon. "I beg to differ," says Gavin Miller, the co-proprietor who grows the grapes and makes the wine. But then in a tasting, he calls Cabernet Sauvignon "the heartbreak grape of the Okanagan . . . but when done properly and cropped correctly, it can be stunning." Later at the same tasting, he admits that "Merlot is what grows best on our site." Hence, my choice.

Gavin is a bit of a Renaissance man who is a sculptor as well as a vintner. Born in Britain in 1965, he was a sales manager in London when he came to Penticton on vacation in 1995. After meeting Shana, now his wife, in Canada, he returned to the Okanagan permanently in 1997. He spent a year as a sign maker and sculptor before studying viticulture. He started his wine career in the vineyard at Lake Breeze, then the cellars at Hawthorne Mountain Vineyards and the tasting room at Sumac Ridge. He became assistant wine-maker at Red Rooster and later worked at Poplar Grove and then at Painted Rock, departing after the 2010 vintage. Shortly after, he teamed up with businessman Wayne Nystrom to buy the bankrupt

Stonehill winery. It resumed production in 2011 as Upper Bench Winery & Creamery; the latter refers to Shana's cheese-making facilities, which were added to the winery.

One of Upper Bench's strengths is its mature vineyard. The winery's original owner planted it between 1998 and 2001 with Riesling, Pinot Blanc, Chardonnay, Pinot Noir, Merlot, Cabernet Sauvignon, and Zweigelt. That last one may be Austria's leading red variety, but it is difficult to sell in Canada. Accordingly, Gavin has grafted half of the one-hectare Zweigelt block to Cabernet Sauvignon.

He produces reds that are fully ripe with juicy concentration by paying close attention to cropping levels. The Estate Merlot is cropped at 3.4 tons per acre, while the Estate Cabernet Sauvignon is cropped at just over three tons per acre. My bias toward the Estate Merlot is based on the figures Gavin reported from the 2012 harvest, a fine vintage. The Merlot grapes were picked on October 7 and produced a big wine with 14.5% alcohol. The Cabernet Sauvignon grapes were picked almost a month later and produced an elegant wine with 13% alcohol. The question is, what ripeness would the vineyard deliver in a cool vintage? However, the answer may not matter that much, given Gavin's expertise at managing both varieties in his vineyard.

2013 ($38)

Merlot. Alcohol 14.9%. Aged 20 months in French oak (30% new). Production 116 cases.

WINERY TASTING NOTES "Nose: black cherry, opulent fruit, cedar, chocolate. Palate: Rainier cherry, blackcurrant, pomegranate, menthol." Drink by 2023.

2012

Merlot. Alcohol 14.5%. Cropped at 3.4 tons per acre, fermented in 700-litre wooden vats, and then aged 20 months in French oak barrels (30% new). Production 154 cases.

WINERY TASTING NOTES "Nose: vanilla, milk chocolate, black pepper, cigar box, black cherry, plum. Palate: Red and black currant, baking spice, mocha, cocoa." Drink by 2022.

Vanessa Vineyard
MERITAGE

This 30-hectare (75-acre) Similkameen Valley vineyard was developed on exceptionally rocky raw land. To prepare it for planting in 2006, the vineyard managers brought in a rock crusher more appropriate, perhaps, to a quarry. The machine wore out two sets of teeth while pulverizing the rock. It is not surprising that the red wines from this vineyard have a spine of minerality that should contribute to their longevity.

The specifications released with the first wines outline this terroir: "The vines grow in rows of rocks, stressing the plants, absorbing the day heat and imparting that warmth during the cooler nights. This gives the grapes their unique and complex character. The west to southwest exposure on which the rocky vineyard sits benefits from the afternoon sun, which contributes to lengthening the growing season and producing low yields of intensely ripe fruit."

Proprietors John Welson and Suki Sekhon did not necessarily have a winery in mind when they bought this property in 2005. Suki is a successful Vancouver developer, while John is a retired stockbroker who is passionate about wine. In his Vancouver business, Suki constructs buildings that are leased to clients. He thought he could develop a vineyard and then lease it to a winery. That is not the wine industry's usual business model. Wineries need to know the quality of the grapes before committing to buying them. When the vineyard produced fruit, Suki and John began selling grapes to Andrew Peller Ltd., the owner of nearby Rocky Ridge Vineyard and also Sandhill Wines. In 2010, Howard Soon, the Sandhill winemaker, added a Vanessa Cabernet Merlot blend made with their grapes to his portfolio of single-vineyard wines.

That wine helped encourage John and Suki to open a boutique winery. "We kind of went into this initially, basically to build a vineyard, and then, as you get into it, the industry just pulls you along," John admits. They arranged to have Howard's colleague, Red Rooster winemaker Karen Gillis, make their initial vintages, beginning with 440 cases of Meritage and 186 cases of Syrah in 2012. This grew to a total of about 3,000 cases in 2014. The intent is to plateau at that level of production of premium wines while continuing to sell grapes.

Except for two acres of Viognier, the Vanessa Vineyard is planted entirely to sun-loving reds: Syrah, Cabernet Sauvignon, Cabernet Franc, and Merlot. Suki had concluded that it is one of the warmest sites in the sunbathed Similkameen and is best suited for red varietals. He will find a cooler site if he and John decide they need white wines in their portfolio.

Old maps show that an easement for a stagecoach road from Osoyoos to Princeton ran by the property. For a time, the partners considered calling the winery Stagecoach Road or Old Stagecoach Road. In the end, they opted for Vanessa, the name of Suki's eldest daughter.

2013 ($36)

Cabernet Sauvignon 44%, Cabernet Franc 32%, Merlot 24%. Alcohol 14%. Production 625 cases.

WINERY TASTING NOTES "A rich Cabernet-based cuvée, our 2013 Meritage is full-bodied and intense, yet elegant and feminine. A wine with excellent structure and concentrated flavour, this vintage is garnet red in the glass and has gorgeous floral aromas with delicate herbaceous undertones. The ripe, silky tannins are balanced by fresh cherry, dark berry, coffee, and licorice flavours. The fruit and oak are particularly well integrated with a smooth, lingering finish." Drink by 2025.

2012

Cabernet Sauvignon 50%, Merlot 27%, Cabernet Franc 23%. Alcohol 14.2%. Production 440 cases.

WINERY TASTING NOTES "Deep purple in colour, the wine gives off a rich bouquet of dark fruits, floral aromas, and notes of sweet tobacco. This Cabernet-based blend is full-bodied and intense [with] concentrated flavours [of] dark berries, fig jam, and cocoa notes . . . over silky tannins and minerality from the soil. The fruit and the oak are particularly well integrated. The long finish shows baking spices, cinnamon and cardamom, and sweet vanilla." Drink by 2024.

Van Westen Vineyards

V, VOLUPTUOUS

The particular conceit of Van Westen Vineyards is that the name of each of its wines must start with the letter V. When Robert Van Westen began making his first two-variety Bordeaux-style blend in 2003, he called it Voluptuous. When he added a second blend in 2009, he called it V, the Roman numeral for five, because it includes five Bordeaux red varietals.

Voluptuous is a single-vineyard wine. The grapes are grown on Robert's 1.6-hectare (4-acre) Boothe Road Vineyard, planted in 1999 near the village of Naramata. The site is a natural amphitheatre with a southern aspect that captures more heat units than many other Naramata Bench sites. The terroir is well suited to making a ripe wine aptly called Voluptuous.

The wine is always a two-grape blend. "That's how the vineyard was planted," Robert explains. "That vineyard is planted two-thirds Merlot, one-third Cabernet Franc." It was a number of years before he was able to source the three other varieties needed to make V. All the fruit is from vineyards near Naramata that the Van Westen family owns or manages.

The family—Robert's father, Jake, emigrated from the Netherlands in 1954—has farmed in the Naramata area since 1974. "We are still 70 percent committed to tree fruits," Robert says. "We are the largest cherry growers on the Naramata Bench." He quickly adds that he does not intend to make cherry wine, if only because the eating cherries lack the necessary balance of sugar and acidity found in grapes.

Robert learned winemaking by studying at Okanagan College and mentoring with other Okanagan winemakers. Experience has led to a refinement in the style of Voluptuous. The first three vintages received extended post-ferment maceration. Because that made the wine more tannic than he thought desirable, he switched to a pre-fermentation cold soak of the grapes, with the wine pressed just as fermentation is ending. "I like to finish the fermentation in tank now," he says. "It makes life simpler. We have enough tannin and enough structure in the wine."

"We have cut back on the amount of new oak," Robert continues. "It used to be as high as 35 percent. Now it is closer to 25 percent. People want a little less of the smoke and oak and a little more fruit in their glass. We also keep it in barrel a little longer." Barrel-aging has been extended to around 20 months, compared with 15 months in the early vintages. Hence, the wine on release is more polished.

Voluptuous and V are structured to still be satisfying at 10 years and perhaps longer. In 2015, after completing inventory in the winery, Robert opened a bottle of Voluptuous 2005. "There is still life left in it," he says. "I wouldn't mind if people cellared the 2005 longer. And I think the 2010 is something I can drink with my granddaughter."

Voluptuous 2013 ($29.90)

Merlot 67%, Cabernet Franc 33%. Alcohol 14.6%. Aged 18–24 months in French oak (one-third new). Production 452 cases.

WINERY TASTING NOTES "A fantastically integrated and intense wine with a complex blueberry, cassis, and plum, with an interesting side of pastry crust, violet, burlap, and pepper. The palate has elegance and freshness while also being bold and rich. The complex mix of dark fruits, savoury cedar, cigar, leather, and spice make for a wonderful long finish." Drink by 2023.

V 2012

Merlot 45%, Cabernet Franc 26%, Malbec 17%, Cabernet Sauvignon 7%, Petit Verdot 5%. Alcohol 14.3%. Production 346 cases.

WINERY TASTING NOTES "Our fourth vintage of this Bordeaux blend has created a complex and intense wine not only to be enjoyed now, but is also built to age. The nose is full with liqueur chocolate cherry, cassis, cocoa, paprika, roasted meat, and a hint of black olive and burlap. The palate is full-bodied, dense, and structured with ripe blackberry, Italian plum, and violets, along with lots of savoury pipe tobacco, clove, charred meat, graphite, and spice." Drink by 2024.

V 2011 ($34.90)

Merlot 49%, Malbec 24%, Cabernet Franc 21%, Cabernet Sauvignon 4%, Petit Verdot 2%. Production 426 cases.

WINERY TASTING NOTES "An intense and savoury wine combining spicy and peppery notes with plum, burlap, dried wild Okanagan sage, and complex cocoa, vanilla, marzipan, and pie crust aromas. The palate is built to age with crisp acidity and firm tannins that will resolve with

two to three years in the cellar to reveal all the cassis, plum, sage, mineral, cocoa, sun-dried tomato, and complex violet notes that lurk beneath." Drink by 2023.

V 2010

Merlot 61%, Malbec 23%, Cabernet Franc 12%, Cabernet Sauvignon 3.6%, Petit Verdot 0.4%. Production 314 cases.

WINERY TASTING NOTES "The nose is like perfectly baked cassis, blackberry, and mulberry pie along with subtle bacon and sweet tobacco. The concentrated and lively palate sings with juicy blackberry, sweet brambly fruit, prune plum, black olive, dusty cocoa, and lingering dried sage flavours." Drink by 2022.

V 2009

Merlot 68%, Cabernet Franc 25%, Malbec 5.6%, Cabernet Sauvignon 1%, Petit Verdot 0.4%. Production 301 cases.

WINERY TASTING NOTES "Elegant yet intense with aromas of plums, currants, orange zest, nut, and chocolate overlaying blueberry and vanilla. The refined palate harmoniously brings together blackberry, plum, blueberry, clove, and allspice with a savoury pastry note that lingers on the finish." Drink by 2020.

Voluptuous 2012

Merlot 67%, Cabernet Franc 33%. Alcohol 14.5%. Aged 20 months in French oak (30% new). Production 341 cases.

WINERY TASTING NOTES "An age worthy, complex, and evolving wine with blackberry, blueberry, violets, black plum, dark chocolate, and paprika on the nose. The palate is youthful with an elegant texture, crisp acidity, and intense black fruits, leather, pepper, and dried sage that will develop beautifully over the next decade." Drink by 2022.

Voluptuous 2011

Merlot 67%, Cabernet Franc 33%. Production 319 cases.

WINERY TASTING NOTES "A wine that evolves constantly in your glass. First mulberry, then damson plum and cherry before the burlap, clove, and cinnamon, finishing with black olive and dried herb aromas. The palate shows structure to develop for years along with intense flavours of prune plum, dried cherry tomato, Saskatoon berry, shortbread, graphite, cocoa, and salty liquorice with underlying burlap, dried herbs, and orange zest that mingle on a very long finish." Drink by 2021.

Voluptuous 2010

Merlot 67%, Cabernet Franc 33%. Production 218 cases.

WINERY TASTING NOTES "Elegance and ageability. Complex aromas of ripe prune plum, blueberry, dried herbs, dusty burlap, tobacco, and bacon lead to an intense and structured palate with great tannin and acidity for aging. The palate constantly evolves through flavours of plum, cherry, sage, cocoa, and graphite that persist into a long mineral finish." Drink by 2020.

Voluptuous 2009

Merlot 67%, Cabernet Franc 33%. Production 204 cases.

WINERY TASTING NOTES "A concentrated nose of prune plums, cassis, raspberry, coffee, Terry's Chocolate Orange and clove. The velvety, rich palate is intensely flavoured with blackberry, ripe black cherry, charred meat, grilled herbs, pepper and a graphite and espresso finish of great length." Drink by 2020.

Voluptuous 2008

Merlot 67%, Cabernet Franc 33%. Production 492 cases.

WINERY TASTING NOTES "A concentrated nose of prune plums, cassis, raspberry, coffee, Terry's Chocolate Orange, and clove. The velvety, rich palate is intensely flavoured with blackberry, ripe black cherry, charred meat, grilled herbs, pepper and a graphite and espresso finish of great length." Drink by 2020.

Voluptuous 2007

Merlot 67%, Cabernet Franc 33%. Production 460 cases.

WINERY TASTING NOTES "Built for aging with structured, ripe tannins and intensity and complexity. Aromas of cassis, damson plum, burlap, chocolate, and orange lead to a full and rich palate of chocolate-covered cherry, brown sugar, mineral, sage brush, coffee, and cassis." Drink by 2019.

Voluptuous 2006

Merlot 67%, Cabernet Franc 33%. Barrel-aged for 18 months in French oak (30% new). Production 630 cases.

WINERY TASTING NOTES "This full-bodied blend is built for aging with structured, ripe tannins giving it intensity and complexity. Tannins start filling the mouth in a distinguished chocolate cassis and rich plum coating . . . chocolate and red fruit such as a succulent covered cherry, brown sugar, mineral, sagebrush, and coffee finishes the well-rounded Old World-style wine." Drink by 2018.

Voluptuous 2005

Merlot 67%, Cabernet Franc 33%. Aged 18 months in French oak (30% new). Production 460 cases.

WINERY TASTING NOTES "This full-bodied blend shows warm dark fruit aromas of plum, cassis, and blueberry laced with chocolate, vanillin, and spice. Tannins coat the mouth in a dusty, cocoa-like texture, forming the background for the complex spice, chocolate, and red fruit flavours. A long, toasty finish completes the seduction of the senses." Drink now.

Venturi-Schulze Vineyards

PINOT NOIR

Collectors who prize wines of originality need look no further than Venturi-Schulze Vineyards in the Cowichan Valley on Vancouver Island. Here, Marilyn Venturi (née Schulze) and Giordano Venturi handcraft intriguing artisanal wines and christen them with charming Italian names. Their aromatic blend of Siegerrebe and Ortega is called Millefiori, meaning a thousand flowers. Other wines are called Primavera, Piccolo, Sassi, and Maranello. The latter, the home of Ferrari, is close to Giordano's birthplace in Italy. For long-term cellaring, however, one chooses the winery's Pinot Noir.

Giordano, who was born in 1941, came to Canada in 1967 and became an electronics teacher. A doctor's daughter, Marilyn was born in Australia in 1951 and immigrated to Canada in 1970. With a degree in microbiology, she also became a teacher. Both found the teaching profession stressful. In 1988, they moved to a Cowichan Valley farm, refurbished the 1893 farmhouse, and began planting vines.

The original planting included just 10 Pinot Noir vines. The nursery did not identify the clone; Giordano believes it is the one the Germans call Spätburgunder. It had been introduced earlier to the Okanagan. "In 1992, we had such incredible success with Pinot Noir because we had budburst in March," Giordano recalls. "We said maybe there is a chance for Pinot Noir, so we started propagating." And they secured additional clones from Oregon State University: Clone 113, the Mariafeld clone, and the Jackson clone.

The Cowichan Valley's growing season is not always long enough to ripen Pinot Noir adequately. Giordano and Marilyn solved that problem in 1998 when they became the region's first winery to tent Pinot Noir. When the vines start growing in the spring, they are covered for up to a month with plastic tents. The greenhouse conditions accelerate plant growth so that the grapes ripen well before the valley's late October rains. In 2003, Venturi-Schulze even overdid it, ripening the Pinot Noir to an astonishing 15.4 percent alcohol, a good two percent above what Giordano considers ideal. They had a similar result a few years later, acquiring a reputation for producing powerful Pinot Noirs.

The winery began making Pinot Noir with more elegance and less extraction in the 2008 vintage, the result of both new equipment and new ideas. A new crusher enabled Giordano to handle the grapes more gently and introduce whole clusters into the fermentation. And he revised some of his winemaking techniques while doing Master of Wine coursework. "It gave me a chance to rub shoulders with incredible people," he says. "I learned quite a few things."

Venturi-Schulze makes just eight to 12 barrels of Pinot Noir each year. So far, reserves have been released in just three vintages: 2006, 2008, and 2009. "It has to be a really special year," Giordano insists. The Pinot Noirs can all age for 10 years or longer.

Pinot Noir 2012 ($45)

Alcohol 13.3%.

WINERY TASTING NOTES "Our 2012 Pinot Noir is characterized by juicy cherry and boysenberry fruit characters with a hint of cinnamon spice. Ageing in two- and three-year-old French oak barrels [Nevers oak] enhanced the development of the wine's smooth 'sweet' tannins." Drink by 2020.

Pinot Noir 2011

Alcohol 14.2%.

WINERY TASTING NOTES "Our Pinot Noir from the cool 2011 season is bursting with lively cherry and berry fruit character. Ageing in two- and three-year-old Nevers French oak barrels enhanced development of its smooth, ripe tannins and contributed to its subtle spice overtones." Drink by 2019.

Pinot Noir 2009

Alcohol 14.5%.

WINERY TASTING NOTES "The 2009 Pinot Noir is a blockbuster [with] rich dark fruit, ripe tannins, and minerality integrated with subtle vanilla and spice from a year in Nevers French oak." Drink by 2019.

Pinot Noir Reserve 2009 ($60)

Aged 2 years in Nevers French oak barrels.

WINERY TASTING NOTES "Selectively harvested from the best exposed slope in our vineyard, the 2009 Pinot Noir Reserve combines four rare clones. The wine from this extremely hot vintage was carefully crafted to showcase the intense fruit character and spice so typical of our terroir. [It has] a seamless, complex, and elegant palate." Drink by 2019.

Pinot Noir Reserve 2008

Alcohol 14.2%. Production 50 cases.

WINERY TASTING NOTES "The 2008 Pinot Noir combines four rare clones. The very cool partial whole-cluster fermentation produced bright fruit characters, while two years in one- and two-year-old French oak barrels resulted in a smooth, complex palate." Drink by 2018.

Wild Goose Vineyards
STONEY SLOPE RIESLING

Hagen Kruger remembers feeling mortified when he was helping his father, Adolf, plant the Stoney Slope Vineyard in 1984. "The neighbours would drive by and yell out, 'Where's the soil?'" he remembers. "And then they would laugh and keep on going." This half-hectare slope is so rugged that a small pit was dug for each Riesling vine. The roots were covered with shovels full of earth and rocks. But when the irrigation was turned on, the vines flourished and produced superb mineral-driven dry Riesling wines.

This is not unusual in the world of Riesling. Some years later, Hagen and his brother Roland visited Germany's Mosel Valley, where many of the world's best Riesling wines are grown. "I was amazed when we looked down the valley and there was no soil!" Hagen says. "It was rock—it was slate and shale. I said to Roland, 'How do these vines grow here?' That brings me back to Wild Goose. I always tell people that this is the closest you will get to the Mosel outside of Germany."

Adolf Kruger acquired a taste for Riesling in his native Germany before immigrating to Vancouver in 1951. He pursued careers in engineering and boat design while nurturing a love of wine as a home vintner. In 1983, he purchased vineyard land in countryside near Okanagan Falls so unspoiled that wild geese still nested there. He planted just Gewürztraminer and Riesling, propagating cuttings obtained from a Sumac Ridge vineyard planted in 1981. The Wild Goose winery opened in 1990. Dry Riesling wines were out of fashion in the 1990s; Wild Goose discontinued making dry Riesling from Stoney Slope grapes in 1995, only resuming production in 2001.

Hagen, after mentoring with his father (who died in 2016), had taken over as winemaker in 1998. He is naturally talented—Wild Goose is among the most awarded Okanagan wineries. He supplemented gaps in his training with winemaking consultants, which has been especially fortunate on occasion. He happened to employ a young French winemaker, a Sauternes specialist, in 2004 when Wild Goose had botrytis in its vineyard for the first time. In 2013, on the second occasion this happened, he was employing a Geisenheim University graduate, Florian Limpur, who had expertise in making noble rot wines. "I love getting these guys here because I can just pick their brains and find out what is new out there," Hagen says.

Florian confirmed to Hagen that Stoney Slope is a premium Riesling site. "I said to him that I want to make the best Riesling in the world," Hagen recalls. "He looked at me and he said, 'Then you should be making it in Germany!'" Hagen, now helped by his winemaking son Nik, is reconciled to aiming for the best Riesling outside Germany.

2015 ($20)

Alcohol 12.2%. Residual sugar 18 grams per litre. Total acidity 7.7 grams per litre. 50% spontaneous fermentation; 25% fermented in barrel and aged on lees for 6 months. Production 200 cases.

WINERY TASTING NOTES "The tasting of this wine starts in the nose, with wonderful aromatics of dried apricot and apple. Intense flavours of flint, clover, and minerality, balanced with excellent crispness." Drink by 2025.

2014

Alcohol 12.8%. Residual sugar 16 grams per litre. Total acidity 7.2 grams per litre. Partial spontaneous ferment. Production 240 cases.

WINERY TASTING NOTES "The wine has flavours and aromas of citrus, lemon zest, Granny Smith apples, honey, and clover with good minerality." Drink by 2024.

2013

Alcohol 13.3%. Residual sugar 12 grams per litre. Total acidity 7.9 grams per litre. Production 420 cases.

WINERY TASTING NOTES "Crisp floral aromas are enhanced by a smell of wet stones and met with flavours of ripe green apple and minerals." Drink by 2023.

2012

Alcohol 12.5%. Residual sugar 11 grams per litre. Total acidity 7.1 grams per litre.

WINERY TASTING NOTES "The pure stone and gravel from this slope come through instantly in this wine. Mouth-watering Granny Smith apples along with minerality, honey, citrus, lime, finishing with a steely crispness." Drink by 2022.

2011

Alcohol 12.5%. Residual sugar 14 grams per litre. Total acidity 8.5 grams per litre.

AUTHOR'S TASTING NOTES "The wine has developed classic aromas and flavours of petrol, along with tangy flavours of lemon and orange rind." Drink by 2021.

2010

Alcohol 13.5%. Residual sugar 15 grams per litre. Total acidity 7.5 grams per litre.

WINERY TASTING NOTES "Spicy aromas of Red Delicious apple along with an earthy minerality, peach and mangoes, finishing with a steely crispness." Drink by 2020.

2009

Alcohol 13.5%. Residual sugar 15 grams per litre. Total acidity 7.5 grams per litre. Tasting notes unavailable.

2007

Alcohol 13.3%.

AUTHOR'S TASTING NOTES "The wine has developed in the bottle a texture with a polished sheen. There are aromas of petrol and orange rind with flavours recalling very good marmalade. The finish is dry." Drink now.

Young & Wyse Collection

BLACK SHEEP

Stephen Wyse, who runs this Osoyoos winery with his wife, Michelle Young, comes from one of the Okanagan's founding wine families. Jim Wyse, his father, launched Burrowing Owl Estate Winery in 1997. That winery is now run by Stephen's older brother Chris.

Born in 1967, Stephen came into wine as a project manager during the construction of the Burrowing Owl winery. From there, he moved to the cellar, becoming winemaker when his mentor, Bill Dyer, left in 2004. Stephen resigned three vintages later to work independently from his family. In 2008, he and Michelle bought a 4-hectare (10-acre) orchard, which they converted to vineyard.

But for a trademark issue, the winery might have been called Black Sheep. "We knew people would be asking why I left the family business," Stephen explains. "It is such a great winery. So we said, 'Because we are the black sheep, of course.' It is just a little spoof." The name, instead, was used for the winery's blended red, starting with the 2010 vintage.

The first blended red in this line was made in 2009 and released as Black Label, with just the percentages of the varietals on the label. It changed to Black Sheep in 2011 when Stephen and Michelle realized the debut label reminded consumers of the numerals on bags of fertilizer.

Collectors will note that Stephen builds the wine around Merlot and Cabernet Sauvignon but keeps other blending options flexible. He also keeps Merlot and Cabernet Sauvignon as stand-alone wines in his portfolio. "It's nice to have people recognize a single variety as well," he says. "It is nice to pick up a Cabernet Sauvignon and say, 'Good, there's a Cabernet Sauvignon, there's that nose I recognize.'"

Cabernet Sauvignon and Malbec grapes are co-fermented because the varieties share a block in the Young & Wyse vineyard. The reds are all barrel-aged for 18 to 20 months before the Black Sheep blend is assembled. "I don't take all of the absolutely best barrels because I keep some of the barrels I really like for single varietals," Stephen says. "I try to make a nice, balanced blend. I like to layer it, so that in the end, you have something that is very harmonious."

Black Sheep 2012 ($31.90)

Cabernet Sauvignon 55%, Merlot 34%, Malbec 11%.

WINERY TASTING NOTES "This luscious wine from Y&W has aromas of ripe raspberry and bold black cherry, complemented by hints of dark chocolate, tobacco, espresso, and spice. Richly layered with fine-grained tannins conveying gorgeous fruit through a long finish." Drink by 2022.

Black Sheep 2011

Cabernet Franc 40%, Merlot 30%, Cabernet Sauvignon 15%, Malbec 15%. Alcohol 14.4%. Production 1,800 cases.

WINERY TASTING NOTES "An inviting and multifaceted nose combining plum and blueberry fruit with coffee, chocolate, tobacco, dried sage, and well-integrated oak. The palate is very intense, full in body with crisp acidity and ripe balanced tannins. Flavours run an intriguing range from juicy red berries through leather, smoked meat, pepper, cocoa, tobacco, ripe blueberry, and violet notes on the long finish." Drink by 2021.

Black Label 33.30.24.13 2009

Merlot 33%, Syrah 30%, Cabernet Sauvignon 24%, Cabernet Franc 13%. Alcohol 14.3%. Production 856 cases.

WINERY TASTING NOTES "This noble blend boasts aromas of licorice, espresso beans, and exotic spices. The texture and silkiness on the palate are seamlessly interwoven with concentrated layers of ripe tannin and fruit." Drink by 2019.

Wines to put on your radar

There are several producers for which full profiles have not been written, for various reasons—for example, the winery is relatively new or the turnover of winemakers and vineyard sources makes it difficult to assess the track record. However, if you are starting a collection, these wines are worth exploring.

ALDERLEA VINEYARDS is based on a Cowichan Valley vineyard developed since 1992 by Roger Dosman. The winery's collectible wines include Pinot Noir and a port-style wine called Heritage Hearth. The big red table wine, made with Maréchal Foch, is sold under a proprietary name because, Roger has said, "It is too good to be called Foch."

Clarinet 2011 ($22)

Maréchal Foch. Aged in French oak. Alcohol 13.5%.

WINERY TASTING NOTES "Dark, ripe, and full-bodied, concentrated aromas of sweet blackberries and a hint of coffee followed by full fruit flavours and a touch of black pepper on the finish."

ANARCHIST MOUNTAIN VINEYARD is an artisanal winery established by Andrew Stone and Terry Meyer Stone. It is based on a small vineyard on Anarchist Mountain, high above Osoyoos, with some vines planted as early as 1985. The two took over the property in 2010 and have produced small lots of sophisticated Chardonnay and Pinot Noir.

Wildfire Pinot Noir 2013 ($35)

Clone 115. Alcohol 14%. Aged in French oak. Production 90 cases.

WINERY TASTING NOTES "The fruit typically expresses itself as cherry with white pepper and reflects the unique Anarchist Mountain terroir." Drink by 2020.

Wildfire Pinot Noir 2012

Clone 115. Alcohol 14%. Aged in French oak. Production 70 cases.

WINERY TASTING NOTES "Cropped to less than 2 tons per acre, it yields deep cherry and vanilla flavours." Drink by 2019.

ANCIENT HILL ESTATE WINERY opened in 2011 near Kelowna International Airport, on one of the most historic vineyard sites in the Okanagan. Here, owner Richard Kamphuys planted varieties he judged well suited to the cool terroir. He has succeeded particularly well with Baco Noir, reviving the reputation of this full-bodied French hybrid red variety.

Baco Noir 2012 ($25)

Aged in barrel. Production 1,000 cases.

WINERY TASTING NOTES "Bursting with dark, rich fruits. Black cherry, plum, spicy, chocolate, vanilla, and butterscotch on the nose. Soft but rich mouthfeel with powerful flavours." Drink by 2018.

⸻

BC WINE STUDIO at Okanagan Falls, as a custom crush winery, has incubated several boutique producers since 2011. However, winemaker Mark Simpson also produces collectible wines under his own Siren's Call label. The winery's big red blend is called Harmonious.

Siren's Call Harmonius 2012 ($35)

Merlot 39%, Cabernet Sauvignon 21%, Cabernet Franc 16%, Malbec 14%, Petit Verdot 6%, Syrah 4%. Alcohol 13.6%.

WINERY TASTING NOTES "Our wines are cultivated from notes of sophistication and unquestionable beauty, with daily punchdowns and 20+ days of skin contact to extract a rich array of soft tannins, big tannins, and fruit notes. Each red has been fermented separately, and lovingly tended with daily punch-downs and 20 days of skin contact to extract a rich array of soft tannins."

Siren's Call Harmonious 2011

Merlot 39%, Cabernet Sauvignon 21%, Cabernet Franc 16%, Malbec 14%, Petit Verdot 6%, Syrah 4%. Alcohol 13.6%.

AUTHOR'S TASTING NOTES "This is a medium-bodied wine with bright aromas of cherry and vanilla leading to spicy, black cherry flavours. The silky tannins make this wine appealing and approachable."

Siren's Call Harmonious 2010

Merlot 39%, Cabernet Franc 20%, Cabernet Sauvignon 20%, Malbec 12%, Petit Verdot 9%. Alcohol 14.1%.

AUTHOR'S TASTING NOTES "This is a blend of the five major Bordeaux red varietals. It is aptly named; the varietals flavours do not override each other but come together in a seamless fashion. Dark in colour, the wine begins with aromas of spice (celery salt) and red berries. The palate presents flavours of blackberry, currants, cherry, and plum."

⸻

BORDERTOWN VINEYARDS & ESTATE WINERY opened in 2015, getting its name from being just north of Osoyoos, the Okanagan town a stone's throw from the border between Canada and the US. The winery is owned by vineyard owner Mohan Gill. Bordertown attracted attention in 2016 by winning a Lieutenant Governor's Award of Excellence in wine with this red blend.

Living Desert Red 2013

Cabernet Franc, Merlot. Alcohol 14.4%.

WINERY TASTING NOTES "It showcases aromas and flavours of red and black fruits, dark chocolate, sandalwood, and the wild herbs that grow amongst this region's vineyards." Drink by 2021.

⸻

D'ANGELO ESTATE WINERY was established in the Okanagan in 2007 by Sal D'Angelo, also the owner of a winery with the same name near Windsor, Ontario, which opened in 1989. Sal was drawn to the Okanagan, with its terroir for big reds. The flagship wine of the Okanagan winery is Sette Coppa, which means seventh measure. It was the nickname of Sal's great-grandfather, who persuaded a local mill in Italy to take as payment for its services every seventh measure of his grain, not the sixth measure that was assessed of others.

Sette Coppa 2012 ($35)

Malbec 32%, Merlot 20%, Cabernet Sauvignon 18%, Cabernet Franc 18%, Petit Verdot 12%.

WINERY TASTING NOTES "This blend is full and ripe with lots of dark fruits, showcasing red fruit with a touch of apple skin and leathery flavours." Drink by 2022.

HEAVEN'S GATE ESTATE WINERY was opened near Summerland in 2011 by Andy and Diane Sarglepp. The winery gained a following for its full-flavoured Malbec wines made with purchased grapes. Andy's Merlot also merits consideration.

Malbec 2013 ($25)

Alcohol 13.2%. Production 115 cases.

WINERY TASTING NOTES "Our Malbec has intense character showcasing flavours of lush blackberry, rich black cherry, and juicy plum with a perfumey toasted almond aroma and a velvety, floral, vanilla finish."

Merlot Malbec 2012

Merlot 77%, Malbec 23%. Alcohol 13.3%. Aged in French oak. Production 192 cases.

WINERY TASTING NOTES "Our blend of Merlot and Malbec is the perfect combination. The boldness from our Merlot together with the smoothness of our Malbec delivers a lively burst of black cherry and blackberry flavours, leaving an intense vanilla finish."

Malbec 2011

Alcohol 13.1%. Production 210 cases.

WINERY TASTING NOTES "Our velvety Malbec has intense character showcasing hints of sweet black cherry, juicy plum, and spicy sage. An explosion of berry flavours on your palate finishes with the delightful, delicate essence of soft, smooth vanilla."

Malbec 2010

WINERY TASTING NOTES "Our 2010 Malbec has intense character showcasing hints of sweet black cherry and juicy plum—leaving an explosion of flavour on your palate and a soft, smooth finish."

KISMET ESTATE WINERY was established in 2013 by Sukhwinder and Balwinder Dhaliwal, who are major grape growers in the South Okanagan; their vineyards support an extensive portfolio. They began producing Mantra, their Bordeaux blend, in the 2011 vintage.

Mantra 2014 ($35)

Merlot 30%, Cabernet Franc 20%, Cabernet Sauvignon 20%, Petit Verdot 20%, Malbec 10%. Alcohol 14.5%. Production 150 cases.

AUTHOR'S TASTING NOTES "The fruit is concentrated, with flavours of black and red currants. Long, ripe tannins give the wine weight and richness." Drink by 2024.

Mantra 2013

Cabernet Sauvignon, Malbec, Merlot, Petit Verdot. Alcohol 14.7%. Aged 11 months in French oak. Production 210 cases.

WINERY TASTING NOTES "Mantra is a well-balanced, full-bodied wine, rich in texture and weight on the palate. Dark berry fruit such as cassis and blackberry, oak and light vanilla in harmony."

MIRABEL VINEYARDS, owned by Doug and Dawn Reimer, launched in 2016 with a super-premium Pinot Noir. However, grapes from what is also called the Reimer Vineyard were also sold to the Meyer Family Estate and to Foxtrot Winery. Those wines established Reimer's Kelowna vineyard as a premier site. Doug, a member of the well-known Winnipeg trucking family, first planted the vineyard in 2006 and, encouraged by the success others have had with his grapes, started this boutique winery.

Pinot Noir 2015 ($70)

Clones 115, 667, 777. Alcohol 13.5%. Production 237 cases.

AUTHOR'S TASTING NOTES "This elegant wine was aged 11 months in barrels (30% new). Gravity was used to transfer it to barrel and then to the bottling line. The gentle handling is reflected in the silky texture of the wine, which has great purity of fruit. It begins with appealing floral and cherry aromas. On the palate, there are flavours of cherry and strawberry, with subtle hints of oak and spice. The wine has good weight on the palate, with a lingering finish."

❧

MORAINE VINEYARDS was opened in 2012 by Russian-born electrical engineer Oleg Aristarkhov and his wife, Svetlana. They completely transformed a winery that had been in receivership, recruiting New Zealand–trained Jacqueline Kemp as winemaker. Her strengths include making Pinot Noir.

Pinot Noir 2013 ($30)

Aged 10 months in premium French oak from the Tronçais forest.

WINERY TASTING NOTES "This wine exhibits aromas of violets, liquorice, cranberries, lingonberries, and exotic tamarillo. Its supple palate is nicely balanced with natural acidity and lingering juicy tannins."

❧

ONE FAITH VINEYARDS began marketing its ultra-premium Bordeaux blend in 2014. At $495 for a three-bottle box, it is the most expensive wine from any Okanagan winery. That is consistent with the ambition of Bill Lui, the Vancouver businessman who owns the winery. "My goal for One Faith Vineyards is to become the First Growth for the Okanagan," he says. His winemaker is a star from the Napa Valley, Anne Vawter, and the grapes are from Sundial Vineyard on Black Sage Road.

Grand Vin 2012

Merlot 45.4%, Cabernet Sauvignon 30%, Cabernet Franc 24.6%. Aged 20 to 22 months in French oak. Production 144 cases.

AUTHOR'S TASTING NOTES "The wine begins with deep and complex aromas of cassis, vanilla, spice, and dark cherry. On the palate, there are layered flavours of black cherry, plum, cassis, chocolate, and tobacco. It is a sveltely polished wine with long, silky tannins." Drink by 2022.

❧

PLATINUM BENCH ESTATE WINERY This Black Sage Road winery was opened in 2012 by Murray Jones and Fiona Duncan, a Winnipeg couple who changed careers from business to growing wine in the Okanagan. The vineyard they bought includes an exceptional block of Gamay Noir. Fiona, formerly a fashion house executive, has also become an accomplished baker. Her artisanal breads are sold in the tasting room to take home and are also paired with the wines.

Gamay Noir Block 28 2014 ($40)

Aged in French oak for 10 months. Production 150 cases.

WINERY TASTING NOTES "This refined, deep, bold wine is an excellent example of a classic Beaujolais Cru–style Gamay. Look for notes of raspberry, strawberry, white pepper, licorice, and chocolate. The wine is a deep violet colour with velvety, smooth tannins." Drink by 2020.

❧

SERENDIPITY WINERY was opened in 2011 by Judy Kingston, a former Toronto lawyer who was attracted to the wine-country lifestyle. The winery's extensive portfolio is crowned by a Bordeaux blend called Serenata.

Reserve Serenata 2010 ($40)

Aged 3 years in oak. Production 456 cases.

WINERY TASTING NOTES "A well-integrated wine with a long finish. This blend of Bordeaux grapes has hints of eucalyptus and smoky notes. It goes on to deliver juicy cherry, blackberry, and dark fruits and finishes with flavours of mochachino."

Private Reserve Serenata 2009

Aged 2 years in barrel.

AUTHOR'S TASTING NOTES "This is the winery's flagship Bordeaux blend, a complex wine with aromas of vanilla, plum, and figs, and flavours of plum, figs, and chocolate. The firm but ripe tannins frame a lovely core of sweet fruit flavours. The structure of this wine suggests it is a keeper with plenty of upside."

Serenata First Edition 2008

Cabernet Sauvignon 60%, Cabernet Franc 30%, Merlot 10%. Aged in French oak barrels for 2 years with extended lees contact. Production 259 cases.

AUTHOR'S TASTING NOTES "It begins with aromas of vanilla, eucalyptus, and red fruit. On the palate, there are flavours of currants, blackberries, chocolate, coffee, and tobacco, with a core of sweet fruit nesting in long, ripe tannins."

THORNHAVEN ESTATES WINERY, since opening near Summerland in 2001, has developed a considerable following for its Sauvignon Blanc. Most collectors, however, prefer to cellar long-lived reds. Of interest is the winery's Syrah. The bright and vibrant style of this medium-bodied wine reflects the Summerland growing conditions, which do not produce jammy Syrahs.

Syrah 2013 ($25)

Alcohol 12.6%.

WINERY TASTING NOTES "[The wine] has aromas of blackberry, cherry, vanilla, and cloves." Drink by 2020.

Acknowledgements

I would like to thank the many winery owners and winemakers who shared their best wines with me, often dipping into rare library stocks to host vertical tastings. It would have been difficult to do this book without experiencing older vintages and recording the specifications of those wines.

I would also like to thank Simon Wosk, formerly the owner of SIP Wines in Richmond, for inviting me to participate in the tasting of iconic red wines that he sponsored. That event gave me the idea for this book.

LOCATIONS FEATURED IN PHOTOGRAPHS

Page no.	Description
i	Springtime in the vineyard
iv–v	Fall view toward Munson Mountain on Naramata Bench
vi	Spring shower in the vineyard
vii	Merlot grapes ready for harvest
viii	Sunshine through the canopy
12–13	Pinot Noir Grapes at Blue Mountain Vineyards
22–23	View over Osoyoos Lake at Nk'Mip Cellars
32–33	Malbec cap during fermentation at Laughing Stock Vineyards
42–43	Looking over Lake Okanagan and the City of Penticton from Poplar Grove Winery
52–53	A rainy autumn day on the Naramata Bench from Laughing Stock Vineyards
64–65	View towards Naramata, Peachland, and Summerland from Corbishley Avenue in Penticton
72–73	Harvest views at Blasted Church Vineyards
80–81	View over Skaha Lake in Penticton, BC from Painted Rock Estate Winery
88–89	Pinotage grapes at Lake Breeze Vineyards
96–97	Vineyard in bloom during magic hour on the Naramata Bench
108–109	Malbec pressing at Lake Breeze Vineyards
116–117	Summer Okanagan Lake view over Lake Breeze Vineyards
124–125	The wine caves at Seven Stones Winery in the Similkameen
132–33	Autumn vines at Tantalus Vineyards in Kelowna
142–143	Grenache grapes from Kiln House Vineyards destined for Stag's Hollow Winery
150–151	Le Vieux Pin Winery in Oliver along the Black Sage Bench
160–161	The barrel cellar at Pentage Winery in Penticton
168–169	Syrah grapes in the press at Marichel Vineyards on the Naramata Bench
178–179	Sleeping vines planted on the Black Sage Bench by Harry McWatters
188–189	Autumn view from Quail's Gate Winery in West Kelowna
198–199	Syrah Grapes on the Naramata Bench
208–209	View over the Golden Mile, Black Sage Bench and Osoyoos Lake from Culmina Family Estate Winery
218–219	Post-harvest remains on the Black Sage Bench
228–229	View over Blue Mountain Vineyard and Cellars in Okanagan Falls
236–237	Fall harvest at Culmina Family Estate Winery
244–245	View of Naramata Bench from Bench 1775 Winery
254–255	Tendrils on the guide wire on the Black Sage Bench
264–265	Pinot Noir veraison in Okanagan Falls
272–273	Summer view over the vineyards at Gray Monk in Lake Country
282–283	The vineyards at Tantalus Vineyards in Kelowna looking over Lake Okanagan
290–291	Grapes ripening at Evolve Cellars in Summerland
298–299	Sunset over Marichel Vineyards on the Naramata Bench
310	Barrels for harvest at Culmina Family Estate Winery in Oliver
316	Sunset at Blue Mountain Vineyard and Cellars
318	Syrah veraison on the Naramata Bench

Editing by Amanda Growe
Cover design by Tree Abraham
Interior design by Pete Kohut
Wine bottle photographs provided by John Schreiner

LIBRARY AND ARCHIVES CANADA CATALOGUING IN PUBLICATION
Schreiner, John, 1936–, author
Icon : flagship wines from British Columbia's best wineries / John
Schreiner, author ; Chris K. Stenberg, photographer.

Issued in print and electronic formats.
ISBN 978-1-77151-207-7

1. Wine and wine making—British Columbia. 2. Wineries—British Columbia. I. Title.

TP559.C3S345 2017   641.2'209711   C2016-907818-3

We acknowledge the financial support of the Government of Canada through the Canada
Book Fund and the Canada Council for the Arts, and of the province of British Columbia
through the British Columbia Arts Council and the Book Publishing Tax Credit.

This book was produced using FSC®-certified acid-free paper,
processed chlorine free, and printed with soya-based inks.

PRINTED IN CHINA

21 20 19 18 17   1 2 3 4 5